W9-BHR-856

THE CASE FOR
RELIGION

Nashville
Public Library
Foundation

*This book
made possible
through generous gifts
to the
Nashville Public Library
Foundation Book Fund*

THE CASE FOR
RELIGION

KEITH WARD

ONEWORLD
OXFORD

For Robert Whyte

THE CASE FOR RELIGION

Oneworld Publications
(Sales and Editorial)
185 Banbury Road
Oxford OX2 7AR
England
www.oneworld-publications.com

ISBN 1–85168–337–2

Cover design by Design Deluxe
Typeset by Jayvee, India
Printed and bound in Singapore by
Tien Wah Press Pte. Ltd

CONTENTS

INTRODUCTION

A Preview of What is to Come

Many writers and philosophers of the first rank, from David Hume to James Frazer, from Auguste Comte to Karl Marx, have argued that religion is obsolete, even if people in general do not seem to have realised the fact. It is, they say, a mass of superstitions and delusions, and it has been superseded by science. It is also intolerant and dangerous, and we are only too well aware that civilisation might yet be destroyed by religious hatred. Only when we get rid of religion, they say, will the world be safe to live in and free from delusion and superstition. As civilisations begin to be liberated from superstition, developing and becoming technologically advanced, they will inevitably leave religion behind. The chief hope for humanity, according to such thought, lies in the advance of education and the extinction of religion, which naturally go hand in hand.

Unfortunately for this theory, the most developed country in the world today, the United States of America, is a living refutation of its claims. There has not been a question about religion in the census for over fifty years. But independent surveys such as the American Religious Identity Survey of 2001, carried out by sociologists Barry

1

Kosmin and Seymour Lachman of the Graduate School at City University, New York, give the proportion of Christians in the population as 76%. There are not insignificant, though very much smaller, numbers of adherents of non-Christian religions, and only 13% of the population described themselves as secular or non-religious. The United States continues to be a standing refutation of the claim sometimes made by European sociologists that religious belief declines in proportion to technological and scientific development – unless, of course, only about 13% of Americans are scientifically developed, which seems unlikely.

Even if we turn to one of the most secular countries in the modern world, Britain, 72% of the population described themselves as 'Christian' in the 2001 census. This was very surprising to the clergy, who had never seen anything like that number of people in church. But it seemed to show that nearly three-quarters of the population identified themselves, however vaguely, with a religion. Again, there are many other religious groups in the United Kingdom, in significant numbers, though there are problems about getting reliable data on those numbers. Social surveys also carried out in the United Kingdom show that between one-third and one-half of all people questioned claim to have had a significant religious experience. So religion still seems to be alive and well, even in a very secular society.

So is religion a natural and important part of human life, which can provide meaning and value and psychological stability? Or is it an intellectual aberration, which gives only false hopes and idle wish-fulfilments, and is psychologically damaging?

We first have to try to find out just what religion is. We want to know how religions have developed, and whether they have any reasonable basis. We want to know what social or psychological functions religions have, or what reasons people might have for being religious. We want to know whether religion has a future, and whether we should oppose it, ignore it, or support it (maybe even participate in it).

In this book I have sought to answer these questions. I begin, in part I, by considering various definitions of religion that have been given, to get a clear idea of just what we are dealing with. Although this is a highly controversial matter, I suggest a general definition of religion – as a set of practices for establishing relationship to a supernatural or transcendent reality, for the sake of obtaining human good or avoiding harm.

Then I go on to consider some of the best-known attempts to explain why people are religious, from David Hume and Sir James Frazer (classicists and early anthropologists) to Emile Durkheim and Karl Marx (sociologists) and to Sigmund Freud, Carl Gustav Jung and William James (psychologists). All except the last two regarded religion as an unfortunate delusion, so that the academic study of religion in the last hundred years has often been a diagnosis of the neurosis of religion and how to get rid of it. I try to show the inadequacy and incompleteness of these explanations, and suggest that it remains an open question whether there is a transcendent spiritual reality to which religions give some access.

Such a reality has been conceived in many different ways throughout history. Part II – chapters 5 through 7 – outlines the way in which religions developed from prehistoric origins to the great canonical traditions we call the 'world religions'. I show how the great traditions developed four basic models of spiritual reality, the idealist (only the spiritual ultimately exists), the dualist (spirit and matter both exist in relative independence), the theistic (the spiritual and the material both exist, but the material exists in total dependence upon the spiritual), and the monist (spirit and matter are different aspects of the same unitary reality). These models are developed mainly in India, the Near East and East Asia respectively, though elements of them can all be found somewhere in the great traditions. So there are four great streams of religious thought in the world. I have called them 'canonical' because they all, in their traditional forms, accept some final and absolute revelation, embodied in one or more holy texts. In these traditions religion comes to consist, not just in relationship to supernatural forces, but in overcoming selfish desire and knowing or realising unity with one spiritual being or state of supreme value. But the canonical religions all seem to offer competing views of that being, and they have got closely involved with different political and cultural systems, and so religions can look as though they are doomed to perpetual conflict.

However, a dramatic change in religious consciousness occurred in Europe in the sixteenth to eighteenth centuries, in a movement often called 'the Enlightenment'. Part III – chapters 8 through 10 – outlines the impact of the Enlightenment on the old religious traditions, especially on Christianity and European Judaism, though the impact has been felt in every religious tradition. At this time traditional religion faced great challenges, and needed to be thoroughly rethought. The two greatest challenges were the principle of evidentialism – that all beliefs should be proportioned to publicly testable evidence – and the principle of autonomy – that beliefs, especially moral beliefs, should not be based on authority. If you accept these two principles religious belief, in its traditional form, cannot survive.

But there is a religious response to these challenges. Religious believers can argue that experience is much wider than publicly testable evidence, and includes experience of a transcendent reality. And they can argue that there is a proper place for authority, based on the teachings of people with special insight into the way of achieving true human fulfilment. The limitation of knowledge to sense-experience and the denial of any legitimate authority in matters of belief turn out to be highly questionable. But the Enlightenment did rightly establish that all religious beliefs are subject to criticism in the light of whatever evidence is available, so they need to be much more tentative about many matters than they have been. And religious beliefs must be assessed by moral criteria, so they have to be seen to be conducive to human well-being.

In the modern world, religions face another change. In part IV – the eleventh and twelfth chapters – I assess the present state of religions, and suggest that the future lies in the growth of a convergent spirituality. Each tradition can accept a distinctive place within a plurality of faiths, as a system of symbols and rituals that seeks with others a convergence on one supreme transcendent reality, in which true human fulfilment is to be found. In this way the modern age offers the possibility, real but uncertain, of seeing religion as a process of spiritual exploration which will be both imaginatively enriching and morally illuminating. Religion, so conceived, will have the function of giving human life an ultimate meaning, as people find ways of living in conscious relation to a supreme spiritual value, which they are to realise in themselves and in the world. They will be able to accept many other spiritual paths as different ways of seeking such realisation, not just as rivals, but as valuable and complementary forms of life.

So, in presenting the case for religion, this book does four key things:

1. It demolishes some influential arguments against religion which are supposed to be based on science, sociology and psychology.
2. It shows just why and how religions differ – they are not in chaotic conflict, but they explore the logically possible set of answers to basic human questions of spiritual meaning.
3. It provides a rational justification of religious belief – showing how religious faith can dramatically change worldviews, attitudes and behaviour. It shows how faith gives experience of a supreme spiritual reality, overcomes egoism and gives a sense of significance and purpose, inner calm, psychological integration, moral motivation and a transformation of awareness.
4. It shows how the established religions must change in the modern world if they are to be forces for good. They must be more provisional and exploratory than dogmatic and absolute, they must have as their central driving force the eliciting of positive experiences of transcendence, they must be conducive to human flourishing, and they must safeguard freedom of belief.

Religions are now faced with a choice between retreating into introverted and competing ideologies which can only increase misunderstanding and mutual antagonism in the world, and moving on to greater humility, tolerance and understanding through acceptance of a global religious outlook. On that choice the future of religion, and perhaps the future of the world itself, depends.

PART I

RELIGION DEFINED
AND EXPLAINED

1

RELIGION AND THE TRANSCENDENT

In Search of a Definition

It is very difficult to know what religion is. That does not stop people being vehemently for it, or against it. But it turns out that they are often for or against very different things. And when it comes to defining religion, almost anything goes.

Many colleges in America and Europe have courses on 'Religion'. These courses usually start with a lecture entitled 'What is Religion?' After running through a few dozen definitions, the lecturer almost invariably concludes that nobody knows what religion is, or is even sure that there is such a thing. The courses continue to be called courses on religion, however, because that sounds better than having a course entitled, 'I do not know what I am talking about'.

The problem became clear when, in the 2001 government census in Britain, thousands of people put down their religious affiliation as 'Jedi Knight'. This is not quite as absurd as it might sound. Jedi Knights wear funny clothes, are in close contact with an invisible Force, and often pronounce platitudes with great profundity. Is that enough to make this a religion? If it is a religion, it has great tax advantages. But how can we decide? Could my grandmother get tax exemption if she started a new religion in her living-room? What about Scientologists, pagans, Druids and X-files devotees?

In recent years many scholars, both in anthropology and in social and cultural studies, have queried whether 'religion' is an appropriate or even an identifiable subject of study. Wilfred Cantwell Smith, in *The Meaning and End of Religion*, argued that the concept of religion is 'recent, Western-and-Islamic, and unstable', and that the term should be dropped.[1] It is recent, because in Europe the word 'religion' at first meant the observance of ritual regulations. Later it most often meant 'piety' or 'worship'. So to be religious was to be pious, and 'true religion' was, in Augustine for instance, true piety or devotion. However, in the seventeenth century, Cantwell Smith argues, the word 'religion' came to have a new meaning, of a system of doctrines, and 'true religion' came to mean the true set of doctrines. This, he suggests, makes religion into a matter of having correct beliefs, whereas it should be, and usually was before the seventeenth century, a matter of personal faith and experience.

The term 'religion' is Western, he goes on to say, because a great many cultures, such as the Chinese or Indian, do not have a word for 'religion', and so the word does not quite capture what they do when they are being religious. Finally, the term 'religion' is unstable, because it can mean so many different things, and it deceives people into asking useless questions such as 'What is the essence of religion?' When they ask that question, they either come up with something suspiciously like what they themselves believe or, if they are atheists, something that is obviously ridiculous. Either way, the question is simply not profitable, and we should stop asking it.

What Cantwell Smith objects to is labelling a whole lot of different things in very different cultures 'religions'. Then each religion is seen as a total isolated system, which competes with others, and is a fixed entity whose essence is clear, precise and exclusive. This, he says, turns a matter of living faith into a set of abstract, 'frozen' doctrines, as though there were a number of 'religions', each with a fixed essence. He recommends that we should speak instead of many cumulative traditions, which are always in flux, always changing, and closely intermingled with their own histories and cultures. We can separate this from the lived experience of faith, of personal relation to the Transcendent. He hoped, when he wrote the book in 1962, that we might have stopped using the word 'religion' by the year 1987. Like most prophecies, this one has turned out to be completely false – and he himself helped to make it false by calling his book *The Meaning and End of Religion*, and writing it so well that it was still on sale well after 1987. There is something slightly paradoxical about a book about religion, the argument of which is that no one should write books about religion any more.

It is an excellent book, and its main argument, with which I wholly agree, and which this book also tries to advocate, is that we should not view religions as discrete and fixed sets of competing doctrines. We should pay close attention to many faiths, seeing each one as a dynamic, fluid and culturally influenced complex, the heart of which is a living personal quality of faith in a transcendent reality. The irony is that, in saying this, Cantwell Smith is precisely advocating a view of what the 'essence of religion' is, as distinct from its many cultural forms. He is not at all saying that there is no such thing as religion.

Other writers, usually anthropologists, have argued that it is artificial to separate religion from the general cultural life of a society. We may speak of the beliefs and practices of various cultures, and the way they change in response to new environmental and economic pressures and opportunities. But cultures are very diverse, and it is not helpful to invent general categories into which we try to force this diversity.

It could be argued that it was only when Christendom began to break up that writers such as Herbert of Cherbury (1582–1648) started to speak of 'natural religion', an essence that underlies all particular reve-lations. Religion, for Edward Herbert, consists of five innate ideas: the existence of God, the duties of worship, of moral conduct, and of repent-ance for sin, and the existence of rewards and punishments after death.[2]

Thus the word 'religion' comes, at a particular point in European history, to stand for an essential nature which is supposed to express the common truth of the many diverse religions, whose particular revelations are all in fact false (except for Christianity, whose essence happens to represent the truth most adequately, according to the European thought at that time). This essence, however, may seem to be only the skeleton of decayed Christian faith. The emphasis on God, on the moral nature of religion, and on final judgement, is what remains of Christianity when its most distinctive dogmas of Trinity, incarnation and atonement have been left behind.

So 'religion' became established in Europe as a post-Christian, minimal notion, allegedly founded on pure reason, which could be used as a criterion in the light of which all particular religions could be found wanting, especially those of foreign, heathen lands. This idea of religion supported the ideology of growing European colonialism, in its mission to bring primitive and savage races under the benevolent shade of civilisation (and to subjugate them economically in the process).

Thus seen, the use of the term 'religion' becomes part of a colonising process, by which all people are persuaded or forced to use a term that subsumes their own culture and belief-system under a European pattern. That in turn subtly undermines their belief-system, by transmuting it into one among many competing 'religions', whose true inner essence turns out to be just that recommended by the colonial powers of liberal democracy. The European colonisation of the savage mind triumphs when religions become options to be freely chosen, and options which in the end must be judged by criteria of reason which in fact embody the bourgeois, liberal, aristocratic morality of capitalist Europe.[3]

There is just enough truth in all this to make any European, and any American too, rather uncomfortable. It is, however, difficult to see what positive alternative is being recommended. It could be that each culture must be studied strictly as a whole on its own terms, without trying to subsume it under general global categories of explanation. But that would be to make any cross-cultural understanding impossible or at least undesirable. The study of religion would be subsumed under

Cultural Studies, or it would perhaps disappear as a politically incorrect subject, which had always disguised a liberal secularising agenda for sanctioning the superiority of the West.

Ironically, it could be argued that Cantwell Smith himself, the advocate of the end of the concept of 'religion', falls prey to the charge of cultural imperialism. He states that the many cumulative traditions are grounds for individual faith in Transcendence. But in using the concept of 'Transcendence', he is focusing attention on a supernatural reality and on the possibility of personal experience of it. A critic could say that he is using what is precisely a liberal, post-Christian term to characterise what he sees as a universal object of human belief. Whereas Lord Herbert had spoken of an innate idea of God, Cantwell Smith goes further in denuding the religious object of content, and is left with the bare idea of 'the Transcendent'. He has thereby left all particular religious traditions behind – none of them worship just the Transcendent. Yet he retains a minimal content, for 'the Transcendent' is that which is beyond and greater than the immanent or the everyday. Thereby he is picking out precisely what he thinks is central to religion. He is himself, an unfriendly critic could say, continuing the secularising liberal programme of viewing religion as a discrete cultural option, suggesting that its real essence is so vague as to be without significant social impact, and thus downgrading all specific revelations in favour of a cultivated, reasonable, tolerant and voluntaristic view of religion as one cultural activity among others, for those who like that sort of thing. The ideology of the West has triumphed, even in the work of one of its chief critics!

DEFENDING 'RELIGION'

In response to such criticism, it must be agreed that speaking of 'the Spiritual' or 'the Supernatural' is vague, and that no actual object of worship is identified simply by that term. But it by no means follows that it must therefore be a decayed remnant of some full-blooded religious belief, much less a Christian one. Any observer, from any culture, looking at the huge variety of human beliefs and practices throughout the world, will naturally be led to see that his or her own beliefs are just one selection from a great number of actual beliefs. That will at once suggest that they should not just be taken for granted, as obvious to everyone. They should be compared with differing beliefs of the same sort, to see what sorts of justification they might have, or what accounts for such differences. This is not simply what happens in a specifically Western culture. It is what will happen to any reflective observer in any culture who takes note of what humans in general believe and do.

For such comparative study to take place, we have to determine what we shall count as 'beliefs of the same sort'. A Christian could talk about differing beliefs in an incarnate God, but that would cover a relatively small range of extant human beliefs. So, like Edward Herbert, one could extend the range by talking about beliefs in God in general. We now know, as he did not appreciate, that many humans have beliefs in a supreme spiritual reality, which they do not know as 'God'. We can extend the range further, and in doing so we gain more knowledge about the varieties of human thought. We may also gain more understanding of and respect for sorts of beliefs that at first seem very different from ours.

There is no reason why understanding should lead to the subsumption of other beliefs as inferior versions of categories we invent. Indeed, we might change our categories precisely because we see that other beliefs discern aspects of things that we have missed, and we might wish to embrace those aspects under some wider term. That is in fact what Cantwell Smith was trying to do in using the term 'Transcendence', and what earlier thinkers such as Schleiermacher and Max Müller had done by using terms such as 'the Infinite'. They may think that their own faith is actually the most adequate conceptualisation of Transcendence. But anyone, from any tradition, is free to think that. It does not detract from the attempt to find a more general term that will express a genuine interest in, a taking account of, and a due respect for, beliefs that differ from our own, but have some important analogy with ours. Once we have put a term like 'the Transcendent' or 'the Spiritual' into currency, we can call 'religions' those sets of beliefs and practices that attempt to relate human thought, experience and practice to the alleged referent of that term.

This is in one sense a liberalising move. It moves from thinking that my local set of beliefs defines what 'religion' is, to seeing a whole set of analogous beliefs throughout the world as widening and extending an understanding of the object of religion. But this does not mean that the term 'religion' is a decayed post-Christian, Western or secularising concept. It need not attempt to pervert local cultures by forcing them to conform to Western imperialist models. On the contrary, it is a term which expresses the desire to see very diverse cultural views not as entirely alien (and therefore possibly as 'sub-human'), but as alternative models of the same world we inhabit, which have the capacity to evoke insights which we may well lack. Herbert was not wrong in speaking of 'religion'. If he was wrong, it was in his limited view of what religion was. It was precisely because he was unaware of many of the spiritual traditions of humanity that his 'essentialist' view failed to capture the flexibility and vitality of the phenomenon of religion.

It may be that anyone who seriously studies a number of religions with respect and sympathy will become less inclined to think that adherence to one religion should be compulsory, or that all its beliefs are quite obviously true. We might come to have a broader and more nuanced interpretation of what revelation is. But that is to say simply that increased knowledge does clearly change beliefs. It ought to produce intellectual virtues, and it is a good thing if it does. The study of religion should produce self-criticism as much as, or more than, criticism of others. There is no disguised liberal agenda, unless one thinks that you have to be a liberal to have sympathetic knowledge and understanding of the beliefs and practices of others. But that is surely not the case.

When people argue that religion cannot be defined at all, they often appeal to Wittgenstein's analogy of 'family resemblances'. People may be members of the same family, though they have no one thing in common, but may resemble each other in a number of different ways – some have the same big noses, some big ears, some blue eyes, but none of them looks just like the others. So we might call something a 'religion' if it has a sufficient number of resemblances to other things we call 'religions', even though we cannot get one definite feature that is found in every case.

This is not in fact a refusal to define religion, however. It is a definition in terms of a set of central features, which is extendable if further resemblances become important. What we want to know is why we should want to group these sets of resemblances together under some one term, 'religion'. In the case of families, the crucial factor is genetic relationship, or upbringing within a particular social group. We want to speak of 'families' because we want to establish special duties of care, or formulate rules of inheritance and responsibility. Is there any such factor in the case of religion? Is there any reason for grouping things together as 'religions'? And is there any reason for picking out specific sorts of resemblance as relevant to this?

One main reason is the desire to say that all, or most, humans have similar basic intellectual and emotive drives, and that one of these drives is the desire to relate to a transcendent reality, or a belief that they can do so. Within each tradition that does seek to relate to such a reality, there is an inner logic that motivates the believer to see at least some apprehensions of that reality in other apparently diverse traditions. That is just an expression of the belief that, if we are not wholly deluded, we must all be in touch with the same world, and must have some knowledge of the same sorts of things. It would be troubling if only a few people had any knowledge of God.

There are religious views that confine knowledge of God to small groups – usually oneself and one's friends, strangely enough. But it is rather an odd sort of God who would not make the divine known in any way to any one else. So reflection on the object of our own belief has a tendency to lead to a wider, 'natural' knowledge of God, or at least of something vaguely like God, God *incognito*. Then a due sense of humility might lead us to seek a term that does not commit others too fully to our own beliefs. We get a term such as 'Transcendent' in the attempt, not to subject other beliefs to our own, but precisely in an attempt to see our own belief in the wider context of basic human forms of apprehension.

Non-theistic views, such as Buddhism, do a similar sort of thing if they say, as they often do, that theistic views are 'lesser paths' to enlightenment. I, as a Christian, have been told by a very senior Buddhist monk, 'I do not think you should change your religion and become a Buddhist.' I was very pleased to think how very tolerant he was. But then he said, 'Christianity is just right for a person at your stage of spiritual development,' and I paused for a moment's thought. Was this really tolerance? However, he was just doing what we all do – thinking that his own view was clearly correct, but doing me the honour of thinking that I was not completely deluded, but was seeing the religious object – *nirvana* – in a rather naive personal guise, which would no doubt be corrected in a few thousand lifetimes.

With real atheists it is more difficult. They do think all believers in a spiritual reality are deluded. There is no spiritual or transcendent reality. However, they too have some interest in tracing the common mistakes and delusions that afflict human beings. A large part of the study of religions in the West has consisted in various attempts to explain how humans are subject to radical delusions, and it is useful to have the term 'religion' for all the delusions that we want to get rid of.

It turns out that the term 'religion' is useful both for people who have sets of distinctive beliefs, and who want to relate in a positive way to many millions of other human beings with beliefs that can be seen as similar, that can be plausibly seen as attempting to relate to the same basic object, and for those who want to get rid of a whole set of related beliefs as superstitious and harmful. One of the biggest cultural battles in the modern world is precisely as to whether these sets of beliefs about a transcendent reality are genuine or delusory.

It may be thought that speaking of religion in terms of 'beliefs' is too intellectual or rationalistic. Ninian Smart has suggested that there are seven main 'dimensions' of religion, seven general descriptive categories under which we can list religious activities.[4] These are: myth or narrative, doctrine, ritual, ethics, social institutions, experience, and the material dimension (buildings, artworks and so on). If we are seeking to describe the phenomenon of religion, these, he suggests, are some categories we can use to get a reasonably adequate description. It might be misleading to focus too much on one dimension, such as doctrines or sets of beliefs. No doubt all religions have some doctrines, but for some the dimension of doctrine will be much less important than for others.

There is something, however, which unites these dimensions or categories. We are not interested in any kind of narrative, any kind of worldview, or any kind of experience. What seems to unite these dimensions is that they all relate directly or indirectly to some description of supernatural reality or realities, to some way of maintaining a relationship with it (or them), and to some way of eliciting typical types of experiences in the context of such a relationship. So it turns out that the element of belief is fundamental after all. However important experiences, stories or rituals might be, if they have no connection to belief in supernatural reality, then neither those who wish to defend the existence of a transcendent realm nor those who wish to deny it will have an interest in the topic. So by focusing on the term 'religion' we can focus on the great debate between those who think that there are spiritual beings, realities other than those in space-time, to which humans can relate in feeling, knowledge and action, and those who deny it. That debate is what I want to focus on. The study of religions is one of the best ways of focusing on it.

The fact is that throughout the world there are practices intended to relate humans to a transcendent or supernatural reality (or realities), and presumably there are some alleged apprehensions of it (or them) by at least some human beings. So it is possible to speak of a distinctive area of human belief, practice and experience, in which humans seek to relate to a supernatural order of being, in ways intended to attain human goods or avoid human harms. We can call such beliefs, practices and experiences 'religious', and they can become the objects of reflective and analytical study. The study of religions may no doubt be part of Cultural Studies – though it will also be concerned with questions of rationality and truth that Cultural Studies often sets aside. But it is primarily a study of those beliefs, practices and experiences in which humans consider themselves to have a potentially fulfilling relation to an objective transcendent reality. There is nothing particularly 'Western', elitist or essentialist about such a study. In fact, one main consequence might be to set Western beliefs in a wider global context, and so undermine imperialist dreams, Western or otherwise.

RELIGION AND THE SEARCH FOR MEANING

People who study religion do not have to believe in it. Indeed, for some years it has almost been a requirement for doing Religious Studies at college that you do not believe any of it. A good example is E.B. Tylor, appointed to the Readership in Anthropology at Oxford University in 1884, who was one of the first writers to consider religion on a global scale as a distinctive human phenomenon. He believed that only if you do not believe in a religious system can you see what it really is, because it is actually a fantasy. When he came to define 'religion', he gave what became a very influential 'minimum definition' of religion as 'belief in spiritual beings'.[5] This simple definition has been criticised in a number of ways. Perhaps it emphasises the dimension of belief or doctrine too much. Perhaps the expression 'spiritual beings' seems rather restrictive for the many sorts of supernatural reality that religions can embrace. But there is a set of stories, beliefs, practices and experiences which are primarily concerned with a reality or realities that are not physical or material (or at least aspects of which have no spatial location) and so can be called 'spiritual', which in some way are greater than physical realities, and which are relevant to human good or harm. It may be useful to call these 'religious', just to catch that element of reference to the supernatural. In a broad sense, religions will indeed centre on belief in spiritual beings, if belief is taken to involve 'commitment to the existence of', and 'spiritual beings' is taken to cover a broad spectrum of spiritual possibilities.

What Tylor did not stress is that religions typically offer a set of social practices for coming to know and participate in the power of the supernatural, for disciplining the mind and conforming the will. They often originate in personal visions, shaped and re-shaped over many years by many minds and cultures. These visions, in diverse particular forms, are evoked in each new generation as types of personal experience that make the tradition a living source of spiritual power. Religion is not just a matter of individual intellectual belief. It also embodies social practices that encourage personal experiences of immense emotional power.

When Tylor says that 'savage animism is almost devoid of that moral element' which characterises higher religions,[6] he implies that it is just a theoretical belief that souls or spirits exist, which has no essential relation to the moral practices of the society, and no relation to any belief in the moral government of the universe. The French founder of sociology, Emile Durkheim, surely rightly, corrected this by pointing out that 'religious forces are ... moral forces'[7] and that 'the first article of any faith is belief in salvation by faith'.[8] By this, Durkheim means, I think, that religious rites mediate a power to make life whole, and trust in that power is morally empowering and efficacious. Religious belief is not just a theoretical hypothesis that there are spiritual beings. It is a practical commitment to receiving creative spiritual power, or to deflecting destructive spiritual power.

The belief that the universe is morally governed, in the sense that it expresses one providential supreme will, is probably not characteristic of many indigenous faiths. But the belief that the universe has a moral order, that it is an interplay of both creative and destructive spiritual powers, which can bring moral good and harm to humans, but whose fundamental orientation is to the production of good, is virtually universal. Religion is primarily practical, and one of its most basic postulates is that the practical task of living well as a human being involves being rightly related to the spiritual power or powers that enfold and interact with human life.

If we are going to have a general definition of religion that covers a reasonably broad range of human practices and beliefs that might help-fully be grouped together, then that definition will necessarily be very general, and will invite the inveterate categoriser to invent many further subdivisions. Proposed definitions range from that of the sociologist M.E. Spiro – 'a culturally patterned interaction with culturally postul-ated superhuman beings'[9] – to that of Max Müller – 'perception of the Infinite insofar as it is able to influence the moral character of man'.[10]

At one end of the spectrum, to speak of the postulation of super-human beings seems to imply a rather negative view of religions, as inventing anthropomorphic superhuman heroes, perhaps to explain why the sun rises or the rain falls (that is very much what Tylor thought). At the other end, religion seems to disappear into the miasma of 'the Infinite', wherein all distinctions are merged into one all-enveloping Romantic conceptual fog.

Specific definitions of religion express the inclinations of their prop-agators. Nevertheless, both 'superhuman beings' and 'the Infinite' refer to a supernatural reality, a reality which is other and, in some sense to be further specified, greater than publicly observable material objects, and which exists objectively – that is, independently of human beings. In the course of human history, there have been many differing ways of con-ceiving such a supernatural reality. Religions can differ greatly from one another, but a central, if not absolutely universal, theme is the existence of a supernatural realm in relation to which some form of human fulfil-ment can be found.

Tylor himself was not interested in questions of the truth of religious beliefs – he rather assumed that they were all false. Tylor's view was that beliefs about supernatural realities are more literal than metaphorical. He therefore assumed that the spiritual beings in question were believed to exist much as they were depicted. He thought in fact that primitive religious belief was a mistaken quasi-scientific belief that the causes of movements in the world were disembodied spirits. He called this view 'animism' – the causes of all things are little invisible people or minds or souls, pushing and pulling things around. This, he thought, is a natural but primitive belief, one that children also have. It arises in the childhood of the race, and attributes false ideas of causality to objects in the world. The gods are just the results of a mistaken idea of causality, essentially a primitive reaction to the world, which sees it as personal through and through.

We do not need to take such a literal interpretation of stories of the gods. The creation stories of many indigenous religions do speak of spiritual beings, and are proposed for belief by worshippers. But there is no reason why we should think of these beings as people in the sky. Perhaps the stories provide images that speak metaphorically of a fundamentally mysterious spiritual reality, which in itself transcends all images. Tylor apparently lacked the sort of feeling that could make this approach plausible, and his assumption was that primitive religion is more like science than like poetry. Such an approach will obviously determine your assessment of what religion is about, and what it is trying to do.

Clifford Geertz provides a more sympathetic appraisal of religious beliefs when he says (in a well-known definition that I here abbreviate) that 'religion is a set of symbols which acts to establish ... moods and motivations in men by formulating conceptions of a general order of existence'.[11] He draws attention to two aspects of religious symbols – they formulate a view of the world, and they evoke or sustain moods and motivations that are appropriate to that worldview.

To say that religious symbols always formulate a view of the world seems rather too systematic and theoretical a programme for many religious systems. Yet it seems true that such symbols do aim to refer to a spiritual order that underlies the perceived physical world. Geertz's definition does not refer explicitly to a 'supernatural' reality. On this definition, an exposition of Darwin's theory of evolution, inducing moods of pessimism and despair, could count as a religion. Darwinism can certainly look rather like a religion in some ways – it is defended with a confidence that goes far beyond available evidence, it is often accompanied by caricatures and stereotypes of competing views, and it offers a total, all-embracing view of the nature of reality. Yet there are no Darwinist churches, no rituals, no prayer or contemplation. Crucially, there is a denial of any supernatural, non-physical element in reality to which humans could consciously relate.

Geertz does actually see this element as crucial, though strangely it is not mentioned in his 'definition'. He speaks of 'an all-pervading vitality', an 'unconditioned end', a 'transcendent truth'. He points to the function of religion as enabling humans to cope with three basic problems, the breakdown of explanation, the existence of suffering, and lack of justice in the world. Religion, he says, affirms that reality is ultimately explicable, that suffering is endurable, and that there is a moral order in reality.

Clearly, not just any old worldview will do. It has to be a view that addresses these fundamental human problems. If it explains the inexplicable, makes suffering bearable and refers to a moral order that is not open to empirical investigation, it must posit an underlying spiritual reality. 'The religious perspective', Geertz says, 'moves beyond the realities of everyday life to wider ones',[12] which are experienced in ritual activity, points at which we worship – commit ourselves to – something that is not ourselves. Darwin's theory of natural selection just will not fill the bill. If taken as a total explanation, it eliminates the credibility of worship, and denies that there is any moral order in reality.

We have to begin by considering the sort of moods that religions try to evoke. Prominent among them are moods of reverence, awe, gratitude, repentance, persistence and hope. Even where religious lives are filled with terror of the gods, rites exist to lessen that terror, not to increase it. Perhaps, like many ancient Greeks, one simply has to learn to bear the yoke of the gods, and resignation is the dominant mood. Even so, there is hope that the gods may be propitiated, and we may share for a while in their more vital life.

These are moods that counter the anxieties to which human lives are prone, not just by a denial that there are reasons to be anxious, but by unveiling a deeper, hidden reality which sets anxiety in a wider context of meaning. It is precisely that wider context that is 'supernatural', beyond the quotidian (the everyday) and the publicly perceptible, and possessing an enduring value – of intelligibility, endurance and justice, perhaps – which, if we can only touch it, can transform our lives.

Religious ritual is a way to touch a hidden reality, which can make the problem of human meaning endurable. So religion provides a system of symbols which acts to establish powerful moods, by formulating conceptions of a hidden, ultimate, supernatural order of existence, to which its ritual practices give access. While Geertz's definition does not quite say this, what he writes about it strongly implies it. Ritual, he says, transports us into another mode of existence, a different way of looking at and living in the world. It is not just a theoretical belief that spirits exist. It is (or is believed to be) a conscious way of relating to a supernatural realm, which enables us to overcome, or at least to endure, the deepest anxieties which mark the character of human existence.

None of this shows that there is such a realm, or that it is reasonable to have such anxieties, or that they can, or should be, overcome. It only claims that some people do have such anxieties, and all of us are capable of understanding what they are. Religion primarily functions to address them, by claiming to make known a level of reality at which their intensity dissolves, and can be transmuted into a more vital and positive form of living.

There does exist a very widespread set of beliefs and practices, varying enormously in their specific character, and in many diverse human societies, which is concerned to alleviate human anxiety by conscious relation to such a supernatural reality, conceived by means of symbols drawn from the culture and experience of each society. It is useful to have a general term for these beliefs and practices, so clearly distinct from those of art, ethics and science, so interesting in both their similarities and their diversities. The word 'religion' seems to be very suitable for that purpose.

Find out more...

It is important to read some general descriptive books on world religions. Good ones are:

Ninian Smart, *The World's Religions* (Cambridge: Cambridge University Press, 1998).

Ian Markham (ed.), *A World Religions Reader* (Oxford: Blackwell, 1996).

Patrick Burke, *The Major Religions* (Oxford: Blackwell, 1996).

John Bowker (ed.), *The Cambridge Illustrated History of Religions* (Cambridge: Cambridge University Press, 2002).

Wilfred Cantwell Smith's *The Meaning and End of Religion* (New York: Macmillan, 1962) is a short, readable and pleasantly contentious book.

Peter Clarke and Peter Byrne, *Religion Defined and Explained* (Basingstoke: Macmillan, 1993) is just what it says, except that it considers and criticises other people's theories of religion rather than propounding one of its own.

2

SICK MEN'S DREAMS?

Explanations of Religion as a Survival
of the Savage Mind

When scholars began to study ancient religions, in eighteenth-century Europe and onwards, many of them viewed early human religions as superstitious, barbaric and absurd. It is probably true that they viewed the religion of their own culture (usually a form of Christianity) as irrational, and they wanted to explain it as a remnant of outmoded and irrational beliefs from earlier times and earlier religions. Needless to say, they had little contact with any such religions, and such contact as they had heard of lacked any attempt at sympathetic understanding. David Hume, in 1757, published *The Natural History of Religion*, in which he pretended to investigate the principles that originally gave rise to religious belief. It goes without saying that he had no way of knowing anything about such origins, though he had a good knowledge of ancient Roman writings, often of a sceptical nature, about their own forms of religion. Armed with these classical sources, his *Natural History* is actually a thinly disguised exposure of the lamentable superstitions of eighteenth-century Scotland (by which he meant the Church of Scotland).

Hume was an urbane and civilised man, and something of a saint, if there can be atheist saints. There is a story that when Dr Johnson visited him on his deathbed, to watch him repenting of his atheism, Hume annoyed him considerably by dying peacefully, if not exactly happily. Nevertheless, one of the strongest impressions that his account of religion gives is of his contempt for the common man. 'The ignorant multitude', he says, 'must first entertain some grovelling and familiar notion of superior powers.'[13] Intellectual theism does not come naturally to human beings. It is 'the incessant hopes and fears which actuate the human mind'[14] that arouse a grovelling belief in the existence of some unknown causes of human happiness and misery, which causes might be personified as beings that might somehow be flattered or cajoled into helping us. 'The primary religion of mankind arises chiefly from an anxious fear of future events.'[15] Its primary mood is fear and anxiety, and its cause is ignorance of the future and of the ultimate causes of things. The tendency to believe in invisible, intelligent powers is 'at least a general attendant of human nature',[16] but that, while it explains, in no sense justifies its existence.

These imagined powers, the gods of polytheism, are, Hume says, 'no better than the elves or fairies of our ancestors'.[17] They are fantasies of ignorance, stupidity, weakness and timidity. When theism arises out of primitive polytheism, it does so simply as the extravagant flattery of one god, in preference to the others. But while theism is rationally preferable to polytheism, it seems indivisible from intolerance and from a tendency to 'sink the human mind into the lowest submission and abasement',[18] which gives rise to all the contemptible 'monkish virtues' which are so unbefitting to human beings. One might think that, if humans are indeed as stupid as Hume thinks, it is quite fitting for them to feel humble, penitent and abased before an all-wise and morally demanding God. Luckily, however, there are a few, like Hume, who have transcended such stupidity, and can bathe contentedly in the knowledge that they are the rational elect, liberated from superstition and the need for humility and grovelling.

Hume considered that almost everyone else was intellectually irredeemable. 'The vulgar, that is, indeed, all mankind, a few excepted, being ignorant and uninstructed',[19] it is hardly surprising that the religious principles which prevail in the world cannot be said to be 'anything but sick men's dreams'.[20]

Strange as it may seem, a person of devout faith might agree with much of Hume's account, while not being quite so sure that he or she was one of the few exceptions to Hume's general strictures on the human race as ignorant, stupid and vulgar. Polytheism probably does precede theism, at least in the sense that many gods and spirits are worshipped in indigenous religions more frequently or intensely than the one High God who is often considered as a rather remote being. It probably is a concern for human happiness and misery that motivates much religious practice. A concern for physical and mental health and integration is central to religious practice, both simple and sophisticated. The gods probably are personifications, founded on a natural analogy from human awareness and will, of the ultimate powers which control nature, and the ultimate values which govern, or ought to govern, personal and social life. Whether such personification is more or less adequate than the mechanisation of nature, which was what Hume took from Isaac Newton, is not perhaps as clear as Hume thought it was. Moreover, humans are ignorant and egoistical; so much of their religion will be marked by ignorance and an egoistic concern for personal happiness at the expense of others. But again, whether these worst cases should be made the standard cases of religious faith is highly dubious.

Why should the primal religious attitude to these posited spiritual powers be one of grovelling fear? And why should the attitudes that belief in God evokes be those of mortification, penance, humility and passive suffering? True, some people fear the anger of the gods, and practise self-mortification. But others love the gods and rejoice in their companionship, and their ritual sacrifices are occasions of joyful feasting and communal celebration. Hume offers no evidence that fear is the origin of religion, or that 'monkish virtues' are the fruit of monotheism – a view which both Jews and Muslims (who have no monks, but are certainly monotheists) would be surprised to hear.

In brief, Hume's *Natural History* is no history at all, but a compendium of the views of some sceptical writers on religion from classical Greece onwards, added to Hume's own dismissal of the views of 'all mankind, a few excepted' as ignorant and vulgar. On his own common-sense principles, we might think that if the religious tendency is a general feature of common human nature, as he says it is, then we might expect to find it about as well established as belief in physical objects, causality or other minds – for which he could find no rational justification either.

Hume was the philosopher who held that there is no rational justification for thinking that the future will be like the past. All we know is that the past was like the past, but that is no reason for thinking that the future will be like the past. After all, the future hasn't happened yet, so how do we know? As Phil Connors, the hero of the film *Groundhog Day*, says, 'There may be no tomorrow. After all, there wasn't one today.' Generations of philosophy students have stayed in bed all day, because they have had no justification for getting up. How do they know that the world outside their bedroom still exists? Since their beliefs have to be strictly proportioned to the available evidence, they cannot get out of bed until they have more evidence. So they are forced to stay where they are. That's their story, anyway.

To all of which Hume replies that we must just let common sense take over and assume without evidence that the world still exists. If we can do that, why can't we assume without evidence that God exists too? Belief in God is widespread and natural. Millions of people think they apprehend God. Admittedly not everyone does. But a great many people do, some of them in apparently intense and overwhelming ways. The fact that other people do not apprehend God does not show that God does not exist. So on Hume's own principles we would expect him to think that belief in God is a pretty commonsense, if not absolutely universal, belief. As such, it ought to be perfectly acceptable. But on the topic of religion the greatest Scottish philosopher of common sense refuses to accept common sense, and prefers the opinions of the very rationalists whom he otherwise loves to refute.

Perhaps all the dispassionate observer can say is that there does exist a common, if not universal, human tendency to personify the powers of nature – i.e. to react to the world as though it expressed quasi-personal or spiritual powers. In early human religions, such personification often takes the form of belief in many gods or spirits, or perhaps in the continuing mediating power of the ancestors. But it also leads to belief in one personal God and to extremely sophisticated spiritual philosophies. What the emotional causes or consequences of such beliefs are probably varies in different places, and with different people. There is little real evidence, however, to show that such a tendency is rooted in fear rather than in reverent admiration and moral concern, or that it conduces to grovelling obedience rather than a sense of courageous adventure. Even a devoted admirer of David Hume must admit that Hume's own principle of having to find good evidence for all one's opinions was cast aside when it came to religion.

All in all, what his *Natural History* shows chiefly is how very difficult it is to give a detailed, informed, discriminating and unbiased account of religious belief. Perhaps, after all, Hume was not quite the purely rational being he, at his least rational, thought he was. He was passionately anti-religious, and the roots of that passion are not in reason, but in his aversion to certain sorts of 'undignified' moral outlook, and in his basic belief in the superiority of the cultivated life of the eighteenth-century European aristocracy to anything else on earth. We might say that he suffered, not from sick men's dreams, but from well-fed men's fantasies about their own freedom from the common human condition of sordid vulgarity and ignorance.

Of course, Hume's strictures do apply to some forms of religion. If religion expresses the deepest hopes and fears of humanity, it will be a blend of light and darkness, of optimism and pessimism, of universal aspiration and particular hatreds. The human concern with spiritual reality will be to use it to obtain human good or to avoid human harm. But what is seen as good and harm may differ widely. To sacrifice a child to obtain fertility harms the child, though it is meant to be for the sake of a greater good. To sacrifice a cock to appease a demon of disease is based on a false view of the causality of disease, but it is meant to orient human lives appropriately to the hidden spiritual powers that underlie all things. It is hardly surprising that beliefs about the supernatural are imbued with the moral and intellectual limitations of specific human cultures. There seems to be no 'pure', culture-free primal revelation of the nature of Spirit. Yet belief in a supernatural reality of some sort seems to be virtually universal in early human societies.

Thus there are shrines to what seem to be goddesses and ancestors in many ancient sites, as well as elaborate burial places, and it is generally thought that ritual played an important part in these human lives. There is unmistakable evidence that by the third millennium BCE the gods were important in human consciousness. The great stone circle of Stonehenge in England, the pyramids of Egypt, the dominating temples of Mesopotamia and South America all testify to belief in spirit protectors, the spiritual significance of the seasons and cycles of nature, and some sort of existence beyond death, whether among the stars or under the earth.

It seems virtually certain that we must regard the origins of religion as rooted in a millennial development of the human mind from pre-linguistic and pre-conceptual forms to the brutal and grandiose structures of the first settled imperial cities. The sense of religion does not seem to have been a sort of clear primordial knowledge. Like all other human knowledge, it grew slowly from a hazy mingling of fact and fantasy, of awe and playfulness, with many false paths and dead ends, but also with unexpected insights and rich imaginative creativity.

Within the general species *homo*, modern man, *Homo sapiens*, probably originated in Africa about one hundred thousand years ago. Whereas the other main branch of hominids, the Neanderthals, did not adapt to the changing environment and became extinct by 35,000 BCE, *Homo sapiens* survived the third Ice Age and went on to dominate the planet. It was this species that developed morality, art, science and religion, and eventually – only in the last fifty years, out of all those hundreds of thousands of years – came to understand the very basis of life itself.

This account of human origins leads us to see modern humans as the descendants of primates, having evolved to a degree greater than any other species a specialised brain capable of abstract thought and decision making. Human religious beliefs and practices have therefore developed gradually over an immense period of time, from ages in which rational thought had not yet developed up to the information explosion of the present.

It is unlikely that our mere five thousand years of moderately civilised life can fundamentally change the deep patterns of thought and response that were laid down in the brains of our ancestors over the long unmeasured aeons of pre-history. We would therefore expect that many basic human beliefs would be pre-rational and pre-reflective, rooted in natural reactions to a largely mysterious environment, and only slowly developing more reflective, systematised forms. Yet there have been moments of sudden breakthrough to a different level of knowledge and understanding. There have been decisive changes in human thought patterns, accelerating over the last five thousand years. So we are looking at traces of a very long pre-rational past, overlaid by a few relatively recent decisive transformations of outlook, which have reconfigured human understanding of the world.

On this evolutionary view, which is founded on the evidence of fossil remains, early burial-sites and caves, geological dating of sedimentary rocks, and now on methods of genetic identification, religious beliefs, like other beliefs, will take shape, not in some supposed original knowledge of hidden truths, but in the imaginative stories told in firelit caves after the hunt, or in ceremonies for helping the first dimly thinking animals to find power for living in a beautiful but dangerous world. It is difficult, if not impossible, to get back to the state of mind of humans one hundred thousand years ago. But it seems certain, if the evidence of the sciences is to be trusted, that religion has a vastly longer pre-rational history than a rational one, and that it has only slowly developed more reflective and sophisticated forms over many thousands of years, though there have been crucial saltations (sudden jumps), especially in recent times. In a word, religion, like life itself, has evolved. Perhaps it is evolving still.

The earliest paintings found on cave walls, mostly later than about 25,000 BCE, represent animals, symbols of the life that must be given, the blood that must be shed, to enable humans to survive. Female statuettes from around the same time seem to be symbols of fertility, of the life-giving power of motherhood. Reverence for the dead, acceptance of the necessity of sacrifice and awe before the powers of fertility and new life are the only traces of their thoughts that our earliest human ancestors have left for us to discover. From all those many tens of thousands of years of human life there is little else that remains to speak to us. From the silence of our prehistory, these symbols of the mysterious powers of death, sacrifice and birth still hold their potency to remind us of the ultimate limiting factors that set bounds to human existence, and unite us in our most basic consciousness with the hunter-gatherers of the third glacial age.

There is little reason to think that prehistoric religion was founded solely in fear and ignorance, which have been overcome by modern civilisation. Why should it not have been founded on a primal intuition that the cosmos expresses, in its forms and rhythms, an underlying spiritual power, or complex of powers, in which human beings can share? As well as fear and ignorance, there was love and understanding, partial and limited but capable of growth. Such a complex affective encounter with the being of the cosmos may embody forms of knowledge and relationship that the impersonal and mechanistic approach of scientific rationalism cannot embrace. In that case, religion may not belong solely to a dead age of superstitious vulgarity. It may retain power to unlock a perception of meaning and value in the cosmos, which is necessary for the realisation of full human cognitive potential. That, at any rate, is a viewpoint that is worth exploring.

THE GOLDEN BOUGH

It is not a viewpoint, however, which is found in one of the best-known accounts of early religion, Sir James Frazer's *The Golden Bough*. To enter into the world of *The Golden Bough* is to enter into a magical world in which an attempt to explain the rule for the succession to the priesthood of Diana at Aricia, an attempt which it might be thought should surely be completed in little more than a short article, grows into twelve volumes of fascinating narrative of ancient customs, bold conjectures as to the origin of human religious beliefs, elegant apostrophisations of the beauties of the natural world and encyclopaedic compendia of comparative anthropology and mythology.

In these magisterial twelve volumes, fortunately for most readers condensed in 1922 into one abridged edition, almost all classical myths and recorded practices of tribal cultures, as well as the superstitions that linger still in the most civilised nations, are to be found. But they are not simply set alongside one another as if in some dusty museum catalogue. They arise and take their place in the narrative, one by one, as successive analyses and ever-expanding explanations of the simple but obscure account of how the priests of Diana met their deaths in the sacred grove of the goddess, and were succeeded by one who had plucked the golden bough of mistletoe from the sacred oak at Nemi.

Enter into this labyrinthine work, and you are in danger of being lost for ever in the rich imaginative thought-world which James Frazer spun out of his training in classics, his skill in romantic descriptions of the natural world, his evident calling to be an anthropological detective, and his monumental assemblage of the best anthropological data then available to him. After reading *The Golden Bough*, you will most likely see dying and rising corn-spirits and tree-gods everywhere. Every sunset and sunrise, every autumn and spring, every cycle of the phases of the moon will display a dying and rising god, calling for propitiation and sacrifice, and reminding you of the primitive though utterly mistaken beliefs which all 'civilised men' carry around beneath the thin veneer of such scientific knowledge as they have.

It is a magnificent work, one that anyone interested in religious beliefs and their origin simply has to read sooner or later. But is it magnificently wrong? Frazer does not present his mass of data in a purely descriptive, neutral way. Far from it. He has an overtly stated theory, by means of which he hopes to explain the origin of religious beliefs, whether these beliefs are about the bad luck caused by walking under ladders or about the creation of the universe by a Supreme God.

His basic theory is simple. It is that humanity has passed through three main stages of thought, each one higher than and superseding its predecessor. First there is the age of magic, then that of religion, and finally that of science. 'The movement of the higher thought, so far as we can trace it, has on the whole been from magic through religion to science'.[21] In magic humans believe that there is an established order in nature which can be manipulated by following certain simple causal principles. These are the principles of homeopathic and contagious magic. By a natural, though mistaken, application of the association of ideas, 'primitive man' comes to think that like causes like, and that two things that are once contiguous continue to influence each other thereafter. 'Magic is a spurious system of natural law',[22] based on the correct recognition of order in nature, and the incorrect hypothesis that this order can be manipulated by using similarity and contiguity as causal mechanisms.

A simple example of homeopathic magic is the scattering of water to make it rain. Another would be the performance of an act of sexual congress on a cornfield to make the corn fertile. An example of contagious magic would be sticking pins into a doll dressed in cuttings from a person's clothes, in order to cause that person pain or even death. In general, the idea is that certain human acts can cause changes in nature, because of their similarity to, or close connection with, the desired occurrences. Primitive man believes in the omnipotence of the human will, and thinks he can control nature, or even that he is responsible for making the sun rise or the corn grow.

This, Frazer thinks, is the original, most primitive stage of human thought. But sooner or later humans discover that it is all a mistake – the sun rises whether or not you sacrifice a young maiden each day, and the spring comes whether or not you perform sexual orgies in winter. Nature goes on its way regardless of human actions. Then, says Frazer, 'in the acuter minds magic is gradually superseded by religion',[23] wherein nature is thought to be governed by 'certain great invisible beings' who need to be propitiated if humans are to get what they desire from nature.

Magic, then, is 'nothing but a mistaken application of the very simplest and most elementary processes of the mind, namely the association of ideas';[24] it is 'the bastard sister of science'.[25] Religion is in one sense higher, because it recognises that magic does not work. But in another sense religion is morally inferior, as well as being just as mistaken. For it supposes, wrongly, that events happen because of the whims of supernatural gods, to whom we must bow in submission and craven fear.

'By religion', says Frazer, 'I understand a propitiation or conciliation of powers superior to man which are believed to direct and control the course of nature and of human life'.[26] The words that Frazer chooses are worth noting carefully. 'Propitiation' is an action by means of which one hopes to appease or placate an offended or threatening enemy. 'Conciliation' is, similarly, something meant to overcome distrust or hostility, to turn aside some dangerous action. In using these words, religion is at once characterised as something concerned with fear and self-abasement, and its object, God or the gods, is seen as an enemy, a dangerous and powerful agent who is yet vain and stupid enough to be placated by various rituals and incantations.

Now it is indeed Frazer's belief that primitive humans were largely lost in 'the jungle of crass ignorance and blind fear',[27] so that the older a belief is the more ignorant and obtuse it is likely to be. Primitive religion, then, will obviously be a mass of ignorance and fear, and the more primitive (the earlier) it is the more benighted it will be – but it is Frazer himself who has decreed that it must be so, by his assumption that 'primitive men' were superstitious and mentally undeveloped.

We might pause, then, to ask whether it is really quite so obvious that our hunter-gathering ancestors were much more mentally undeveloped than Cambridge classicists, and whether we can be quite so sure that the 'primitively scientific' approach of magic preceded the first contemptible and ridiculous efforts to placate the hidden and arbitrary gods which saw the birth of religion.

A fairly typical passage from Frazer reads as follows:

> If in the most backward state of human society now known to us we find magic thus conspicuously present and religion conspicuously absent, may we not reasonably conjecture that the civilised races of the world have also at some period of their history passed through a similar intellectual phase, that they attempted to force the great powers of nature to do their pleasure before they thought of courting their favour by offerings and prayer?[28]

It is the unfortunate Aborigines of Australia who were usually selected as the most backward humans available, and whose practices were then projected back to the universal childhood of humanity. In assessing such comments and comparisons, it must first be granted that an evolutionary account of human origins is almost universally accepted by natural scientists. So presumably for hundreds of thousands of years there existed humanoid beings with mental abilities somewhere between those of modern *Homo sapiens* and chimpanzees. In other words, the human race, or its immediate evolutionary predecessor, has passed through stages of mental development, and any beliefs and practices such beings had would be much less abstract and certainly much less informed than those of typical modern Cambridge classicists. If we could discover the practices of early humanoids, they would be much simpler and less sophisticated than those of the best-educated members of the species as it now exists.

Sir James never met any of these savages – when he looked for their nearest counterparts, he looked among the superstitious peasantry of Europe, or the more backward parts of the Scottish Highlands. He did not actually ask them for some account of their beliefs and practices, but relied on the vast store of information, which he gathered from classical texts, the reports of missionaries and businessmen, and folk-tales of the world. And his principle, put rather crudely, seems to have been this: what is superstitious and absurd among civilised nations now is what is completely normal among the primitive races and was universal in the early history of humanity. It is by looking at folk-tales and rustic rituals that we can discover, admittedly by a great deal of reconstruction and detective work, the origins of religion in the earliest history of the human race.

It is indisputable that there is a great deal of deceit, superstition, manipulation, and credulity in matters of religion, as there is in matters of politics, art, morality, and anything touched by human thought. Today's astrology columns testify to the persistence among large numbers of people of a scientifically unfounded belief in some sort of ability to predict the future from the position of the stars at the time of a person's birth. Perhaps some far future historian, from a study of some newspapers that somehow survived the great disaster that destroyed our civilisation, would surmise that the foundation of our religious beliefs was a false scientific theory of how the stars cause things to happen by magical influence.

So in religion there are many well-attested accounts of human and animal sacrifice, of the burning of witches, and of gruesome rites of self-torture and flagellation. These occur not only among 'primitive tribes' – the Aborigines know few things of that sort, in fact – but among the so-called 'higher' religions, where they tend to recur from time to time. It would be agreed by all that such practices go against the spirit of the great religions, and far from being their foundation are aberrations of a wholly reprehensible sort. Their occurrence may be adduced by the mythological detective as evidence for the survival of earlier, more primitive strands of religion, through a later, more ethically developed, faith. But why should they be the more primitive and original, rather than what they might more naturally seem to be, degradations from a quasipersonal relationship of reverence and awe before the great spirit or spirits who is known in and through the immediate apprehension of the human environment?

The evolutionary anthropologists E.B. Tylor and James Frazer both opposed the 'degradation' theory as an unsubstantiated theological dogma, which depended on there being some supernatural and original revelation, from which humans had subsequently declined. Against it they set the evolutionary view that human thought had developed greater sophistication and ethical insight as time went on. On the other hand, they did admit that humans had not in fact progressed morally to a great extent, as the devastating wars of the twentieth century were to prove.

On evolutionary principles, at least as understood in a roughly Darwinian sense, there is no reason why things should progress in any uniform direction. We are familiar with the fact that great civilisations, such as those of Egypt, Greece and Rome, can fade away and be succeeded by ages of barbarism. So, in the long history of human development, is it not possible that some abilities and sensibilities may degrade, or remain unused, and by their lack of use atrophy?

Shifting attention from the Aborigines, consider a safely extinct religion, that of the Aztecs, which most people would consider truly horrible in its extravagant reliance on human sacrifice. No doubt this is based on a belief that the sun god requires human blood to give warmth and heat. But what evidence is there that such a belief is a truly ancient one, which the Aztecs have preserved intact, while other cultures have given it up long ago? I think the plain answer is that it is simply so repugnant that it seems to call for a less cultivated, and therefore less evolved, moral sensibility than that of Cambridge professors.

Frazer himself thinks this to be a degraded belief, in the sense that it is 'religious' propitiation of the sun god, which has morally degraded from a simple magical mechanism for keeping the sun going, though it has intellectually upgraded in seeing that the magic does not work automatically. But might it not be degraded from a prior properly religious belief that the sun god was not to be placated by human blood, but adored by reverence, love of nature, and hard work? Why, in other words, should the bloody, repugnant and immoral be the original?

Few would today maintain that God really walked in the Garden of Eden with Adam and Eve, and that the original revelation, from which all else has degraded, is to be found there. But might it not be true that the requirements of bloody sacrifices and sexual orgies, which characterise some ancient cultures, represent the triumph of the will to aggression and lust over an earlier, or at least over an equally ancient, set of rituals which were much gentler, and concerned with establishing harmony with the natural world and good relations among humans and animals?

Perhaps at a very early stage there existed a matriarchal society, which was later overturned by male militarism and the corruption of religious ritual by imperial ambitions. I would not insist upon this, though some feminist anthropologists and archaeologists have adduced some evidence for it. What I would suggest is that we simply do not know enough about the pre-literate origins of religion to be sure. And if you were inclined to think there actually is a creator God, it might seem reasonable to suppose that the earliest humanoids were able to relate to that God – probably not explicitly known as one creator – as a beneficent power. Since most theists would also say that at an early stage in history humans followed a path of egoism and the will to power, when they need not have done so, it would then follow that human religions, too, would reflect the egoism and lust to power of their adherents. It is not at all absurd to think of many degradations in religion, and to think that the earliest ritual practices might have been as much concerned with ideas of harmony and balance in nature as with gratifying selfish human desires by appeasing wrathful gods.

What I chiefly want to point out, though, is that Frazer does appear to assume that the earlier a practice is, the bloodier, more repugnant, absurd and immoral it must be. That sort of evolutionism does not seem to be well evidenced, and it evinces a view of human nature that might be counteracted by the reflection that the early stages of human evolution may well have shown traits both innocent and benign, as well as the cruder dispositions that came to dominate human history.

Frazer also assumes that the study of primitive religious practices will reveal the essential nature of religion most clearly. As Durkheim, who disagreed that primitive religion was based on fear and propitiation, put it, in primitive religion 'all is reduced to that which is indispensable'.[29] 'In the primitive religions, the religious fact still visibly carries the mark of its origins.'[30] So the earlier you get, the nearer you come to the essential core of religion. That was an agreed position among the early investigators of religion.

It is, however, a very odd position to take. Suppose someone said, 'In primitive chemistry, you discover what is really essential to chemistry. In fact, alchemy is the essential core of chemistry. That is what chemistry really is.' Or you might say, 'Astronomy began in Babylon with astrology. Therefore astrology is the core of astronomy.' These statements are clearly absurd. The earliest beginnings of any human activity are likely to be the least adequate or satisfactory, and to pre-date all the advances which define that activity at a later, more mature stage. So you might think that religion, too, begins with speculations and practices that were to be modified enormously in the course of history, and which are a very misleading guide to what religion essentially is – if, indeed, it is essentially anything. It is of interest to know that the earliest humans of whom we know had beliefs and practices which seem quite close to what we call religious beliefs and practices, and also that present-day undeveloped tribal societies have recognisably religious practices. This suggests a certain common human inclination to form religious beliefs, to have a religious orientation. What is odd is to think that the study of such beliefs will reveal what is central or most important to the present religions of developed technological societies. The very opposite is more likely to be true.

AN EXCURSUS ON THE HEBREW BIBLE

It is indeed hard to deny that there has been a certain sort of moral and spiritual development in the recorded history of humanity. The Hebrew Bible (the Old Testament) is one of the earliest and most complete records of the religious history of a human culture, and it shows clear signs of developing insights over many years.

In the written Torah, which is everything from Genesis to Deuteronomy, including, by tradition, 613 commands of God given through Moses, one command is the extermination of those citizens of Canaan who refuse to accept Israelite domination. Men, women, children and even cattle are to be wholly exterminated, 'devoted to God', and nothing is to be taken as booty.[31] Such a command, given today, would be regarded with horror, and no modern Jew would believe that God would issue it now.

Moral advances have been made from time to time in human history. Within the Bible itself, there has developed a greater sense of individual responsibility, of humane punishment and of protection of the innocent. These are advances, and they have sometimes been made in the face of opposition and with difficulty. But that is not to say that religion began in fear and cruelty, which were overcome only as the sense of religion weakened.

There was fear and cruelty, but there was also kindness and compassion, expressed in the Old Testament laws enjoining compassion and mercy, and setting out times of celebration of the joy of life and of liberation. It was the great prophets who deepened appreciation of what justice and mercy requires, and insisted that ancient tribal taboos be interpreted in ways that made for human flourishing.

Such progress as there was did not move from religious fear to secular responsibility. It was a development within the religious tradition, highlighting the elements of reverence and love of neighbour that had always been there, and discarding old interpretations which were more clearly seen to be in conflict with the basic religious principles of *chesed*, loving-kindness, and *chokmah*, wisdom.

Thus the prophet Ezekiel uttered a new injunction, in about the eighth century BCE, that only the guilty are to be punished for their own crimes.[32] This is a definite advance on the earlier view that whole families could be punished for the crimes of one of their members.

There are also many rules in Torah which are concerned with ritual uncleanness caused by such things as menstruation, and again this provides evidence of a time when issues of blood were regarded as dangerous manifestations of holy power, against which people needed to be protected by taboos.

Many of the rules of Torah seem totally obscure to contemporary believers, whether they are Orthodox or not – they are often called 'inexplicable ordinances'. It is one of the major insights of early modern anthropology to find parallels to such rules in the practices of undeveloped and pre-literary tribal cultures in the modern world, and so explain their origin in earlier stages of Hebrew culture. Whereas few, if any, members of European societies would seriously think that eating pigs was actually dangerous, one can find tribal cultures in which the ordinary eating of pigs, or other animals, is prohibited, precisely because they are regarded as receptacles of holy power, which may break out and harm the populace. A study of primal cultures can show the widespread incidence of rules of 'holiness' or 'sacred power', which set apart animals or things as powerful and dangerous vehicles of spirit force, to be surrounded with prohibitions and rituals of various kinds. This illuminates many of the rules of Torah, and gives a high probability to the view that they are survivals of earlier beliefs that have been superseded.

The Bible also shows beliefs being superseded within its own pages. Whereas Yahweh was regarded as one among many gods, the god of Abraham and his descendants, it was the great prophets of Israel who firmly established Yahweh as the one and only creator of all things, the only god, before whom all other gods were unreal. In the history of Israel, we can trace a development from polygamy to monogamy, from punitive punishments of whole groups to the idea of proportional retributive punishment, from a world of many national gods to the idea of one creator, and from rules for ritual purity and elaborate animal sacrifice to the idea that the true worship of God is found in the pursuit of justice and mercy.

So in the Hebrew Bible we can see a development of beliefs about moral conduct and about the character of God, which is associated very largely with a series of critical reforms in the eighth to the sixth centuries BCE, and the rise of the major prophets – Isaiah, Ezekiel and Jeremiah. The Bible itself, which was once thought to speak of a primal perfect knowledge of God in Eden, followed by a degradation of beliefs through sin, actually illustrates very well that moral and religious beliefs in some ways changed as moral principles were more clearly seen as rules for imitating God's justice and mercy. The Bible, while it may at first sight suggest a degradation view of religion, actually manifests an evolutionist view, of a progress, made through a series of reforms, from the existence of sets of taboos associated with a tribal war god (the Lord of Hosts or armies) towards a more moral and rational concept of God. Possibly the fairest view to take is that there is both progress and degradation in the biblical record, in differing respects. But that there is some progress seems clear.

PRIMITIVE SCIENCE AND RELIGION

The two great contributions of Tylor and Frazer, the comparative method of seeing religious beliefs and practices in a global context and the evolutionist method of tracing many beliefs as survivals of or developments from earlier and simpler beliefs, greatly helps the understanding of biblical belief. I think we may take it as established that 'wherever there are found elaborate arts, abstruse knowledge, complex institutions, these are results of gradual development from an earlier, simpler, and ruder state of life. No stage of civilisation comes into existence spontaneously, but grows or is developed out of the stage before it.'[33]

The evolutionist method leads us to see present religion as a development from earlier, simpler forms. And we can find evidence of those simpler forms in extant documents from ancient cultures such as Egypt and Mesopotamia, in archaeological remains of even earlier states of human existence, and in the practices of non-literate societies throughout the world. Of course present non-literate traditions cannot immediately be assumed to be the same as those of Stone Age humans, for instance. But their practices are remarkably similar to many of those recorded in ancient documents, including the Hebrew Bible, and they are certainly less intellectually articulated and simpler than most literate forms of religion. So they are suggestive of earlier stages of religion, even if they cannot be taken as actually showing us what earlier religion was like.

All this Frazer shows us. But problems begin to appear when he develops his own theory that magic preceded religion, and that religion is the placation of angry gods. Frazer thinks of early humans as primitive philosophers, seeking to explain and control their environment. He assumes that the most elementary form of explanation is the association of ideas, found in homeopathic and contagious magic. Religion, involving the more abstract hypothesis of a controlling spirit, arises only when that elementary theory is found to fail.

There are two hugely questionable assumptions here – that early religion was a matter of theoretical, quasi-scientific explanation, and that religious practice is a matter of getting things to happen in the way one wants, either by magic or by obsequious pleading. It is at once obvious that these assumptions could only be made by one who does not belong to any living religious tradition, and who in fact regards religion as some sort of theoretical mistake.

Frazer does not disguise this fact. As he concludes *The Golden Bough*, he compares magic, religion and science to 'a web woven of three different threads – the black thread of magic, the red thread of religion, and the white thread of science'.[34] He says, 'There rests on the middle portion of the web, where religion has entered most deeply into its texture, a dark crimson stain'. And then he asks, 'Will a reaction set in which may arrest progress and even undo much that has been done? Will it [the web] be white or red?'[35] Clearly, religion is now a reactionary, anti-scientific force, which should be encouraged to fade away as rapidly as possible.

Now if religion is what Frazer thinks it is, a mistaken series of immoral and irrational beliefs, we can understand his point of view. But might it not be better to ask sophisticated modern adherents of some religious tradition what they think religion is and what it means to them?

One immediate result of such an enquiry would surely be to suggest that people are not primarily interested in trying to explain why events happen, and their practice is not primarily intended to make things happen as they wish. The contemporary Christian does not go to church to find out how televisions or transistors work, or to make sure that she gets a good job. Appeal to God is so far from explaining anything that it is more often a puzzle than a clarification. The query, 'Why does God allow suffering?' never explains it; it intensifies the problem. So it seems very odd to suggest that the motivation for belief in God is a desire for explanation. Similarly, Christians are usually castigated by preachers for trying to use religion as a means to worldly success. Abandonment to the divine will is more often recommended than attempts to get God to do what one wants. Of course, in prayer people often do ask God to do what they would like to see. But it again seems very odd to suggest that this is the primary reason for their practice, when it is so frequently and vehemently criticised by most Christian teachers as mislocating the primary importance of the adoration of God as a being of supreme value.

Is what is going on, then, an interpretation of religion in terms of its worst features – those features that religious teachers themselves criticise – and a complete neglect of the question of how religious belief differs from scientific, moral or aesthetic belief and practice? If we could isolate something distinctive about religious belief, we might seek its roots in some more elementary forms at the dawn of human history. But we would not be compelled to think that these roots are going to be a complete compendium of all the worst features of present religion, which are assumed to have been its total content in the cruder and simpler days of savagery.

The most questionable part of Frazer's analysis, then, is his thesis that magic is prior to religion, and is an attempt to explain nature in a quasi-scientific way. The beliefs that the cosmos exhibits an unchanging order, and that the human will can control this order by homeopathic or contagious practices, are really quite sophisticated, as is science. Would it not seem simpler, more elementary, for humans to take nature as representing the same sort of personal forces that they find bodies, themselves small parts of nature, to represent? The personalisation of natural forces and events suggests itself as readily as the acceptance that human bodies are those of persons. As far as simplicity goes, Frazer's 'religion' seems to be simpler than his magic. But this might also lead us to think that such personalisation is not an attempt to explain the occurrence of events. It is rather an attempt to enter into certain sorts of personal relation with natural powers – relationships of awe, reverence, gratitude and, yes, intercession. This is not a scientific hypothesis, but the adoption of a basic reactive attitude to the natural powers that surround us, and of which we are part. This supposal could well seem as arbitrary as Frazer's conception of the savage as a very naive empiricist philosopher. But there is overwhelming evidence for it in the 'primitive' religions that exist in the world today, and that Frazer uses as the evidence for his theory.

THE NUER AND HOPI

It is possible to see this by examining a case that can easily be thought to give support to a Frazerian attitude to 'primitive' religion. The case can be found in the work of Edward Evans-Pritchard, Professor of Social Anthropology at Oxford from 1946 to 1970, who published a classic anthropological study of the African tribe the Nuer.[36] Their religion could easily be seen, and has been seen, as an almost wholly superstitious, animistic and terror-inspired religion of fear. The Nuer have whole rafts of sacrificial and propitiatory rites to appease the spirits who bring disease and misfortune to the tribe, and they seem ideal candidates for a Frazerian treatment. But Evans-Pritchard gives a much more sympathetic account, in which he points out that the primary motivation of the Nuer is to drive away sickness and evil, and achieve wholeness of life and well-being. There are many spirit powers, both good and evil, but they all relate to – or are forms of – Kwoth, the great 'spirit in the sky', who is a friend and presence as well as a distant and fearsome creator. The spirits are imaginative constructions that present particular ways in which Kwoth, Spirit, is apprehended in events in tribal and personal life. In the end, Evans-Pritchard claims, 'Nuer religion is ultimately an interior state ... externalised in rites'.[37] It is not a theoretical attempt to explain the world, and it is not simply a set of magical techniques to avert evil. It is centred on 'a strong sense of dependence on God', even though it involves many beliefs about spirit influences, which complicate the understanding of how people can achieve right relationship to Kwoth. Many aspects of Nuer religion – its acceptance of witchcraft and demon-possession, and its taboos and rituals for appeasing ghosts of the dead – might appear undesirable, psychologically harmful and pre-scientific. But we would misunderstand the religious life of the Nuer completely if we simply saw it in such terms. More important is the idea of Kwoth, Spirit, as expressed in personal experiences and historical events, and as evoking personal attitudes of reverence, gratitude and dependence in its devotees.

Donald Hughes, in his work on American Indian ecology, takes an even more positive attitude to Native American beliefs, which Frazer would undoubtedly have dismissed as savage and superstitious. Indians, says Hughes, see 'a community in nature of living beings among whom the Indians formed a part, but not all. There were also animals, trees, plants, and rivers, and the Indians regarded themselves as relatives of these, not as their superiors.'[38]

He points out that the Hopi spend about a third of their waking lives in ritual dances, prayers, songs and preparation for ceremonials. But these are not scientific experiments to cause changes in nature. They are celebrations of 'the mysterious interrelatedness of all that is, and attempts to stay in harmony with nature and maintain its balance. 'The offerings made ... are not so much sacrifices as things given in exchange for other things taken or killed, to maintain the balance. A ceremony is one way in which people contribute to maintaining the world as it should be.'[39] 'Indians regarded things in nature as spiritual beings, not because they were seeking some explanation for natural phenomena, but because human beings experience a spiritual resonance in nature.' The ceremonies are not, as Tylor and Frazer supposed – never having asked a

Native American – attempts to bend nature to the human will, but ways of subordinating the human will to natural rhythms. Black Elk said, 'with all beings and all things we shall be as relatives'.[40]

One may sometimes feel that tribal religions are here being given a Romantic and sentimentalised makeover, tailored to an ecologically aware and rather guilty audience. Nevertheless, these accounts give a much better idea of what tribal believers might say – and it is interesting that primal religions throughout the world are experiencing a revival, in opposition to what are seen as the destructive, patriarchal and repressive tendencies of the 'great religions', and of Western liberal imperialism. The marks of that revival are a reiteration of reverence for the natural world, in contrast with the Western tradition, which has seen nature as just a means to human dominance and comfort. The revenge of the savage mind is to see Frazer as cut off from his roots in nature, as having a radically self-deceived view of the superiority of rational human thought to feelings of unity with nature, which the primal traditions celebrate.

Native Americans do regard everything in nature as powerful, able to help or harm. Things mediate *wakan*, sacred power that permeates all its forms (in this it is similar to the Nuer idea of Kwoth). *Wakan-Tanka* is the great Mystery of which nature and human alike are parts. Indian life is a 'constant conversation with the sacred universe'.[41] Is this to be seen as an infantile personification of impersonal laws and forces, a projection of the human mind onto the external world? Or is it a recognition, not formulated in any systematic way, that nature herself is a sacred power, the giver of life, to be revered as well as respected, the Power which embraces humans as those called to respect and further her inborn potencies?

Tylor and Frazer were right in saying that there is a fundamental divide in human thought, between those who see nature as an ordered and impersonal system in which one event follows another necessarily and invariably without the intervention of any spiritual or personal agency, and those who see nature as a system of signs and symbols of an underlying quasi-personal reality.

What we call 'religion' seeks to evoke an intuition of such spiritual power, and that is its most fundamental role. To overlook that fact, which is testified to by religious believers themselves, is to overlook the central distinctive feature in religious belief, and to assume the truth of materialism – and can such an assumption really underpin an 'explanation' of what religion is?

With hindsight, it is easy for us to say that the evolutionism of the early anthropologists erred in assuming that the more elementary and primitive a belief the more stupid, fearful and morally crude it must be. We need to be much more discriminating in our treatment of primal traditions. They may indeed embody pre-scientific worldviews and morally limited perceptions. But they can be seen as responses, from particular cultural settings, to what is perceived to be of transcendent, objective and commanding value. That value may not be clearly identified and fully reflected upon – it would be hard to say that our current notions of value have been! It may be mixed, as much religion is, with cruder ideas of human sacrifice and magical rituals. But a theist might expect that early religion is founded basically upon reverence and gratitude, upon self-examination and moral commitment, upon the celebration of value in symbolic forms taken from the environment and from crucial events in tribal history. They were right to look for an evolutionary account of religion, but highly dubious in assuming that it was originally founded on fear and on mistaken attempts to explain why things happen.

In a rather similar way, the comparativism of these thinkers is groundbreaking in its insistence on treating religion as a global phenomenon, and in looking outside one particular religious tradition to find what is characteristic of religious thought and practice. But it is also restricted, in finding the common basis of religion to lie in a quasi-scientific search for explanation. Is it at all plausible to think that the elaborate genealogies of the gods, the highly imaginative descriptions of their powers and properties and the narratives of their quarrels and exploits are attempts to explain natural phenomena? Stories of the gods are more like literature than like physics. That is what Tylor and Frazer missed – and at least in Frazer's case, that is very ironic, as *The Golden Bough* is one of the finest literary fairy-stories ever told.

If these religious stories explain, it is in the sense that art explains, and it might be wondered whether that should be called 'explanation' at all. They do, or they do hope to, tell us something about the world. But what they tell us is that there is a transcendent depth, underlying the visible and tangible, to which we can relate, knowledge of which will bring a distinctive sort of fulfilment. That is not explanation. It is revelation, in the true sense – drawing back the veil of space and time to reveal what is hidden, what is beyond, what, among all the concerns and cares of every-day life, might easily be missed.

Who draws back the veil? Those with the ability to penetrate beyond, whether that is by being taken up into the world of the gods, or by the attainment of wisdom and enlightenment through long self-discipline. Thus Moses and Muhammad hear the gods, or God, speak. Jesus is claimed to be a unique mediator between God and the world. The Buddha attains *nirvana* through meditation. Confucius apprehends the Tao through wisdom. And Plato works it all out by pure thinking – or so his followers say. All of them bring back to this transient world metaphors and images, which glow with the mysterious light of eternity, which resound with a beauty and power which time-bound understanding can never match. On their words are founded traditions which seek to re-evoke the origina-tive insight which they express, so that other, more mundane lives can, in a form and to an extent that is possible for them, share in eternity.

All of this may indeed be a mistake, a deep and ineradicable human illusion. Proponents of the secular worldview would say that it is. But there is no way of establishing on neutral grounds that it is so, and it is largely prejudice that leads some to think that the systematic study of religions must assume it to be so. Secular worldviews are as ideo-logically committed and value-laden as any religious worldview, and methodological atheism, far from being necessary to the scientific study of religions, may plausibly be thought to impede the understanding of religious belief.

Find out more...

James Frazer, *The Golden Bough* (abridged edn 1922, republished Harmondsworth: Penguin, 1996). Still a classic, though anthropologists would regard it as archaic. Reading chapters 1–4, 16, 23, 27, 28, 49, 68, 69 and the conclusion will give a good impression of the overall work.

David Hume, *Dialogues and Natural History of Religion*, ed. J.C.A. Gaskin ([1757] Oxford: Oxford University Press, 1993), is one of the first (but very prejudiced) accounts of the nature of religion in English.

E. Evans-Pritchard, *Nuer Religion* (Oxford: Clarendon Press, 1956), is a good case study of one African traditional religion. The same author's *Theories of Primitive Religion* (Oxford: Clarendon Press, 1965) is a hilarious critique of early theories of religion.

Daniel Pals, *Seven Theories of Religion* (Oxford: Oxford University Press, 1996), presents excellent expositions and critiques of seven major theorists of religion, including Tylor and Frazer.

J. Samuel Preus, *Explaining Religion* (New Haven: Yale University Press, 1987), gives a very clear exposition of Bodin, Herbert, Fontenelle, Vico, Hume, Comte, Tylor, Durkheim and Freud – all important writers on religion. Preus has an axe to grind – religious studies must be committed to naturalism. He dislikes talk of 'the transcendent', holding it to be superfluous and vacuous.

3

THE SIGH OF THE
OPPRESSED

Explanations of Religion as a Social Construct

Religious believers think that there is a transcendent or supernatural reality, that some knowledge of it is possible, and that such knowledge will help to achieve human good. There is an important claim to truth in religion. Believers think that their images speak, however inadequately, of that which is most truly real, and of ultimate significance for their lives and for the human future.

The strange thing is that many of the best-known writers who have studied religion as a global phenomenon in the last one hundred and fifty years have denied this fact. Or at least they thought that religious believers were deceived about the real nature of what they were doing. Believers may think they are speaking of an objective spiritual reality. They may indeed be referring to something. But that thing is not what they think. It is incumbent upon unbelievers to give some account of how religious beliefs arise and become so very important to vast numbers of people, many of them intelligent and morally sensitive people. The believers' account is, of course, that since there is such a reality, it will become known, or will even make itself known, to those who seek it. The 'making known' may not be immediate, definite, and unmistakably clear. It may be, as most human knowledge is, a gradually developing matter, involving many imaginative hypotheses, much culturally influenced experience, and a cumulative tradition of wisdom. But basically, the hope is that humans will gradually grow in knowledge of what spiritual reality is like.

For the unbeliever, this whole religious quest must be based on an illusion. The trouble is that the illusion does not seem to be fading away. It seems firmly rooted in human nature. That does require some explanation. Atheists who have studied religion have obligingly come up with explanations, though it is questionable whether they are very convincing. The fact that there are so many different explanations, each claiming to be the truly explanatory one, is not a very good start.

Such explanations fall into three main groups. There are explanations such as those of Tylor and Frazer, which see religion as a primitive form of science, long outdated. There are explanations in psychological terms, showing how religious beliefs originate in various states of mind, usually subconscious, which rise to consciousness in dreams or visions. There are explanations in social terms, seeing how religious beliefs help to consolidate certain forms of social order, or perhaps compensate for the inability to gain social satisfaction. A modern variant, evolutionary psychology, tries to show how some beliefs have been conducive to survival in human prehistory, and have continued to be selected because of their efficacy in sustaining specific sorts of society.

The import of all these forms of explanation is to show how such a false system of beliefs could become so important and enduring in human life. If the beliefs were not false, the best form of explanation, and the only adequate one, would show how humans could become acquainted with the spiritual reality that such beliefs postulate. Other forms of explanation could be significant parts of a total explanation. Intellectual forms of explanation might be, not in terms of primitive science, but in terms of a metaphysical vision of reality as fundamentally based on mind or Spirit. Psychological forms of explanation might not show the growth of neuroses in religion, but ways in which religious belief can contribute to mental health and stability, or to personal integration. Social forms of explanation do not have to be in terms of reinforcement of the status quo or compensation for social disadvantage. They could be in terms of the reinforcement of social ideals and personal empowerment for moral action. These forms of explanation can, in other words, give a much more positive interpretation of religion. But the success of a positive account would probably depend on the claims of religion being accepted as true by the believer. It would be difficult to accept a religious view solely on the grounds that it would provide a coherent metaphysical vision of reality, that it contributes to mental health, or that it reinforces social ideals. We might be very happy that it does these things, but we would also need to think that it was true, if all these positive effects were not to be undermined by our knowledge that they were based on illusion. I might be very cheerful if I could make myself believe that I had won the lottery. But if I also really knew that there was no lottery, and that I had not won it, it would be hard to maintain my cheerfulness for very long.

EMILE DURKHEIM

Anyone who seeks to give a purely naturalistic explanation of religious belief is compelled to say that believers are deluded. There is then a tendency to look for the more negative types of explanation, since delusions are hardly a good basis for positive psychological and social attitudes. A major exception to this tendency is found in one of the great founders of the study of religion in its modern form, Emile Durkheim, who surprisingly asserts that all religions are true. The surprise is mitigated, however, when we discover that this is a rather confusing way of saying what he really means, which is that all religions are false. Religion, he says, is 'an essential and permanent aspect of humanity'. It is so universal that 'it cannot rest upon an error and a lie'.[42] What is true about it, however, is that it fulfils important functions in human life. 'Religious representations are collective representations which express collective realities.'[43] Rituals excite, maintain and recreate states of mind that subordinate the individual to the group, which make the moral ideals of the group dominant in the consciousness of its members. As he puts it in his best-known formulation, religion is a 'unified system of beliefs and practices relative to sacred things ... which unite into one single moral community called a church, those who adhere to them'.[44]

Durkheim insists that religions are social phenomena. Religion is not what an individual does with his solitude, as Whitehead and William James claimed. It is a way of shaping communal life. In the rites and stories of religion, individuals come to apprehend a way of seeing and responding to the reality theyexperience.

Further, religion is a moral phenomenon. It places ideals before individuals, and evokes strong passions of attachment to them. It is not, as Hume and Frazer claimed, based on fear and propitiation of angry gods. Its characteristic moods are reverence, joy and social harmony. These are the mental states that rituals seek to inculcate, as the individual is coaxed into subordinating himself to the collective consciousness of the group. The particular symbols and images of faith are not as important as what they symbolise. They symbolise what Durkheim calls 'the Totemic principle', which he describes as an immaterial force diffused through animals, men and things: 'Totemism is the religion of an anonymous and impersonal force.'[45] The idea of such a force precedes personal theism. It acts for good and evil, can be possessed, and shows itself in power and excellence. It is, he thinks, the power of the clan, in its well-being and its ill-being.

This supernatural (immaterial) power may seem to be morally ambiguous, but it has strong moral overtones, and is rapidly moralised: 'The great tribal god is only an ancestral spirit who finally won a pre-eminent place. The ancestral spirits are only entities forged in the image of individual souls whose origin they are destined to explain. The souls are only the form taken by individualised impersonal mana.'[46] We must be on our guard whenever this word 'only' is used, and also when a confident account is given of the order of events that happened long before recorded history. Durkheim posits an increasing personalisation of the totemic principle. With that personalisation goes a move from seeing transcendence as a sort of blind energy or force to seeing it as a personal agent, with purposes that must at least seem good to the agent. The totemic principle becomes no longer blind or undirected, and it comes to have purposes that are directed to some desirable goal.

In fact, the totemic principle was never entirely blind, for it is aware of human acts, punishing infringements of taboos and responding to prayers and ritual acts of sacrifice. It represents some sort of rudimentary moral order. Indeed, it is more closely connected to morality than that, for 'the god of the clan, the totemic principle, can be nothing else than the clan itself, personified and represented to the imagination under the visible form of the animal or vegetable'.[47] It is a moral authority that demands self-sacrifice and co-operation, and evinces respect in the individual.

It is at first hard to see how the totemic principle can be both a morally neutral energy and also the moral authority of the clan. The point is that, insofar as it is seen as an impersonal power, it refers to the causal bases of events, and they can be catastrophic and destructive as well as beneficent – this is moral neutrality. Insofar as it is seen as a moral ideal, it refers to the obligations that raise individuals above themselves to a higher state (in Durkheim's phrase). For Durkheim, there is no causal power of a spiritual nature, so this part of primitive belief is false. The group consciousness is not an objective personal being, but simply the power of the group, which has no physical causal power at all, and which might be oppressive as well as beneficent.

But the moral power of the totemic principle is extremely strong. Durkheim holds that 'moral remaking ... is the principal object of the positive rite',[48] and that the object of religion is 'to raise man above himself and to make him lead a life superior to that which he would lead'.[49] The totemic principle can be misused, but its proper use is that of internalising the group consciousness in the individual, which is a positive and dynamic power. It can even be spoken of as divine: 'There really is a particle of divinity in us because there is within us a particle of these great ideas which are the soul of the group.'[50]

Thus Durkheim holds that there is an immaterial power which, though it can be misused in repressive and frightening ways, can also be properly channelled, through group rituals, to evoke reverence and joy in individuals, and fill them with the desire to sacrifice themselves for the sake of great moral ideals, thought of as greater than any personal desires, and immensely worthwhile. This power is symbolised in various ways, but its reality lies beyond the symbol, and has its own life. It is essential to the good of communal life that this power should be effectively symbolised and become the object of reverence and the source of power for living well, for raising human lives to a divine level through the performance of ritual.

All this seems to me a good description of how religious life, even in its allegedly most primitive forms, is centred on reverence for a morally transcendent immaterial (and that means spiritual) reality. The specific ways in which this Transcendent is symbolised and ritually mediated arise from the history and practices of the clan or tribe. They are local, and often specifically exclude or oppose the practices of other clans, who may well be seen as enemies. But they do have the capacity to raise individual humans to a superior level of morality, as they see it, and creative power. Religious life is centred on the idea of a spiritual or divine reality (which does not have to be imagined in a very personalistic way), and on human participation in the divine life.

But then Durkheim goes on to spoil the whole thing by saying 'the god of the clan ... can be nothing else than the clan itself'.[51] Why can it be nothing else? Why cannot it just be a god? Durkheim seems to think that, because societies are so various, there are many differing, and often conflicting, ideas of God. They cannot all be correct, and it is not fair to privilege one set of beliefs above another. So the fairest thing is to admit that none of them refers to an objective cosmological reality at all. The object of reference must therefore be a social construct, differing from clan to clan. It is objective, but the objectivity is that of the social mind of the clan, not of some truly external cosmic or supra-cosmic object.

Since religion is necessary, valuable and true, there must be some religious object. Only the group mind is left to be such an object. But isn't it obvious that the group mind is even more of a mythological projection than god? If you tell any religious believer that what they are really worshipping is the collective consciousness of their society, the response is likely to be one of alarmed and vehement denial. If I look at a hypothetical Mrs Smith and Mr Jones, who are members of my society, with all their quirks and oddities, I certainly would not worship them. Now if you tell me that I should worship society, which is made up of hundreds of Smiths and Joneses, the whole thing gets a hundred times worse. To worship Mr Smith is bad enough. But to worship Mr Smith reified, magnified and multiplied is a truly horrifying prospect. Why should I worship my group? Religion is critical of group mores as often as it is supportive of them. Were the prophets of Israel supporting the group mind of the Israelites? They certainly had an odd way of showing it, and their condemnations of group behaviour were in general not well received.

Sometimes religious rites may generate social enthusiasm and commitment to shared ideals. But the mass rallies of nationalist political parties seem even more effective in this respect. There often is a connection between ethnic or nationalist identity and religious identity – to have a 'Christian nation' or a 'Muslim nation' is often thought to be desirable. But the situation is usually very complex. People who think there should be a Christian state think that because they think Christianity is true, and its rules should be sanctioned by the state. They do not think that the state, whatever it is, should be sanctioned by Christianity, or by some religion invented especially for that purpose. They certainly do not think that Christianity should support whatever the state says. On the contrary, the state should do what Christianity (in its locally preferred form) says. And the same is true of Islam. To put the group before the religion is to put the cart before the horse.

So even in religious states, it is accepted that the religion can be critical of the state, and has normative superiority in the final analysis. The belief that a nation should conform to the moral ideals of some religion is at the opposite extreme from the belief that a religion should express the moral ideals of some state. Durkheim has turned things completely upside down.

He is right, of course, in saying that religions do not descend in a pristine state from some supernatural realm. They do relate to the beliefs and interests of the societies in which they originate. The insights they bring are often, perhaps always, limited by the horizons of those societies. One of the most obvious ways in which this is true is the patriarchal nature of most religions. It is assumed that males will be the teachers and leaders of the religious community, and so priests or religious scholars are almost always male. Women are often excluded from public religious rituals, and given roles held to be better suited to childbearing and domestic life. This could be seen as a mandate of heaven, and it often has been. It is more likely, however, to be just an unreflective adoption of the male-centred attitudes of most human cultures. Since I cannot think of one good reason that now exists for such male-centredness, it might well seem one of the tasks of a morally oriented religion to countermand it.

If a religion did decide to promote female equality, however, would it be expressing moral ideals that reinforce the unity of the community? I fear not. It would simply cause more divisions and arguments. It would be wholly implausible to say that this religious insight expressed the mind of the society. Would it, then, reflect a conflict and change in the wider society, wrestling with moral problems of gender? Indeed it would. In Christianity, for example, those who rely on the literal teaching of the Bible would probably support male superiority. But it would be too simple to say that the 'reformers' are simply adopting a liberal secular agenda. Rather, general critical attitudes to the Bible came first, which led to the demand to justify acceptance of particular moral norms advocated in the Bible. Once this process began, it was easy to see much in the teaching of Jesus and Paul that commends equality of respect and consideration, and freedom from social conventions – and thus suggests sexual equality.

In other words, it was not just an 'Enlightenment' or secular notion of equality which was brought in to oppose biblical teaching. It was an exploration of diverse biblical teachings, plus the need to justify particular interpretations. That did result from the 'Enlightenment' view that biblical authority needed to be critically examined – though not wholly rejected.

What is going on here is a reasoned consideration of how a religious text is to be interpreted, together with reasoned consideration of how moral principles can be justified. To suggest that all this is no more than the reflection of social, economic and power relations in a given society is to suggest that reason plays no important part in the process. What reason does is to test biblical statements against well-established historical or scientific statements for coherence, or look for coherence among biblical documents themselves. Reason asks how moral principles can be justified in ways that can stand the test of public scrutiny. Is it seriously being suggested that we should not seek such coherence, or seek justification for our beliefs?

There can be a (not very) thinly hidden agenda in the sociology of knowledge, which might, rightly or wrongly, claim Durkheim as its ancestor. That agenda is to show that human beliefs are the results of deeper forces of a search for power, or of economic processes that are beyond rational control. It is to downgrade reason by suggesting that reason itself is only a disguised appeal to power. So no view is objectively more 'reasonable' than any other. What you have to ask is not what the rational view is, but whom does your view oppress, and whose interests does it support?

That is a most important question to ask. The 'deconstructors' of reason raise it in intense form. But, taken on its own, it suggests that no moral ideals are any more reasonable than others. If I want to be sexist, racist and colonialist, that is no less rational than being egalitarian with regard to sex, race and nationhood. How then can I choose? What the deconstructors of reason show is not that reason is used too much, but that is not pressed far enough. Sexism flourishes because it is not seen that it cannot be rationally justified – i.e. there are no good reasons for giving males superiority, simply because they are male. Racism flourishes because it is not seen that there are no relevant differences between races that would justify inequality of treatment. European or 'Western' ideas of liberty, equality and democracy are not aggressively exploitative and colonialist. Regrettably, they have been espoused by people who are exploitative and colonialist, and who have limited their ideals to white males, who were taken to be the only truly civilised or rational beings to be included in the egalitarian community. What is wrong with that view is not the ideals, but the fact that they have not pressed far enough the question of what a rational being is, and what the limits of equal consideration truly are.

All this is just to say that morality, and religion too, is subject to rational consideration – to the demand for consistency, coherence and justification, a demand extremely simple to state, but hugely difficult to implement. Durkheim apparently would accept this, since he holds that religious beliefs must agree with science – and that requires precisely the sort of rational reflection just mentioned. But in that case one must allow that religion is not just expressing the social mind. It is also playing a part in forming the social mind. Or it may be challenging that mind, and introducing conflict into society on moral grounds. Durkheim's view seems to place religion in an inherently conservative position, as an expression of the status quo. Much religion is conservative. But much is radical, and seeks a reformation of society. It is hard to see how a Durkheimian view can cope with the fact of radical religious groups that seek to transform or even overturn the present social order. If they do so, is their belief-system not playing an important part in the process of social change?

FROM DURKHEIM TO MARX

This was a point the social historian Max Weber was concerned to make, that religious ideas could play a part in social change. They are not simply a causally ineffective, extrinsic feature of social life. Once in place, they have their own internal trajectory, which may either challenge or support particular social policies. There may be no direct causal relationship between a religious belief and social change. But there are what Weber called 'elective affinities' between some religious ideas and some social principles. When circumstances are right, such affinities can become co-operating causes of change, sometimes for better and sometimes for worse. Weber thought that the Protestant ethic and early capitalism was just such an elective affinity. It could be that certain forms of radical Islam and the political ideal of 'martyrdom' (which the rest of the world sees as terrorism) is such an elective affinity. Clearly, there is no real affinity between Islam and terrorism. But in particular situations, some strands of religious thought reinforce some social trends. In other situations, the peaceable and compassionate strands of Islam may find affinity with a liberal and humane social framework. Or Christians may discover teachings about equality and service of the poor in their tradition, which reinforce socialist teachings in their society. The web of causality is complex and diverse.

Religious ideas can take on many different complexions in different circumstances. They form a coherent set of meanings and readings of significance and value, which need to change and adapt as a whole, rather than by piecemeal adjustments. But it is positively misleading to think of the belief-system out of relation to any specific society, and equally misleading to miss the fact that how such religious systems change will be in large part dependent on the social and economic circumstances of particular societies.

It is for this reason that we cannot sensibly speak of 'religion' as being good or bad, or of it having just one sort of function in society. Religion is just more varied than Durkheim's analysis suggests. And most sociologists would agree that attention to particularity and the very complex interaction of local causes of many different kinds – economic, social and religious – is required if we are to say what the function of religion is in a particular society.

Sociology of religion has developed enormously since Durkheim, and few would now accept his ideas about group consciousness and the objective existence of social facts. But sociological analyses of religion are still important, and some of them pursue the Feuerbachian programme of seeing the gods as projections of social ideals, or as mechanisms of social control, defending particular conceptions of social power.

A major problem with the sociological study of religion is that it has often been closely bound up with a form of 'left-wing', non-theistic Hegelianism. Hegel brought to attention the way in which human beliefs have a history, and are integrated into complex social systems. 'Primitive' societies regard human social life as changeless, and rituals are often intended to preserve social order in a world that basically remains the same, or is continually in danger of disintegrating. In nineteenth-century Europe, however, the revolutionary changes that had been epitomised by the French Revolution engendered an evolutionary and optimistic view of social change. Human societies, by their increased mastery of the natural world, could for the first time order their lives on rational principles to increase the sum of human happiness for all.

Hegel's vision was of progressive historical change as expressing the self-realisation of Absolute Spirit. No longer was the world a realm of competing powers – life and death, light and darkness – in precarious interaction. Nor was it the medieval Christian world dominated by the Devil and destined for destruction, within which the Church was a ship riding the floods of time to rescue those who turned from chaos to its inviting light. For Hegel time became something positive, opening the possibility of progress and future fulfilment. The Divine Spirit itself entered into time, and there created its own perfection in and through the history of humanity.

Those who came after Hegel, and were known as 'left-wing' Hegelians, accepted his picture of history as an instrument of social change and improvement. But Absolute Spirit fell out of the picture. For them, there was no objective reality working in and through humanity. There was only humanity itself, bearing the banner of a future society of justice and happiness, to be forged by an iron will which would ruthlessly overthrow the restrictions of the past, and create itself as the coming perfected Spirit.

Thus Feuerbach postulated that 'God is merely the hypostatised and objectified essence of the human imagination'.[52] Man is not the expression of perfect Spirit. Rather, Spirit is a projection of the human will to self-realised perfection. Feuerbach speaks of the illusory, fantastic, heavenly position of God which in actual life necessarily leads to the degradation of man. Man conceives of the infinite potential of his own nature, not as a future goal to inspire positive revolutionary action, but as an actually existing perfect being. The existence of such a being 'degrades' humanity, since by comparison with it all humans are imperfect, nothing but worms alongside the perfect beauty of God. The worship of God fills man with the idea of his own unworthiness, with self-loathing, and an ultimate pessimism about his own ability to change anything for the better. Unless that God is dethroned, and replaced by the conscious idea of the future perfection of humanity itself, we will not be able to realise human destiny.

Karl Marx built on Feuerbach's idea that the idea of Spirit, or God, is a projection of an alienated human ideal. The idea comes to have two main functions, consolation and justification. 'The abolition of religion as the illusory happiness of the people is required for their real happiness.'[53] Those who are prevented by poverty and oppression from obtaining happiness find an illusory happiness in religion, and in the idea of a better life hereafter. On the other hand, as an agent of the state (as it was in Prussia and, in a different way, in England), religion functions to justify the status quo, an oppressive social order, by condemning as evil any attempt to overthrow state authorities, and by advocating humility and submission as primary virtues of the individual.

Religion is thus both the 'sigh of the oppressed creature' and an agent of social alienation and oppression. When humans are able to find their fulfilment in a just society of free and equal persons, the need for religion will simply disappear. The projection of God can be relocated where it belongs, in the fully realised social nature of humanity. Worship can be replaced by reverence for humanity, which is what it always secretly signified, though in a perverse and alienated fashion.

None of this can possibly qualify as an objective, 'scientific' study of religion and its many diverse forms. It is an ambitious worldview that sees history as a teleological process, culminating in a future perfection. This is an odd sort of teleology, a purpose that is not actually envisaged by any being, but just happens to come into existence. To believe in such a thing requires a faith at least as paradoxical as any theism, which at least posits a cosmic mind capable of envisaging and realising some purpose.

Moreover, the Marxian postulate that humans have infinite potential, which only needs the right social conditions to produce total fulfilment, is both theoretically dubious and highly value-laden (one might even say wish-fulfilling). Even if we do not like the idea of 'original sin', it seems clear to many that human nature, the result of a chequered evolutionary past, is far from perfect or perfectible. Lust and aggression are basic features of human life, and the idea that changing social conditions might eliminate them has no evidential basis. The history of Marxist experiments in the twentieth century provides no positive evidence in its favour.

Nor is it obvious that belief in a perfect God, just as such, is bound to degrade humans. There may be elective affinities in certain forms of religion, with which Feuerbach and Marx were acquainted, which lead to a sense of self-loathing. But if God is really supposed to be perfect, we might think this should lead to a view that God is loving and forgiving and encouraging, and will help us to realise our natures rather than repress them. Moreover, since for Jews and Christians humans are said to be made in the image of God, human nature is to be respected, not disparaged. For such believers, all innocent human life will be morally inviolate. By contrast, Marxist political regimes often show no reverence for the bourgeoisie, who are to be eliminated and ridiculed, as opponents of the true faith. It often seems as if Marxists advocate the worship of a perfected humanity, but hate and oppose almost all examples of actual humanity, particularly if it possesses property. This is as good an example of 'false consciousness' as any examples Marx ever claimed to find in religion.

The Marxist analysis requires us to see religion, like art, philosophy and science, as a superstructure that reflects the social conditions of its time. Weber, however, in his analysis of Protestantism and the capitalist ethic, proposed that it was precisely some new Protestant ideas that helped the cause of capitalism, not the economic situation that caused Protestantism. It does seem as though ideas and beliefs can have a causal part to play in the development of social life. They are not just by-products of social processes. Marx has successfully drawn attention to the close and complex relationship between social and economic facts and human beliefs and activities, but he has not shown that cultural artefacts are just by-products of specific societies.

Probably Mozart could only have written music as he did because he wrote for aristocratic patrons in a hierarchical society. But does that throw doubt on the value of his music? Or reduce it to a projection of aristocratic tea-parties? Probably not. So, in religion, it is worth reflecting on the socio-economic affiliations of particular religious views, which may sometimes be other than we think. But questions of coherence and spiritual insight remain which, however closely connected they are with specific social conditions, can never be seen just as reflections of those conditions.

Marx believed that if we could achieve a 'perfect', classless society, that would bring about the disappearance of religion. But will religion disappear in a socially fulfilling society? One reply might be that we cannot know, since we have never had such a society. But it seems likely that the question of meaning, of what value and purpose there is in life, will continue for many to have a transcendent dimension, to require some reference to, or hope for, fulfilment in relation to one supreme and unchanging value which cannot be destroyed by time. Perhaps religion, in its present forms, would not exist in a society of fulfilled, happy humans, just as religion as we know it presumably does not exist in heaven. But that does not mean there would be no belief in a transcendent spiritual reality. The forms of religion may change, but the supposition that there is an objective reality of supreme value, in knowledge of which human fulfilment can be found, might well be part of what would make humans happy and fulfilled in any case.

Of course it might still be true that belief in God is a projection. It is apparent that ideas of the Transcendent are based on concepts and images current in specific societies. It would be very odd if this were not the case. The Transcendent is always apprehended (or alleged to be apprehended) in a particular historical situation, and the form of its appearance often becomes a symbol of its reality. Spirits may be conceived as animals, or more remotely, as 'masters of animals', reigning spirits of the species. If, as in ancient Greece and Rome, they are imaged in human form, this is a way of representing them in terms of the highest life-form we know. Even when concepts of Transcendence become more abstract – as, for example, a being of pure intelligence and bliss – the ideas of intelligence and bliss are taken from human experience of the greatest values we can think of.

What is happening is an attempt to depict an apprehension of a reality of great value or power in terms, however inadequate, which we have available in our ordinary experience. Why not call this a projection? The only reason for hesitation is that a projection is assumed to be a pure invention, a figment of the imagination; whereas those who believe in Spirit are seeking adequate concepts for something apprehended, not imagined. It is not that we invent something that is meant to be a perfect human person. On the contrary, even perfect human persons are inadequate images for Spirit. The ideal we posit is far superior to human persons, even if personhood can be ascribed to it in some way. Perhaps we can conceive of a human person as embodying the divine ideal (as in the case of Jesus for Christians). But even then, the Godhead is far beyond the humanity of Jesus. That postulate of another, supra-human, reality is essential to the idea of Spirit. God is not a projection of an ideal of humanity, because humanity is, and always will be, so far removed from the perfect reality of God.

The idea of a God can be, and has been, used to console the oppressed, and to justify oppression. But that is not always its function, by any means. The prophets of Israel condemned oppression, and the liberators of Israel (the Judges) called on the oppressed to rise up against their oppressors, not simply to accept humbly what was meted out to them. There are many functions that ideas of an ultimate transcendent Ideal may have. But the primary one, by its interior logic, which in the end will outlive any elective affinities it may have, is to function as a goal to be striven for, imitated or participated in, to inspire and challenge rather than to console and justify inequality.

The gods play many roles in human society, from demanding human sacrifice to inspiring altruistic moral heroism. They embody limited and diverse human images, and all particular conceptions of them are open to rational and moral criticism and revision. But in all their forms, admirable and horrific, they are imaginative attempts to capture diverse facets of an objective moral ideal which is beyond that of any particular human society, which compels our attention as something not purely invented, but discovered by human enquiry, and always capable of calling in question current understandings of what a proper human life should be. Durkheim and Marx see the connection of religious belief with the postulation of a moral ideal, which may also be an object of human striving. Neither of them, however, is able to accept that such an ideal could exist apart from any human belief in it. Marx was unable to see how the postulation of such an ideal could be other than oppressive.

The question for religion is whether we can reasonably believe in a spiritual dimension of reality, and if so, how such belief can be made a vital positive force for human good. Sociological explanations of religion succeed in showing that religions have important and sometimes unexpected or undesirable social functions, which vary with specific cultures and histories. Such explanations cannot resolve the question of whether religions also have transcendent reference, and attempts to show that religion can be adequately explained in purely social terms need to assume that such transcendent reference is neither necessary nor possible. It is not clear that such an assumption is justifiable. Indeed, it seems to beg the main question at issue. Religion does seem to be partly a social construct. But it also seems to be something more, and that 'more' is the most important part of it.

Find out more . . .

Emile Durkheim, *The Elementary Forms of the Religious Life*, trans. J. Swain (New York: Macmillan, 1963), is the foundational text of a sociological approach to religion.

Karl Marx's thoughts on religion are scattered throughout his works, but a good guide is David McLellan, *Marxism and Religion* (New York: Harper, 1987).

For wider reading in the sociology of religion, Roland Robertson (ed.), *Sociology of Religion* (London: Penguin, 1969).

Peter Berger, *The Sacred Canopy* (New York: Doubleday, 1967), is an influential essay on these themes.

4

VOICES FROM THE
UNCONSCIOUS

Explanations of Religion in Terms of Psychology

Social and anthropological analyses of religion range from views that
seek to see the gods as projections of social classifications and structures
to accounts which simply note how religious beliefs, beliefs about transcendent reality, take on particular forms and emphasise particular
values or doctrines in diverse social circumstances. In a similar way, psychological or psychoanalytic analyses of religion may either see religious
concepts as projections of unconscious needs and wishes, or they may
be content to note correlations and affinities between specific psychological states and specific types of religious belief.

The former interpretations are reductionist, seeing the gods as supernatural and imaginary shadows of the real structures and values of various human societies or minds. The latter give to the gods an objective
reality, while accepting that the precise way in which they are conceived
depends on many cultural and historical factors.

Is there any way of deciding between these interpretations? There is
certainly no agreed way – the battle between belief and unbelief looks set
to continue indefinitely. Nevertheless there is a range of good reasons for

preferring the non-reductionist interpretation. One of the strongest and best-known reasons is the perception that our consciousness cannot be reduced to or fully explained in terms of matter. We understand at least to some extent what the universe is like. We feel the intricate beauty of existence, and the subtle interweaving of fear and love, of despair and of hope, that forms the fabric of our lives. We feel ourselves to be free and responsible to act in ways that will harm or help the world in which we live, and the people among whom we live. The inward awareness of our own being is the most immediate thing we know, and so we know in ourselves the transcendence of the material world, the irreducible reality of something that is not bound by the limits of space, the primacy of awareness over objectivity, in which religious apprehensions of a supreme consciousness are rooted.

Moreover, humans have a strong moral sense, which leads them to think of morality as objective and demanding, and a strong aesthetic sense, which leads them to think of beauty in sound, colour and words, as conveying intimations of objective value. Many of the wisest and most morally heroic people have a strong sense of the presence of God, or of a transcendent reality of ultimate value. Sometimes that is discerned in the events of history and of their lives, as a guiding, liberating or enlivening power. Sometimes it is discerned as a wider spiritual reality in which one feels oneself to be enveloped, or which one finds silently within, in the innermost cave of the heart. So in morality, in beauty and in religious experience we sense the immediacy of the Transcendent in and through the particularities of the finite world.

Moreover, as we regard the cosmos more widely, we find that it has an elegant and intelligible structure, precariously and precisely dependent upon sets of improbably correlated physical constants, which almost irresistibly suggests intelligent design. If we are seeking to explain why things are the way they are, the most comprehensive and ultimate form of explanation is one which would show all things to exist for the ultimate purpose of realising states of great value, and indeed that the cosmos arises by a combination of necessity and freedom from a reality which embodies supreme value in itself. That ideal of ultimate explanation stands before us as something yet to be attained, but as the final ground for accepting that the cosmos has a rational basis, that is oriented towards the values of beauty, understanding and love, and that it is somehow necessary for realising a purpose of great worth, a realisation in which we have a small but important part to play.

Before that sense of the ultimate meaning of being, any attempted reduction of all things, of all truth, beauty and goodness, of all human striving and endeavour, of our attempts at greater understanding and love, of our awareness of the miracle of existence, of our conscious questioning of our own existence, and the search for a meaning which will give sense to our lives – the reduction of all this to the blind purposeless blunderings of bits of matter seems desperately inadequate and superficial. Add to all that the implausibility of most of the reductionist accounts which have been proposed, and which claim to reduce all the rich complexity of experience to the random wanderings of a few simple material particles (or strings, however super) – a claim which has never been worked out in more than the sketchiest of ways – and the superiority of a spiritual interpretation of human experience in the cosmos can seem overwhelming.

Or so it seems to me and those who think like me! I am of course aware that some people disagree with me, and that for some strange reason reductionist materialism has become a fashionable doctrine, even though no one is quite sure what matter is. One eminent atheistic scientist with whom I sometimes have public debates in Oxford explains my beliefs by suggesting that they are due to an excess of oxygen in my brain. One response might be to deplore the lack of oxygen in his. But my own explanation for my beliefs is that they are very largely correct.

Of course I then have to explain why he fails to agree. But that is fairly simple – the prestige of the natural sciences has led him to think that only quantitative measurable publicly observable phenomena, the phenomena with which the hard sciences deal, really exist. His distaste for 'romantic', touchy-feely, sentimentality has led him to deny that he has any feelings at all. And his dislike for the sorts of religion he has come across – very literalist and judgemental believers who tell him he is bound for Hell unless he sings hymns and waves his arms in the air – has led him to reject any views which could possibly lead to hymn-singing and arm-waving. As Dr Johnson said of the early Methodists, 'Enthusiasm – a very horrid thing.' So he avoids reading any proper theological or philosophical books, and avoids all problems raised by the existence of spiritual (immaterial) things by looking the other way very hard, and denying any such things do or even could exist.

I suppose he would think this is a very prejudiced way of putting the matter. But the plain fact is that each of us thinks the other is slightly mad – either I see things that are not there, or he fails to see things that are right in front of him. Either I am deluded or he is blind. What can we do about this? Nothing. We just have to go on being as reasonable as we can, within the limits of the way we ultimately see the world – which we cannot help and do not choose. The fact that other people disagree with me does not mean that I am irrational or that my beliefs are incorrect. Neither does it mean that there is nothing to choose between them and me, as if all the arguments were roughly equally balanced. No, each of us will think our arguments are better (the only difference is that I happen to be right!). We weigh things differently, we stress different aspects of reality, and we form different conscientious judgements – just as we do in matters of law, politics and morality.

The best we can do is to work out our own basic view as reasonably and carefully as possible, and seek to be fair to other views, while saying what we find unconvincing about them. That is what I am doing now. I am definitely not a reductionist – if anything, I am an expansionist, with an inbuilt tendency to see everything as basically spiritual in nature. But some of the best-known analysts of the phenomenon of religion have been reductionists. Their views have been influential and they are worth studying for the insights they bring. I hope to show that their analyses are inadequate, if not downright wrong. But I do not seriously expect to convince everyone, especially not those who are invincibly ignorant (that is my return insult to those who think my brain is over-oxygenated).

PSYCHOANALYSIS: SIGMUND FREUD

Sigmund Freud, the father of psychoanalysis, best represents the reductionist strand in the psychology of religion. Like many other students of human behaviour at the end of the nineteenth century, he assumed that 'primitive' societies parallel infantile stages of human development. By an imaginative reconstruction of early human history, he attempted to trace the genesis of religious beliefs as an expression of infantile neuroses. Freud found, through conversation with male neurotic patients, that there was a widespread repressed desire to possess the mother and to kill the father. This murder, however, completed in imagination if not in fact, produced a paralysing sense of guilt, which had to be appeased by offering deferred obedience to the imagined father-figure, now conceived as an invisible and possibly hostile power. This was accompanied by a strict prohibition (a taboo) on incest, which represented sexual congress with the mother. In primitive society, Freud hypothesised, the primal slaying of the father is ritually repeated, together with an attempt to gain the father's power (by eating him), and an expression of contrition by renouncing many kinds, and perhaps all kinds, of sexuality. Thus 'the sacred was originally nothing but the perpetuated will of the primeval father'.[54]

Freud's imagined reconstruction of history is that early humans lived in a 'primal horde', ruled by one dominant male (their father), who possessed all the females. The sons banded together to kill and eat the father, so that they could possess the females. Then, however, overcome with remorse, they deified the father, creating an animal totem to represent him, which they worshipped. They erected about the totem the first taboo, 'Do not kill the totem' (never repeat the original crime), as an expression of the ambivalent hate (jealousy of his sexual power) and love (filial affection) they had for the primal father. But they nevertheless do repeat the original crime ritually over and over again (reinterpreting it as the free sacrifice of the father for them). And they repeat the second primal taboo, 'Do not fulfil your sexual desires', as a perpetual expression of hated renunciation and also an expression of loving obedience. All this complex interplay of emotion takes place in a disguised way, in the unconscious, and it is meant to relieve or at least control the neurosis that results from the unacceptable facts of each new humans' father-hatred and mother-love, repeating the real primal murder which was the beginning of the obsessional neuroses of religion.

There are no historical records to substantiate Freud's view of early religion, and his evidence is taken from analyses of neurotic patients. He seems to have successfully uncovered many deeply disguised emotions of love and hatred towards parents in nineteenth-century Europe, which led to obsessional neuroses of various sorts. Not all such neuroses took a religious form, and it is hard to see why all religious believers should be thought to be neurotic, when their behaviour shows no particular signs of neurosis. Some believers may always have to light candles in a specific order, but others do not care very much either way. So why should one not say that Freud successfully uncovered the emotional roots of some obsessional forms of religion among nineteenth-century Europeans in the unresolved desires and experiences of their early childhood? To generalise from this to explain all religion in that way is more hazardous, and less convincing. Religions that do not have a father-god or rituals of sacrifice seem particularly hard to explain on Freudian lines.

What Freud is trying to explain is the sense of repression of desire and feeling of absolute obligation that goes with some forms of Christian religion. Why should one repress natural desires, and why should one have feelings of absolute obligation, which cannot be justified in terms of rational self-interest? The traditional religious answer is that human desires are disordered, and obligations are the objective principles of moral action that God upholds. But Freud is looking for a purely psychological mechanism that can give rise to feelings of obligation and counteract natural desires. Whereas Durkheim finds the explanation in terms of social conditioning, Freud finds it in infantile experience, which lays down forces of repression and compulsion, which subsequently control behaviour.

The general principle is similar. All so-called 'higher' feelings – moral obligation, shame and guilt – are to be explained in terms of their genesis in pre-rational imprinted behaviour. The problem is simply to decide what does the imprinting. In more recent times, evolutionary biology has entered the scene with a new candidate, the genetically imprinted behaviour that was once successful in the competition for survival in the far past history of the species. Human behaviour and beliefs are to be explained from the bottom up. Their basis is blind, unconscious, biologically or psychologically determined behaviour, which leaves us with obsessive and compulsive beliefs for which there is no rational basis.

Religion, according to Freud, is not rationally justifiable and in its ritual activities is clearly obsessive. So we must look for its origin in unconscious forces, which still determine much of our behaviour, though we do not know why. Just suppose, however, that there is a spiritual reality whose effects upon the physical universe, and especially upon created and at least partly spiritual beings, are real. Part of the explanation for human behaviour would then be the pressure or influence of that spiritual reality upon human lives. One might expect the influence to draw human awareness gradually towards an apprehension of that which is good, true and beautiful, encouraging the development of a distinctively moral consciousness, a capacity for intellectual understanding and for aesthetic sensibility. What might otherwise seem compulsive beliefs might be insights into the claims of objective goodness. What might seem pointlessly obsessive rituals might be techniques for coming to greater awareness of such claims. This would be a top-down explanation for human religious behaviour, accounting for it in terms of an interaction, only partly conscious, with a greater spiritual reality.

What is basically at stake here is the sort of explanation that is felt to be appropriate and sufficient for human religious behaviour. Freud sees such behaviour as very like neurotic behaviour. It is disabling, making one unable to cope rationally with everyday life, or with ordinary problems that arise. Some religious behaviour, however, might be enabling, helping people to cope better with problems, making them more integrated and happy. It might be important to try to explain why religion could have such diverse effects on different people. Explanations in terms of sexual repression and imagined father-figures are illuminating for some religious conditions. But such explanations are simply too general to cover more than a tiny number of religious attitudes.

Some people see the world as a purely material reality. What explains that fact? It can seem that there is a sort of materialist neurosis, which drives people to seek just one sort of explanation for the whole range of diverse phenomena, and to reduce all sorts of realities to just one basic kind. This would be a monothematic neurosis, possibly due to fixation at an anal-retentive stage. We seek to exercise control over the universe by subordinating it to one simple and fixed scheme that is our own product. Control is absolute (the theory wholly orders the world), and nothing 'dirty' or messy is allowed to exist. The scientific cosmos is the perfectly potty-trained neurosis.

I suppose any scientist would protest that such a psychoanalytical diagnosis of science is not only irrelevant to the truth or falsity of scientific theories, but it is demeaning of the intellectual struggles of high-minded, truth-oriented scientists. Quite so. The same is true of religion. In both cases, there are individuals who seem to be fanatically obsessed with the truth of their own theories, and with establishing the omnipotence of thought, and indeed of the one magic all-explaining theory, over the whole of reality. There are strange mental mechanisms at work here, which might benefit from a psychiatrist's attention. But most scientists, and most religious believers too, have no such dreams of the omnipotence of thought. They just want to see if particular hypotheses work. In the case of science, the question is usually, 'Do they predict correctly?' In the case of religion, it is more likely to be, 'Do they help us to see life in terms of objective goodness, and enable us to apprehend and be empowered by such goodness?'

For Freud, the super-ego, the source of a sense of absolute moral obligation, was a non-rational introjection of a fantasised father-figure. Might it not rather be the call of a truly transcendent, morally demanding

Spirit, who wills the fulfilment of personhood and abandonment of ego? In other words, there can be a rational morality, one that is justifiable in terms of an appeal to universal principles making for human flourishing. It will have the central characteristic of a taboo, in its peremptory demand upon individual loyalty. For some individuals, it will be wholly reasonable to feel a sense of guilt, and to attempt to allay it by seeking some way of obeying the moral demand more effectively. We do not need a story about father-killing and subsequent attempts to appease the fantasised father in order to make sense of such feelings. And, of course, there are religious views that do not stress the element of guilt at all, but concentrate instead on feelings of unity with the divine, and of positive benevolent action. We must conclude that Freud's analysis applies only to a restricted set of religious views, and within them, to a group of people who do have problems with relating to their fathers, and within that group to a smaller group of those for whom those problems issue in troubling neuroses.

It is vitally important to dissect the pathologies of religion, which are no more or less than those of humanity in general. Freud has helped to begin such a process. His work might then also help to devise a non-pathological version of religious beliefs, which would be both reasonable and personally integrating. That task has been partly carried out by Erich Fromm, though with regard to morality rather than religion. Fromm suggests that what Freud opposed was 'obedience ethics', in which people simply obey non-rational obligations out of a sense of compulsion. What should replace that is 'rational ethics', in which people work out a set of principles for obtaining human flourishing and realising their desires in a mutually fulfilling way. Even rational ethics needs a sense of obligation if it is to have any effect on human conduct. So a place remains for training children to have a sense of obligation. All that is reprehensible is to let such a sense lose touch with the construction of a set of truly fulfilling principles for action.

The same is true with religion, though Fromm does not draw that conclusion. We should not obey God for no reason. But we would be wise to reverence true goodness, to seek a power to enable us to be good, and to aim to participate in goodness, so far as that is possible for human beings. We need to ask what a non-pathological form of religious beliefs is: it is one that does not contradict any known and well-established facts, and which justifies its beliefs by considerations of what makes for supreme goodness, and of how humans can achieve it. We then need to commend practices that will centre the mind on goodness, and bring human lives to a fulfilment that intrinsically relates to such goodness. Freud writes that religion arises 'from the filial sense of guilt, in an attempt to allay that feeling and to appease the father by deferred obedience to him'.[55] He has in mind guilt for the primordial killing of the king, and imaginary obedience to his re-embodiment as an invisible god. But we can give a less fantasising interpretation to these religious images and emotions. If a sense of a father-god helps us to love the good, helps to allay the feeling of guilt at failing to realise the good, and helps us to strive for goodness out of love and not merely out of a sense of abstract duty, then the religious image will be a help, not a hindrance, to a way of being truly human in the world. It may well be, however, that other images will help those who interpret the world in different ways.

Such a view of religion would pay attention to human fulfilment as a primary condition of rational religion, and in this respect Freud has done a great service in pointing out how some religious views diminish the human personality, and in pointing, if only by implication, to the sorts of view that would help it to flourish. This does not turn religion into simply a means to human fulfilment, but it draws attention to the close connection between positing an objective ideal of goodness (the religious object) and the pursuit of such an ideal, realising valuable states in human life.

Freud himself saw that religion can have such an integrating and morally motivating function in *The Future of an Illusion*, in which he outlined a view of religious beliefs as 'illusions, fulfilments of the oldest, strongest and most insistent wishes of mankind'.[56] He suggests that humans need to imagine some external power or powers which will authorise morality, compensate for their self-renunciations, and exorcise the terrors of nature, which humans are unable completely to master.

On this suggestion, religion is not a neurosis, but it is a wish-fulfilment, founded on no objective evidence, and therefore destined inevitably to be eroded by the soft but insistent voice of reason. He here concedes that religion is something that could be reasonably desired, and that may even have an essential part to play in human life – since 'every culture must be built up on coercion and instinctual renunciation',[57] and it is often religion which sustains a sense of moral authority and prompts renunciation of ego.

Freud's whole case here rests simply upon the claim that, regrettably, there is no evidence for such highly desirable wish-fulfilments: 'Scientific work is our only way to the knowledge of external reality.'[58] This can sound rather odd to a later generation which is very sceptical as to whether Freud's own work, with its extravagant hypotheses of super-ego, ego and id, thanatos and eros, can be called properly scientific. Was he not seeing human nature with an immensely jaundiced Viennese eye, obsessed with sex, and determined to trace all human motivations to their fundamental unacknowledged basis in lust and aggression?

We need to ask what exactly 'scientific work' is. Presumably what Freud primarily had in mind is the formation of theories, founded on public and repeatable observations under controlled conditions, which can be verified by their high predictive accuracy. Very few religious assertions conform to such conditions. But then very few historical assertions, or assertions about disputed facts in criminal law cases, conform to such conditions either. It does not follow that they give no information about 'external reality'.

Assertions about historical events are certainly in the public domain. They can in principle be seen by many observers. But different observers are liable to give different accounts of what has been seen. There are not many cases of precisely observed and widely agreed events in history. No one doubts that something happened, and that most people probably got it roughly right. But historical events cannot be repeated or controlled, and they rarely give rise to predictions. We can only seek to record the facts as well as we can.

If an explanation is attempted, it will not be anything like a 'law of nature'. We may appeal to common human motivations – Adam Smith's rational egoism, for example. Or, as is the case with Freudian analysis, we may claim to uncover general patterns of behaviour, caused by crucial formative events. But Jung and Adler may describe different motivations – a need for integration or a drive for power, perhaps – and they may describe human behaviour in very different ways.

Two main factors distinguish such public observations from those of physics or chemistry. The crucial observations are unrepeatable and not susceptible to precisely controlled experimentation. And ways of describing basic human motives and desires seem to be ineliminably evaluative – expressing an underlying view of human nature which incorporates beliefs about what is 'normal' and 'proper' to human life.

Religious beliefs are even further removed from the 'paradigm' beliefs of natural science. The crucial experiences of transcendence, which help to give rise to religious beliefs, are not repeatable or controllable. But more importantly they are also limited to a small group of prophets or sages, so that they do not typically fall within the arena of generally available observation at all. Moreover, they seem to require a special kind of susceptibility to that sort of experience, a special sort of mentality, which embodies an underlying view of human nature as oriented to transcendence. Atheists and materialists do not usually have religious experiences. The characters and predispositions of the religious shape their experiences in a way that the characters of scientists do not. Anyone can make observations in a laboratory, given the right training, whatever their beliefs. But not anyone can have a religious experience.

For Freud this only corroborates his view that religious experiences cannot give knowledge of external reality. The only mode of reliable access to such reality is public sense-experience. But why should that be so? If there is a spiritual reality, non-physical in nature, sense-experience could not be a means of access to it. It might well require a particular sort of mental disposition to make cognition of it possible. We might say that the more knowledge is of distinctively personal or spiritual factors, the more the nature of the knowing agent is important to the sort of knowledge which is available, and the more personal variation there will be in the interpretation which is given of any apprehensions which are felt to occur.

That is why it is not absurd to say that neurotics may have peculiarly aberrant sorts of religious experiences, and that their mental state may be such as to make them open to experiences of transcendence, albeit of a negative and partly disabling kind. It is also not absurd to suppose that there are non-neurotic forms of similar experience, which may disclose aspects of reality – spiritual aspects – that will remain opaque to those whose personalities are closed to neurotic and to transcendent experience alike.

RELIGIOUS EXPERIENCE

The idea that there are specific sorts of personality which are predisposed to religious experiences, that there are many varieties of religious experience and that there is an affinity between some kinds of neuroticism and some varieties of intense religious experience is one that has found classical expression in the work of the psychologist William James.

In *The Varieties of Religious Experience*, he limits his investigation to 'the feelings, acts, and experiences of individual men in their solitude, so far as they apprehend themselves to stand in relation to whatever they may consider the divine'.[59] This should not be taken as a definition of religion in general. As a psychologist of his time, James is concerned with inner experiences, and defines these experiences in two main ways – in terms of their qualitative 'feel', and in terms of the object to which they are directed.

In both aspects, he wishes to cast his net fairly widely. So he does not limit the 'religious object' to God. Indeed, he is temperamentally

opposed to dogmatic theology, to which, he says, 'we must ... bid a definite good-bye'.[60] The object he is concerned with is a 'spiritual' or
'higher' universe, 'an unseen order', 'a larger power' or 'something
larger than ourselves'. He has in mind a non-physical realm of being,
which has causal effects upon the physical universe, and which is greater
in power and/or value than we are.

His own personal hypothesis he calls 'pluralistic', meaning that there
may be many higher selves, of many different sorts (not just one God), of
which we can have some experience. There is real 'work done' by those
higher selves, in that they have definite effects upon human lives. To establish 'harmonious relation' with them, to let those effects upon us be inten-
sified is, he thinks, the true end of humanity.

What are the effects? He refers to the inner quality of religious
experiences in various ways – they are solemn, serious and tender. They
fill us with enchantment and enthusiasm, with happiness, love, humility,
serenity and peace. This is all, as he says, very 'healthy-minded'. But
there is also a place for the 'sick soul' in religion, a soul that knows its
inadequacy and the need for forgiveness and deliverance. Even here,
however, the characteristic religious feelings are those of grace, reconciliation and liberation. If Rudolf Otto's terrifying and uncanny sense of the
numinous occurs, it does not do so to any great extent in the accounts
James examines. William James's religious believers have breathed the
gentle and beneficent New England air, and their religion brings them
more exuberant and vibrant life. But that life consists in walks and edify-
ing conversations among plane-trees rather than the heroic adventures
of conquest.

The value of James's book is that it provides a record of many human
experiences which seem to the experients to be of a supernatural and
benevolent power, and which have increased their happiness, energy and
moral commitment. It is an antidote to a Freudian preoccupation with
neurosis. As James repeatedly says, it does not prove anything about the
existence of a God or gods. As a good pragmatist, he thinks that 'the true
is what works well'.[61] Religion works if religious experiences produce

good fruits. If a person's life is filled with new happiness and energy, then there is some object that produces these things. But what that object is remains under-determined by the experience. It is presumably a 'power for good', but it may be the unconscious self, or many higher selves (perhaps bodhisattvas, in the Buddhist traditions?), or one supreme God, or something as yet unimagined. How could we tell, just from experience of a higher power for healthy-mindedness?

Mystical types of experience are, he says, pantheistic and optimistic. They lead experients to see the self as part of one all-inclusive Whole, whose character is good. Saintly experience is slightly different. It leads to a sense of self-abandonment and surrender. This can lead to extremes of self-immolations, but it always focuses the mind on a reality that is of a goodness far outshadowing one's own. Purely healthy-minded faiths tend to be unduly optimistic and sunny. 'The completest religions', he says, 'seem to be those in which the pessimistic elements are best developed' – but also overcome by a greater spiritual power.

Despite his dislike of abstract speculation, James is here proposing with suitable tentativeness a categorisation of experiences in terms of their adequacy to embrace the whole of known reality, in all its aspects. The reality of evil and the unacceptability of extreme asceticism lead him to make value-judgements as to the character of the experienced spiritual reality. It must, he thinks, have real psychological effects, and those effects must be for good, as measured by a broadly humanistic code of happiness, serenity and compassion. Some sort of theology is at work, however vague. And indeed it is probably unavoidable.

What do James's investigations, limited as they are, suggest about the religious object? His studies suggest that religious experience is not rare, but that it is very diverse, and does not yield one unequivocal truth about the supernatural. Subsequent psychological studies corroborate these suggestions. Apparently about a third of the population of Britain, America and Australia report having experiences of 'a powerful spiritual force that seemed to lift you out of yourself'.[62] Many more people report having experiences of transcendent meaning or significance while listening to music, looking at a beautiful landscape, or even examining the structure of DNA. An interesting small-scale survey in London carried out in 1998 found that 70% of people approached said that they had had 'an experience that [they] would call religious, spiritual, ecstatic, sacred, paranormal or mystical'.[63] This question is extremely broad, and the sample (forty respondents) very small, so not too much should be read into it. Yet it suggests that the supernatural, broadly conceived, is believed to be personally apprehended by many people on occasion.

In other words, most people have some sort of 'supernormal' experiences during the course of their lives. But most do not have what they would describe as intense religious experiences, though quite a large number do, and most people recognise and value the sorts of things they are, and the effects they have. The occurrence of such experiences cannot be correlated with any special personality types (certainly not neurotics). If we take these data seriously, it seems that we cannot identify religious experience with any one religious tradition or set of particular beliefs. People with all sorts of diverse religious beliefs record experiences that are similar in a general way. If there is a spiritual reality, it seems to be apprehended in a significant way by a large minority of the human population, in all sorts of cultures and places (it may indeed be apprehended by a much larger number, though not recognised for what it is).

This suggests that there is a capacity for spiritual apprehension, varying quite widely in degree, which does not correlate with any other specific personality type, and which is spread widely throughout the human race. It is interpreted in many different ways – and James says that this is a wholly good thing, since 'a god of battles must be allowed to be the god for one kind of person, a god of peace and heaven and home, the god for another'.[64] This is a good example of James's form of pluralism. There really are lots of divinities, one for every sort of person. Whatever our conception of divinity, the thing itself is known primarily in 'feeling', as a living interaction with a quasi-personal object that 'freshens our vital powers'.[65] If we call this 'God', then it seems that God is neither clearly known nor completely unknown. God is known as a transforming power throughout the world, but in varying degrees and in very different ways.

It is for this reason that reliance on religious experience can be regarded as dangerous by orthodox religious believers. It comes up with so many divergent interpretations that it is hardly a reliable guide to ultimate truth about the divine. People get messages from spirit guides, are given secret information on the inner nature of the universe, have visions of Buddhas, Virgin Marys and Archangels, and receive psychic powers with tedious regularity. Since so much of this information is contradictory, we badly need some way of sorting out the genuine (if any) from the spurious.

Orthodox believers appeal to revelation at this point. But of course that is secret information too, just like the messages given to spirit mediums. So it begs the question to use it as a test of genuineness. There can be no doubt that the majority of spirit experiences are incorrectly interpreted – this is simply because if any of the interpretations are correct, all the others (and there will be more of them) must be incorrect. So a good first principle is that you cannot trust any information just because people say it was revealed to them.

What sorts of tests might be available? One obvious one is the provision of checkable information. If someone foretells the future accurately, or predicts consistently who will win a horse race, that will increase their credibility. Regrettably, religious predictions are not so precise or lucrative. Still, we can distinguish 'crazy' information from sensible. If there is good reason to think there are no UFOs, revelations about them will have low probability. If we think people do not reincarnate, revelations of past lives will fail to convince. Of course some really good evidence might change that. But the vagueness and untestability of most revelations lessens their credibility. They simply do not provide good evidence of reliability. Like most reported psychic phenomena, there is a great deal of data, but none of it stands up under precise testable conditions.

Well, the religious will say, that is not their function. God does not provide knockdown evidence for the divine existence and purpose. We really knew that anyway, but it is surprising how often believers speak as though they did have knockdown evidence and theoretical certainty. We might even say that the more specific revealed information claims to be, the less it is to be trusted. The end of the world has been specifically predicted, down to the month and day, at least four times in the twentieth century, and we are still here.

It looks as though James is right – the reliable information content of religious experiences is very small. It suggests a higher power (or powers) making for goodness, and that is about all. We might begin by hoping that the more precise information the better, but if we make an extensive and thorough investigation of claims to religious experience we will end by admitting that the less precise information the better. The risk of deception is then smaller. The best rule for religious experience is: make modest claims, and keep them vague. Best of all perhaps is James's own characterisation of 'mysticism' – mystical experiences have noetic content, but they are ineffable. They tell us something, but we do not know what it is. Or more exactly, we cannot say what it is.

Some, like W.T. Stace, have argued that there is one ineffable core experience, which forms the basis of all religious doctrines, and that these owe their diversity to cultural and external factors. R.C. Zaehner, among others, has argued against this. In *Mysticism, Sacred and Profane* he distinguishes three different types of mysticism: panenhenic (oneness with nature), monistic (interior unity) and the mysticism of loving union.[66] Steven Katz argues, more radically, that experiences are wholly diverse and very different in character because presupposed beliefs and dogmas dictate the sorts of experience believers will have.[67] So experiences cannot be the source of specific religious beliefs at all.

The best hypothesis seems to be that many people have experience of spiritual powers, but the specific information provided – whether in the form of visions or of 'heard' messages – depends very much upon cultural expectations, general background beliefs and the imaginative ability of the human mind to construct vast edifices of ontology from the merest hints of mystery. The omens are not good for the very specific claims that many religions make about God, spirits and the afterlife. Each cultural tradition builds up an increasingly detailed set of such claims.

For instance, belief in purgatory, if it existed at all in the early Christian Church, was extremely tentative. But in a few hundred years the Church had learned quite a lot about it. Purgatory was born in 1170, according to one of the major scholars on the subject, Jacques LeGoff.[68] At least that is when the first written references to it occur. Soon afterwards, however, the Church was able to divide the time spent in purgatory into days, and issue certificates granting a few days' holiday for various pious reasons, and Dante could describe its inhabitants and its many-levelled geography in fascinating detail. Muslims also issue geographies of the afterlife, but they differ from Dante's, since Dante insensitively placed Muhammad among the pigs in purgatory, whereas Muslims naturally do not place him there at all. It seems altogether more natural to allot these details to imagination, working on the basic thought that souls are destined for greater knowledge of God. Once purgatory is in place, the souls therein can appear in visions and speak to entranced hearers. Underneath the imaginative detail, what is there but the sense of a higher human destiny, and of some sort of dim contact with spirits of that imagined realm in which it can be realised? Is that wish-fulfilment? It is, I think, something that arises from the sense of a higher power with which some sort of personal relationship is possible, yet which is remote and demanding, as well as near and consoling. From such essentially vague but immensely powerful feelings the hypotheses of religious orthodoxy grow, becoming strangely more definite and defined in each generation.

It may seem that a good test for the genuineness of religious experience is the provision of testable information not obtainable by normal human modes of knowledge. But it turns out that almost the opposite is true – the most reliable experiences are those which are most reticent about informational content, and simply register apprehension of a higher power, understood in the imaginative forms of one's own culture. The sense of mystery and ineffability is more appropriate than the provision of the exact date of the end of the world.

Religious experience is not really about the provision of additional secret information. It is about a personal apprehension of spiritual reality. This will be person-relative in a strong way. That is, the way in which we come to know another person depends very much on the sort of persons we are. It is well established in psychology that we project onto others the hidden, repressed or 'shadow' sides of our own personalities. We might also project onto them our own ideals and desires. We see others as demons or heroes, as fantasy figures who interact with our own complex goals and fears. It is not, of course, wholly projection. Other people really exist, and we can have more or less accurate assessments of them. But to make an accurate assessment requires maturity, self-confidence, self-knowledge and sensitivity. Some people have lots of these qualities, some conspicuously lack them, and some are immature, self-deceived, fearful and deeply prejudiced. If religious apprehension were like personal knowledge, one would expect that religious experiences would range from wildly fantastic projections of personal inadequacies to positive and life-enhancing transformations of personality by encounter with a wider and deeper personal reality.

It follows that a large part of sorting out reliable religious experiences will be an assessment of the character of the experients. If they are well balanced and integrated, and if their experiences increase their wisdom, insight and sensitivity, it might be sensible to take their reports of encounters with a spiritual reality seriously. If they show a depth of insight into human problems, and an extraordinary degree of creative power; if they have powers of mental and physical healing and a profound sense of well-being; if they show compassion for the sufferings of others and delight in beauty and friendship, then their reports of a transforming awareness of spiritual reality are of significant worth. On the other hand, if they have a sharply exaggerated sense of their own importance; if they place enormous value on relatively insignificant facts; if they manipulate others and seem obsessed with particular beliefs or rituals, their reported experiences are likely to be based largely on projections of their own fragmented personalities.

So the sense of mystery, which is central to genuine religious experience, should be associated with some degree of intellectual insight and moral power, which changes the experient's life in the religious apprehension. The higher power disclosed by religious experience is closely related to some idea of an objective human good, something ultimately worth striving for. In some forms of religious practice, people may seek the help of that power to obtain things they consider to be good, such as wealth or victory in war. But in other forms the very idea of what is truly good is disclosed in the experience of the power itself. It is seen as a standard of goodness by which human lives are judged and in union with which the highest human good can be obtained.

There are two aspects to this. One is that a trustworthy religious experience must at least meet the highest standards of moral goodness we are aware of. It must increase compassion and love for others. The other is something that goes beyond morality, in the sense of concern for others. It is the realisation of a specific ideal in our own life. As James puts it, 'Life, more life, a larger, richer, more satisfying life, is in the last analysis the end of religion.'[69] Religion is not, like morality, primarily concerned with others. It is concerned with the self, and with a journey towards the fullest realisation of the self.

However, to speak of self-realisation here is paradoxical, for religious practice usually requires an abandonment of self. 'The abandonment of self-responsibility seems to be the fundamental act in specifically religious, as distinguished from moral practice.'[70] The self that is realised in religion is beyond the conscious ego; it is a wider self, often experienced as a power from beyond the ego, bringing as a gift a quality of life unobtainable by purely self-conscious effort, which both enlarges moral sensitivity and also brings a sense of serenity and mindfulness to the knower.

For William James, the 'discovery' of the subconscious mind (which he dates to 1886) was 'the most important step forward that has occurred in psychology since I have been a student'.[71] James thought that 'the fact that the conscious person is continuous with a wider self through which saving experiences come' was 'literally and objectively true'.[72] This wider self is a manifestation of 'the higher faculties of our own hidden mind'.[73] Religious ideas, insofar as they are real and powerful, come from the subconscious. Whether or not, and how far, that subconscious is the transmitter of influences from an objective, extra-mental reality, James leaves undecided as a psychologist – though his own hypothesis as a member of that suspect species, the philosophers, is that there are a number of such extra-mental realities.

JUNG

Carl Gustav Jung (1875–1961) is the person who, more than anyone else, has sought to explain religious beliefs and experiences in terms of influences from the subconscious mind. Whereas Freud ideally wished to account for the unconscious in terms of brain physiology, Jung always maintained that there is a psychic realm that really exists, and is no less real than the body. The exact status of this psychic realm is something of a mystery. The personal unconscious can be thought of as an area of the mind in which autonomous psychic complexes exist, consisting of lost and repressed memories and broken-off and unacknowledged parts of the personality. There is good evidence for the existence of such complexes, which can be expressed in dreams, which are found in schizophrenic states, and which have definite effects on behaviour, though they are not consciously recognised by the ego. For Freud, such repressed memories were largely sexual in nature, but Jung saw them more widely as parts of the personality the ego was not prepared to acknowledge. Jung's notion of libido was of a life-energy, not of a sexual urge.

Jung postulated that there is also a collective unconscious, in which lie primordial images derived from the prehistory of the race. These form what he called 'archetypes', primordial psychic forces apprehended through symbolic forms. There are a number of main archetypes, which are found in religious symbols throughout the world, and which come to expression in dreams and in Jungian analysis.

The psyche is a self-regulating system, which seeks to balance the conscious and unconscious minds. 'The psyche is a world within which the ego is contained.'[74] It contains a number of polarities – anima and animus (the feminine and masculine principles), the God-symbol of perfect goodness and the shadow or Satan, introversion and extraversion, thought and feeling, and sensation and intuition.

As the psyche develops in the growing person, the personality moves to increasing differentiation, which usually involves the repression of parts of itself. In the second main part of life the person seeks to achieve individuation by reintegrating these dissociated parts of the personality into the self. The goal of analysis is integration, or the reappropriation and acknowledgement of the repressed parts – perhaps particularly of 'the shadow' or dark side, and the anima or animus, the contra sexual side – so as to move to a new centre of wholeness, the self which is other than the conscious ego, and balances unconscious and conscious minds. The self should not be confused with the ego. Jung says that it is 'a compensatory ordering factor which is independent of the ego and whose nature transcends consciousness'.[75] It is represented for many by the 'God-image' or by a Christ image of wholeness and integration.

Jung was much more sympathetic to religion than was Freud, though he thought that Christianity was unable to perform the psychic task of personal integration any longer in the modern world. In particular, the feminine had been repressed, so that God was wholly masculine. Jung spoke approvingly of the papal declaration of the Assumption of Mary, and held that, instead of speaking of a Trinity, Christians should go further and speak of a Quaternity, with the feminine as a fourth principle. He also held that the shadow had been repressed, caricatured as Satan and cast out of the Godhead, where it belonged. The shadow, too, should be reintegrated into God, so that God has a 'dark side', mischievous, arbitrary and non-rational, even violent and unjust, from which the possibility of evil necessarily springs. Michael Argyle wryly remarks: 'This part of Jung's writings is not popular with theologians.'[76]

Jung's theories are based on his work with patients in analysis, and he insisted that he was an 'empiricist', sticking just to the evidence he had, not to abstract theories. So he would not comment on whether God objectively existed, but spoke of 'God' simply as an archetype or psychic complex, a symbol for integration or for the perfection of the integrated self. Jung's patients seem to have been remarkably different from Freud's. They were all apparently on a quest for personal integration – whereas Freud's patients were relieved just to get rid of their most persistent delusions. Jung's work clearly offers a more positive explanation of religious experiences. They can be seen as stages on the life-task of integrating personality, and as messages from the unconscious, which lead one further on that task. They seem to be of objective powers from beyond the ego, and indeed they are. 'These images are involuntary spontaneous manifestations and by no means intentional inventions,' he wrote.[77] They are psychic complexes located within the collective unconscious.

One has the suspicion, however, that if a person becomes wholly integrated and balanced, the religious task will be complete, and there will be no further need for religion. The myths and symbols of religion will have done their job, and the true object of belief will be seen always to have been some aspect of the human psyche.

Psychologists in general find Jung's idea of the collective unconscious at least as controversial as the idea of a supernatural reality. If it is supposed to be based on the physiology of the brain, then most biologists would say that it is not possible to inherit acquired characteristics. So the experiences of primal humans could not be genetically passed on in any form. If it is supposed to be some unconscious mind shared by all humans, it is as metaphysical as a straight-forward supernaturalist account. So what exactly is its status? Some would hold that we do not need to posit an actual shared unconscious mind to explain the existence of archetypes. They are, after all, based on universal themes such as motherhood or fear of chaos, and so it is not surprising that they arise throughout the human race. What Jung discovered was that such universal images are constructed from often repressed or forgotten experiences, and express deep fears, desires and hopes common to most humans. It would not be surprising if contact with an objective spiritual reality were by means of such images, drawn from past human experiences. If the spiritual is a rich and complex reality, with virtually limitless potentialities and aspects of being, then human minds may become aware of many different aspects, frightening as well as sustaining, all of them mediated through the often forgotten or unrecognised repertoire of experiences in the human mind. The virgin mother, the Devil, Christ and Muhammad, as well as compassionate liberated souls, can all be apprehended as aspects of spiritual reality, taking form from the data existing in memory. Whether such apprehensions come as visions, as words 'heard' in the mind, or as enhanced states of feeling and awareness, they may be points of contact with the realm of Spirit, perceived in ways governed by the dispositions, fears and desires of the apprehending mind.

Such a possibility does seem to fit the fact that religious images are constructed from the resources of human imagination, and that they often express deep-rooted fears and ideals. It also suggests that religious experiences are symptomatic of a personal inner journey towards (or away from) integration, and that their nature will express particular points on that journey. Most people are very uncomfortable with the idea that there exists a world of demons and angels, of gods and goddesses. It is perhaps more acceptable to see demons and gods as images that well up from below the conscious ego. While expressing psychological forces within us, they seem to carry their own objectivity, and they may well express some encounter with that infinitely complex spiritual reality which is the source of religious experience. Dreams still convey revelations, but of the hidden recesses of the mind, both good and bad, as it encounters the spiritual realm, rather than of some quite dispassionately perceived separate realm that we enter when we sleep.

The sorts of dreams and visions we have reflect our own stage of our inner journey, the problems we encounter and possible ways of resolving them. What we discern reflects both what is within us and the way in which we are able to cope with that or integrate it into our conscious lives. And here again the fundamental question arises: is our discernment only of what is within, or is it of some external reality, as we filter it through our imaginative and emotional repertoire, with all its limitations and perspectives? Both James and Jung are officially agnostic about the answer. But both are in practice often more positive. James speaks of 'a more spiritual universe', union with which is 'our true end'.[78] And Jung, in a much more personal book, developed his own myth of the universe as developing consciousness so that God can through it integrate the opposites which are inherent in the divine being.[79] In one letter, he wrote, 'There is as little doubt of the existence of a supreme being as of matter.'[80]

Jung saw integration as a calling or task set for human persons, and the symbols that exist in so many religions as images which make present repressed unconscious realities, and which enable the ego to participate in and integrate those realities into consciousness. Thus religion itself becomes a sort of therapy. Its aim is salvation in the sense of healing and wholeness, and it sets out a path of self-discovery and self-acceptance that leads towards integration.

He thought that the religious traditions he was best acquainted with, Catholicism and Protestantism, had largely lost the ability to perform this therapeutic role adequately, having turned symbols into dogmas and being compromised by social and political agendas. But he was hopeful that religion might develop to become an overtly therapeutic path, in which symbols would again play their role of mediating the real and objective powers of the unconscious mind, and leading people on an intensely personal journey towards the conscious integration of all aspects of the psyche into one fully individuated personality.

THE QUESTION OF TRUTH

Social explanations of religion can be either negative (as in Marx, hoping for the dissolution of religion as society becomes more able to meet real human needs) or positive (as in Durkheim, seeing the permanent need of religion as a means of articulating the ideals of the group). In a similar way, psychological explanations of religions can be negative (as in Freud, who saw religions as manifestations of neurosis) or positive (as in Jung, who saw religious symbols as necessary for personal integration and mental health).

These forms of explanation are all functional, setting out what religious systems do, socially or individually. Religions are seen as a means to some other end, whether that is the symptomatic expression of conflict and dissatisfaction or the attainment of harmony and health. Surveying the leading writings in this field, it looks very much as if some religious views will be symptoms of social and individual disorder, and others will be helpful for social and individual fulfilment. There is, in other words, both neurotic religion and integrating religion. We would obviously prefer the latter. But it is rather odd to think that religions exist simply in order to express neuroses or advance integration. Believers, both neurotic and integrated, think they believe something that is true.

There is, in other words, a question to ask about the content, as well as the function, of religious beliefs. Are there supernatural realities which are not part of the content of some human mind, not even part of a 'social mind' or collective unconscious, but which exist in their own right? What functional explanations suggest is that the way in which such realities are apprehended is partly a result of the nature of the minds that apprehend them. There is, perhaps, no neutral way of apprehending the spiritual. It is not like seeing a table, which is there whatever mood one happens to be in. The spiritual is apprehended as a dynamic power in relation to a human perceiver facing particular problems and working out specific solutions to them.

It is misleading to ask whether religious beliefs are true, as if that was a neutrally ascertainable matter of fact. As Jung put it, 'Only that which acts upon me do I recognise as real and actual.'[81] The 'truth' of a religious belief is known in some definite psychological response to an active power, the form of whose activity itself depends upon the predispositions and receptivity of the human mind.

A dim analogy is our relation to other people. If I have a headache, have just had an argument with my partner, and am worried about doing my job properly, then when I meet my boss I will be in a complex emotional state, which will affect my interpretation of what she says to me. It will probably also affect what she does say to me, as she will perceive my confused condition and act in response to it. Maybe she will misinterpret my condition as laziness, and then things will really get complicated. This is the stuff of which novels are made. Personal knowledge cannot be divorced from feelings and interpretation.

How the spiritual acts in relation to me may similarly depend upon my psychological state, and how I respond to those acts, also depends on my state. There is a twofold subjective component of such apprehension, my initial predisposition and my quality of response. Whether religion is psychotic or integrating may depend upon what aspects of the spiritual I am predisposed to apprehend, and how I respond to such apprehension. I may attract the dark forces of unbalance and chaos, and respond to them by seeking to use them for my own selfish purposes, perhaps to injure my enemies or supposed enemies. Or I may be open to powers of harmony and equanimity, and use them to help me overcome selfish desires. Both forms of religious practice, typified in 'black' witchcraft and devotional prayer respectively, are commonly found throughout the world.

Are there such varied powers, which exist, in a spiritual realm? To believers, it seems that there are. But they see them in different ways. A practising witch among the Azande may seem to apprehend a variety of spiritual forces, which can be used by humans in various ways for good or ill. A Christian or Vaishnava devotee will seem to apprehend a loving supreme Lord, who asks only for love in return. The former may discern no supreme Lord, and the latter may discern destructive spiritual powers, if at all, only as demons which are subordinate and ultimately doomed powers.

As far as the phenomenology of religious experience goes, it is the case that malevolent powers are apprehended as well as beneficent powers. Spirit can be apprehended as destructive and fragmented, or as creative and unified. As far as a consideration of reports of intense experiences throughout the whole range of religions goes, Jung seems correct in saying that Spirit has a shadow side as well as an integrating power. How this experienced fact is to be theoretically articulated is another question. In the next chapter I shall illustrate how some of the earliest recorded religious views, from Babylon and Egypt, think of a cosmic conflict between many spirit powers of chaos and order, wilderness and city. But they also show commitment to some underlying moral order in the universe, and to the requirement that humans should serve the gods in order to achieve some higher fulfilment or goal. The intellectual history of religion is in part the history of how cosmic conflict and cosmic moral purpose – both expressed by symbols rooted in the visionary experiences of seers and prophets – are to be harmonised.

Perhaps it cannot be done. The idea of a greater moral purpose may have to be renounced, and the idea of cosmic conflict can be relocated in purely physical forces of the natural world that carry no spiritual or moral overtones. That is an attractive option with all the appeal of economy of thought, but its cost is the relegation of all religious experiences and teachings to the realm of the illusory. Perhaps an idea of Spirit can be devised that can plausibly suggest how its destructive and creative aspects are blended together, and how there can be a moral goal in a universe that makes its attainment so difficult. The main problem is that any such theory seems hugely under-determined by the experiences that give rise to it. That is why both James and Jung renounce the theoretical enterprise, and claim only to be recording psychologically evident data. They take the data seriously, and refuse to reduce it to illusion or neurosis. But they postulate no grand theory.

Or so they say. In fact, however, James goes on to write about his philosophy of spiritual pluralism, with many higher minds in communication with the human. And Jung advocates the idea of a fourfold God (masculine and feminine, light and dark), and of human integration as consisting in an acceptance of the dark and contra-sexual sides of human nature, in a cosmic journey towards complete integration of the fragmented cosmic consciousness itself. These are both recognisably religious, though rather unorthodox, views.

Religious experiences may be the ultimate origin of religious beliefs. But such experiences need to be interpreted by means of a general conception of reality, which they (or some of them) can then be taken to confirm. The theoretical enterprise cannot be renounced. The question is whether any such general conception can be formulated which is consistent, plausible, coherent with other knowledge, and which enables experiences to be assessed and sometimes accepted as confirmations of the conception. That is not a question psychology can answer. It is a question that haunts religion still.

Find out more . . .

Sigmund Freud, *Moses and Monotheism, The Future of an Illusion* and *Totem and Taboo* are short, readable and provocative books, and are available in many editions. They can all be found in Sigmund Freud, *The Standard Edition of the Complete Psychological Works of Sigmund Freud*, ed. James Strachey and Anna Freud (London: Hogarth Press, 1953).

William James, *The Varieties of Religious Experience* ([Gifford lectures, 1901] London: Fontana, 1971) remains a classic in this field.

Carl Jung, *Psychology and Religion* (New Haven: Yale University Press, 1938) is a small book on the general topic. Many other pieces, including those referred to in the text, can be found in *The Collected Works of C.G. Jung*, trans. R.F.C. Hull and others (Princeton: Princeton University Press, 1953–77).

Michael Argyle, *Psychology and Religion* (London: Routledge, 2000) is a very clear, short introduction by a psychologist who is unimpressed on the whole by psychoanalysis.

Eric Sharpe, *Comparative Religion: A History* (London: Duckworth, 1998), is a good clear history of the comparative study of religion, introducing virtually all the major thinkers in the field.

PART II

THE GREAT WORLD RELIGIONS

5

RHYTHMS OF THE SPIRIT
The Beginnings of Religion

Religion is a combination of a theoretical conception of reality and of claims to experience, and to participate in the power of, a transcendent reality. This is a state or being which is other and greater in power or value than things in the world of space and time.

In the earliest prehistory of humanity, the cave paintings, burial chambers and carved figures that survive seem to many to suggest some awareness of a spiritual dimension of reality, seen as pluriform and diverse in its expressions, under many symbolic forms, both dangerous and life enhancing. We can trace religion back to the earliest forms of humanity we know about. Even though it is not true that knowing the origins of religion tells you what its 'true essence' is, it is still important to trace how the religious sense developed from elementary beginnings to the sophisticated forms it takes in the modern world. Those elementary forms are probably with us still in disguised ways, and knowledge of them may still give valuable clues about the role and scope of religion today.

However, the fact is that little is known about the earliest stages of human religious history. It is only with the growth of agriculture and village settlements that we begin to get a few more definite clues. After many thousands of generations of living as hunter-gatherers, the first evidence appears of humans cultivating cereals in the Fertile Crescent, between Egypt and Mesopotamia, in about 9000 BCE. By 5000 BCE, three main areas of agriculture existed on earth: the Fertile Crescent, the Indus valley in India, and the Yellow River valley in China. In two or three thousand years, the nature of human life radically changed. Animals were herded, not hunted. Wheat was sown and harvested, not found as it happened to grow. Villages and towns, with mud-brick and even stone houses, began to develop. Humans began to shape nature – but were still almost wholly dependent on the vagaries of climate and disease, on the seasons of dormant winter and revitalising spring. A delicate symbiosis of cherishing and control, of respect and mastery, grew between humans and their natural habitat. Humans planted and watered, fed and sheltered. But they also ploughed and consumed, killed and devoured. And in all this, they contended continually with the wilderness powers, human and non-human, whose savagery, if unchecked, lays waste to all human endeavour.

It was probably at this time that ideas such as those of dying and rising agricultural spirits developed, reflecting the sowing (burying or descent to the underworld) of the seed in the dark earth, its growth in the warmth of the sun (resurrection or return to life), its harvesting and threshing (slaying) when the crop is ripe, and its eating (communion) to enable human life to continue. The vegetation gods of the first planters express that reality through the rhythms of spring and autumn, seedtime and harvest, and the inter-woven themes of love and death that mark the genesis of life on earth. These themes still live, often in a disguised form, in many contemporary forms of religion.

It is not hard to see the concern of these early myths with discernment of a spiritual reality that is known in and through the elements and processes of the material world. In sharing in the cycles of nature, its dormant waiting, its sudden rising to new life, its brilliant flowering and long, beautiful fading, we share in the rhythms of the spirit. Rituals do not make the crops grow so much as allow us to participate in the natural processes of germination, generation and growth, in which by a massive breakthrough to a new form of human life, namely agriculture, humans are able to play a responsible part. Rituals do not control nature as an object to be manipulated – that might be seen as a very unreligious attitude. They celebrate nature, as the expression of a vital power that is to be responded to with reverence and gratitude, with awe and appreciative attention. It is not that religious rites are reminiscences of past stupidities. Rather, the earliest rites we know of in human history are precursors of participation in spiritual reality, appearing to us in its many material forms, which is still the mark of the religiously inclined mind.

It is hardly surprising that these ancient forms also carry traces of practices that seem to us barbaric and unjustifiable. Evidence of human sacrifice, the mutilation and confinement of women, the use of malevolent spells and self-flagellation, the practice of orgiastic fertility rituals and the often violent exorcism of demonic powers alleged to cause disease and death are found in many ancient societies (they are found in many modern societies too). The Spiritual is not necessarily friendly or universally benevolent. It is often seen as a force of fertility and power which is indifferent to moral concerns, and which can be used for the dominance of one tribe over others. Many forms of religion are tribal or restricted in their search for human good, and it is only some forms of religious life that become either moralised by considerations of global humanity or rationalised by considerations of consonance with the carefully observed nature of the universe.

ENUMA ELISH

With the invention of writing, the first evidence of which is in about 3250 BCE in Sumeria, we begin to gain a clearer idea of what early humans thought and believed. The stories, or fragments of stories, that have come down to us from around that time speak allusively of the powers of wilderness and the natural order, of conflict and sustenance, of sacrifice and care, powers that set bounds to human existence in the long ages of unrecorded time.

The earliest written fragments we have are from Sumeria and Egypt. One of the earliest stories we have is the *Enuma Elish*,[82] from the early civilisation of Babylon, between the Tigris and Euphrates, in what is now Iraq. Here the early settlements of agriculturists had developed into cities of stone, with strong defences and hierarchies of power, and temples to the gods, the liminal powers (powers at the boundaries) of human being in the world. When we read the fragmentary records of these ancient people, we gain our first definite insight into the religious thoughts and feelings of humanity. Here, more than anywhere, we see how they conceived the cosmos and the place of human beings within it, how they related to the gods and what such a relation meant in their lives. It is interesting to read this early creation story partly because it makes a change from the book of Genesis. More importantly, it suggests a way of reading religious stories (myths) that gets away from literalism and shows how profound spiritual teachings can be conveyed in imaginative stories. It also suggests a good way of making sense of the early chapters of the book of Genesis, once we see the Hebrew myth in the context of other early creation stories from the same part of the world.

In the *Enuma Elish* all things originate from primal chaos, a world without diversity or form, the boundless deep, the Unconditioned. This is signified by water, an element without apparent form, immense and powerful. Water is what gives life. Indeed, it is what we are mostly made of, and need to survive. But it is also what threatens life, its storms and floods taking all things down into its silent depths. Water, fresh and salt, depicts the ambiguity of the world, giving and taking life with seeming indifference, an object of gratitude and fear, the primal power of creation.

It was not a bad guess that all things came from water. Thales, one of the first philosopher-scientists, made the same guess. They had not heard about electrons, much less quarks or superstrings. But the point is not really what came first, in the order of time. It is about how one can symbolise the ultimate powers of being, what effective symbol one can find for the origin and depth of all the things of time. Water symbolises the formless abyss of primal being, the ambiguities of creation and destruction that characterise the cosmos, and the opacity to human reason of the primal origin. From this abyss, human reason, which works by dividing things into categories and abstracting essential natures, falls back in bafflement. The primal deep, the unlimited ocean of being, without name and form, defeats all intellectual enquiry.

Yet from the formless forms arise. In the Babylonian story, they arise in pairs, brother and sister, again expressing the balance, the potential conflict and the interrelatedness of all created being. From these many pairs arise two great gods, Anu the sky-god and Ea the god of wisdom. The sky-god is the god of order and authority. In Greece and Rome he was to be named Zeus or Jupiter. He brings just order to the things that are, maintaining all things under one rule of cosmic law, and ensuring that the times and seasons pass in regular succession. The god of wisdom, Ea, is a god of creativity and imagination. Having magical power, he brings about new and surprising events, and into the ordered cosmos he introduces particularity and originality. He is the god of surprises and of wonder, sometimes mischievous and unruly, the spirit of the new.

All these things happened long before human time began, in what Australian Aborigines call the Time of Dreams. Decoding the story, one can discern the ultimate mystery of the unknowable source, and the principles of order and originality that characterise the cosmos in which humans came to have their origin. But in the aeons before human history there was to be a cataclysmic conflict among the gods, the powers of being.

In Milton's *Paradise Lost* there is a dramatic account of war in heaven. That war is between God and Satan, an angel who rebelled against God, and was cast down to Hell. The war of the Babylonian gods is not such a straightforward story of good versus evil. The problem was that all the young gods were running about making a row, and disturbing the rest of Apsu, the old father god. Apsu, who must have been extremely short-tempered, decided to destroy them all. So the war was between the young, active, ebullient gods and the old, tired and sleepy god. In that war it was Ea who cast a magic circle of protection around the gods, sent Apsu to sleep, slew him and took his crown. In that war, it is hard to tell who is good and who is evil. But the young gods, energetic and active, conquer the old god of primal sleep.

In Greece, too, there was war between the gods and their ancestors, the Titans. There, it was Zeus who castrated and imprisoned Chronos, his own father. This theme, of a war among the cosmic powers, is widespread in many archaic societies. The cosmos was seen as a place of conflict, as well as of order and wisdom. Yet the conflict is itself a creative one. Ea fashions out of the dead body of Apsu a realm in which he lives. That realm is born out of the slaying of the god. Wisdom carved out of the primal deep a habitable world. The primordial creative power threatens to re-absorb its own children, back into that formless deep from which they came. It is not a set of evil, rebellious gods who are to be overcome by the power of the all-good king of gods. Rather, the king must be dethroned by his children, and from his corpse a world must be woven in which activity and community can thrive. Neither Apsu nor the young gods are unambiguously good. They are the powers of form and formlessness, activity and rest, sound and silence, from whose continual conflict, in a vast non-moral cosmos, the universe is formed.

The conflict between Apsu and his children was only the prelude to the greater conflict between Tiamat, the salt-water sea, spouse of Apsu, begetter of all the gods, and Marduk, son of Ea, who became the greatest of the gods. Tiamat was roused by one group of the gods, led by Kingu, to seek revenge for the death of her husband. She brought into being eleven kinds of monsters, including serpents, dragons and scorpion-men, all with 'irresistible weapons'. Again, the cosmic chaos from which all things originate becomes a threatening immensity, generating myriad terrible forms of destructive power. Generated from her, and indeed living and moving within her, the gods develop greater and more personal attributes and powers, generation by generation. Authority, wisdom and, eventually, the stupendous might of Marduk, come into being. These gods are not good, but not wholly evil either. They are properly regarded as beyond, or perhaps as prior to, morality, as diverse and active energies, carving out particularity and order within a wilderness of chaos.

Marduk is the one who would become the god of Babylon, god of the city, of humanity. Before the formless dragon of the deep, the terrifying Tiamat, only he can prevail where appeals to reason (Anu) and to magical wisdom (Ea) fail. In single combat, he ensnares her in his net. As she opens her mouth to engulf him, he drives a mighty wind into her belly, shoots fiery arrows into her heart, and ends her life. From her body, Marduk shapes earth and sky. He places three hundred gods in the sky, and three hundred on the earth. So the powers of sky and earth are ordered on the great division of the primal sea. From the blood of Kingu, the leader of her armies, Marduk formed the human race. And upon humans he places the responsibility of providing food for the gods.

So at last, in this Babylonian story, the human race finds its origin and role. Beyond this earth there lies a vast and terrifying realm, where the gods play and fight, their ways beyond human imagination. But in that vast cosmic drama, the primal generative chaos is held captive, and becomes the encompassing ocean of being within which human life is played out. Among the many divine powers Marduk, king of gods, holds all destinies in his hand, and requires of humans obedience to his rule of justice and order. Humans are made to serve the gods by cultivating the wilderness of earth. Formed of demon's blood, ruled by the all-powerful shaper of worlds, men and women act out a shadowy reflection of the life of the gods, their vocation servitude, their destiny, perhaps, the approval of their hidden masters – even, possibly, an entrance after death into that hidden world, if the gods will it.

This Babylonian story accompanied rituals played out in the temples of Sumeria and Babylon, rituals which represent, make present, the perpetual battle between chaos and order, wilderness and city, the triumph of the king and the divine requirement of justice in an ambiguous and largely amoral universe. You, the story says, are a mix of chaos and creativity. Serpent and warrior both live in you. It is for you to rise from the formless ocean of being to serve the gods of order and wisdom, both revering Nature as your ultimate begetter, within whom you live, and yet sacrificing her to form new life and consciousness.

STORIES OF THE GODS

In ancient Egypt there is a similar creation story, in which the gods arise in pairs from primeval chaos. Seth becomes the force of darkness and violence, while Horus is the king of gods, and the divine counterpart of the Egyptian Pharaoh. His mother, Isis, is goddess of wisdom and magical knowledge, and her consort Osiris, murdered by Seth, becomes lord and judge of the dead. In Egypt there was a much greater concern with death and afterlife, but the themes of human participation in a cosmic conflict, in divine sacrifice and through it the generation of new life, are common. In these ancient polytheisms, long since extinct, a great narrative of participation in a wider spiritual reality, which can support and strengthen the incipient empires of the earth – and control the powers of chaos and wilderness – is fashioned in the service of warrior-kings by priests and poets, by visionaries and the guardians of oracles.

What these stories evoke is a sense of human life as essentially related to superhuman powers, objectively existing powers greater and other than human, which dictate the proper way in which humans should live. Every part of the world both hides and discloses a god, a personal presence with its own distinctive form and mood. All emerge from primal chaos, and all live under the rule of a god like the warrior god Marduk, who sacrifices the primordial dragon of the salt-water sea in order to bring wisdom, friendship and joy – but also ignorance, envy and discontent – into being. Under his harsh yet just rule, the supernatural powers of the world fight, forge friendships and feast, and their servants, men and women of the earth, find their fulfilment in pleasing and honouring the gods.

The stories have been moulded over many generations by human imagination, prompted perhaps by dreams, visions and reflections, which seek to probe the mysteries of existence. Some people see them simply as fantasies, vain attempts to make sense of a universe of which humans have as yet no true understanding. Perhaps no one today would see them as factual accounts of how humans came into being – these are long-dead religions, with no fundamentalist defenders left alive. They are without doubt imaginative stories, and literally false. Yet might they not portray the character of something like a personal reality, expressed yet also concealed in the finite forms of space and time, in relation to which humans can find the deepest meaning of their own being? And might they not tell us something important about the roots of religious imagination and devotion even in modern religion?

In the Babylonian stories, spiritual reality is seen as manifold – there are many gods, many moods and aspects of personal being – and as dipolar – a constant interplay of darkness and light, chaos and order, city and sea. Out of that dialectical conflict, out of the sacrifice of primal being, new life and creativity emerges. The blood of the slain gods gives food for the world, and the world provides food, harvested by human beings, for the gods. Humans are bound into the cosmic order as those responsible for making the earth fertile, so that the personal being of the cosmos may thrive and increase. So humans enter into conscious relationship with the manifold and dipolar reality of Spirit, helping to realise its potential values, to make them actual, to give them particular form and vitality – and that is what it is to 'feed the gods'.

If we look reasonably impartially at a whole range of creation stories in many societies throughout the world, it is clearly impossible to take all of them as literally descriptive. Their diversity suggests a strong element of human imagination, local historical and geographical colouring, and tribal tradition, in each set of stories. Their presence in officially sanctioned, and expensively maintained, cultic practices counts against their just being fictional narratives. So we are led to seek a symbolic interpretation. And, as far as believers in these stories are concerned, what is symbolised is some objectively existing reality. The believers may be mistaken, but at least we have to say that they genuinely thought the stories depict spiritual reality in a way that is appropriate, if not entirely adequate.

What is spiritual reality? The phrase is intentionally vague, but it points to something more like consciousness than unconsciousness, more like mind than matter, more like something purposive and valuable than like something accidental and value-neutral. So if you ask whether a spiritual reality exists, you are asking whether there is something (or some things) conscious, with purposes and values, underlying the objective world. That reality might be conceived in personal terms, as a god or gods. Or it may be conceived less personally, as an objectively existing, immaterial value or principle of order, underlying the material world. If you think there is such a reality, then you may think that the Babylonian stories are giving a set of images for thinking of spiritual reality – and that does not commit you to saying the images are adequate or even appropriate. It just says: that is what the images were meant to be doing, and that is most basically what religion is.

A survey of the earliest written records of religion suggests two major facts: that humans were concerned for relationship with a real and objective spiritual reality, and that this reality could only be expressed in symbols, originating in dreams, visions and poetic imagination. From the very beginning religion swings between literalising the gods and seeing them as only projections of human ideals. Perhaps we need a little of both. Our projections govern what we experience and how we describe it, but there always remains that obstinate resistant reality, just beyond our descriptive reach, inviting our projections and perhaps shaping them to particular forms by its diverse relationships with us. Maybe our projections themselves are drawn out by the insistent attract-ive power of a transcendent spiritual reality, occasionally disclosing a dim outline of its being, but then continually withdrawing again into mystery. If so, no religious account can just be dismissed, but we might be cautious in giving any one account a uniquely literal interpretation.

That is a good reason for studying religion as a global phenomenon, and for seeing the history of religion as the history of developing apprehensions of an objective yet elusive spiritual reality.

THE AXIAL AGE: MODELS OF SPIRIT

After the archaic religions of the hunter-gatherers, the agriculturists of the great river-valley civilisations and the warrior-heroes of the first human cities, a decisive saltation occurred in the evolution of religion, in the six hundred years from 800 BCE to 200 BCE, in what Karl Jaspers called 'the Axial Age' of religious thought.[83] In the main great ancient centres of culture – the Fertile Crescent, the Indian subcontinent, China and the Greek city-states – the multiple symbols of the Transcendent were integrated and unified around central normative images. These integrations gave rise to the major religious traditions in our present world, in their traditional forms.

If we are to think of the spiritual realm as integrated around the idea of one central normative image, there are six basic general possibilities for thinking of the relation of that imaged reality to the material cosmos (see diagram on next page). First, spirit and matter may be seen as distinct and independent, though related to each other in various ways. Matter is not created by spirit, and is eternally existent without any spiritual cause. This can be called **dualism**. If humans are mixtures of spirit and matter, the spiritual goal for human life is usually seen as liberation from matter. Some forms of ascetic religion originating in India, such as Jainism and the Sankhya and Yoga traditions, see liberation from the wheel of material rebirth as the goal of religious practice. Some forms of Theravada Buddhism, also, are dualist, in distinguishing a 'material' realm of atomistic elements from the realm of spirit – *nirvana* – which is distinct from all such elements, and is unconditioned and the goal of the spiritual life, but is certainly not the creator of the material world.

Second, matter and spirit may be seen as different aspects of one unitary reality. This can be called **monism** – there is only one reality, but

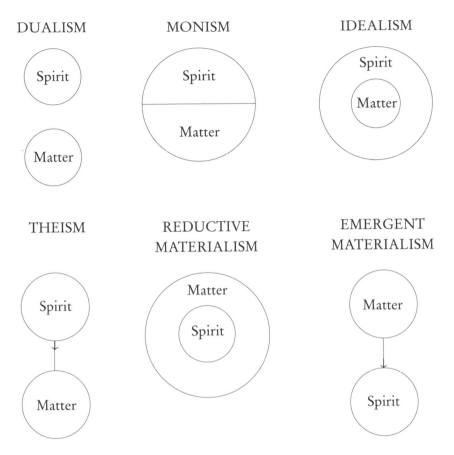

DUALISM

Spirit

Matter

MONISM

Spirit

Matter

IDEALISM

Spirit

Matter

THEISM

Spirit

Matter

REDUCTIVE
MATERIALISM

Matter

Spirit

EMERGENT
MATERIALISM

Matter

Spirit

Six models for understanding the relationship of spirit to matter.

it has two distinct aspects. What is common to this view is the denial that there is one supreme creator of the material universe, together with an affirmation that there is an important spiritual dimension to reality. Chinese traditions such as Confucianism and Taoism are variations on such a view, seeing the material cosmos as having an inner spiritual dimension, the Tao or the Way of Heaven. Some schools of Buddhism fall into this general category, in seeing *samsara*, the wheel of rebirth, as another aspect of *nirvana*, the realm of liberated existence. The emphasis for such traditions is on attaining harmony and balance between the spiritual and material aspects of existence.

Third, spirit can be seen as the only reality. Matter can then be seen as an appearance of spirit, and that appearance can be seen either as a positive self-realisation or as an illusion. Matter is a realisation of spirit if it is an objective manifestation of what spirit is. We might see the human body, or better, the human face, as the expression of a particular personality. The face, we might say, is how the person appears to other people. When the person is angry, the face is contorted, and the contortions express the anger. So the body could be how what is in reality a purely spiritual person appears to others, or what enables the person to express their feelings. In a similar way, the material universe could be how spiritual reality appears, how that reality expresses itself in a specific way.

Matter is an illusion if it is rather like a mirage in the desert. You think you see a pool of water, but it is not really there. It just seems to you as though it is there. Or I might dream that I am lying on the beach, and even enjoy the dream. But it is not real. It is a figment of my imagination. So perhaps the whole world is the dream of spirit, something that seems to be real, but is not real at all. When spirit wakes up, or knows itself as it truly is, the dream will disappear. These are forms of **idealism**, a view that says that only spirit is truly real, and matter is only an appearance. It is characteristic of the Indian tradition of Advaita (non-dualism), which some people wrongly think is the only Hindu philosophy – though it is a major religious and philosophical tradition in India. Some schools of Buddhism, such as the *cittamatra*, or 'mind only', school, fall into this category, since they see our sense of individual identity as an illusion disguising a basically 'non-dual' reality – though one made up of an infinity of separate elements, not of one supreme Self, like Advaita.

Fourth, spirit and matter can be seen as distinct, though matter depends for its existence upon spirit. Matter may be generated by spirit either unconsciously and by necessity, or by a conscious act of will, and spirit may either determine all that happens in the material realm, or permit it a relative autonomy of its own. These are all forms of **theism**, which is associated most clearly with the Semitic religious traditions, which go back to early Hebrew religion. Many Indian religious traditions are also theistic, though they tend to see the created universe as existing 'within' God, rather than as absolutely distinct.

Fifth, matter can be seen as the only reality, and consciousness is an illusion, or an epiphenomenon or by-product of material processes. This possibility, of **reductive materialism**, is not popular with religious believers, and usually represents an anti-religious possibility.

Sixth, spirit and matter can be seen as different, while spirit depends for its nature and existence upon matter. This may be called **emergent materialism**. There have been materialists of this sort in most parts of the world, but as a school it is found most explicitly in ancient Greece, where philosophical schools competed with traditional religious cults, and in Aristotle a basically materialist philosophy posited the increase of consciousness and intelligence as a basic goal of the material process. Much later in European history, some types of Hegelian and Marxist philosophies are materialist in this looser sense, and some evolutionist views posit a God who is the result of an emergent cosmic process. Of these six possibilities, however, only the first four – dualism, monism, idealism and theism – were seriously explored by the developing traditions of the Axial Age.

The early civilisations explored these different models of Transcendence, as they sought to bring some sort of integration and unity to the many gods, spirits and ancestors of earlier cults, and sought a supreme value that would define a final human goal and be an exemplar and inspiration for human life in the world. This process of rationalising (constructing an integrated systematic spiritual unity) and moralising (positing one supreme spiritual value) was inevitable as humans began to reflect systematically on the nature of the world in which they lived and on the sort of human life that was most worth living.

The distinctively religious data for such reflection was given by experience, and in particular by the paradigm experiences of the great teachers and founders of traditions. It could be a great ascetic who claimed to have experienced the wisdom and bliss of the liberated state. It could be a wise teacher who found in his own experience the way to live a just and compassionate life in society, or who was able to penetrate the delusions of sense to apprehend a more fundamental and rational order. It could be one who claimed to experience union with an Absolute Reality of intelligence and bliss, one who experienced in an intense and overwhelming way the presence of a personal Lord, or one who seemed to hear the very words of the Lord resounding in his mind.

It would, I think, be quite wrong to see these different ways as totally different apprehensions of totally different and contradictory things. We need to see here a blend of experience and reflection, and of modes of interaction with Transcendence, which are shaped both by a long cultural tradition and by attempts to develop a basic model for interpreting Transcendence. The development of the 'great traditions' of religion can be seen as experiments in exploring interpretations of Transcendence, and of course part of this process is the assessment of claims that the Transcendent has revealed or disclosed itself in a specific way to human beings.

Find out more . . .

The main Babylonian creation myths can be found in A. Heidel (ed.), *The Babylonian Genesis* (Chicago: University of Chicago, 1963). It is interesting to read it in conjunction and comparison with the biblical Genesis, chapters 1–11.

There is no general agreement on the nature and development of archaic religion. Joseph Campbell, *Primitive Mythology* (London: Penguin, 1969) conveniently collects a huge range of sources, and interprets them from a Jungian point of view. Excellent short collections of myths from various part of the world can be found in the series The Legendary Past, published by the British Museum Press.

Keith Ward, *Religion and Revelation* (Oxford: Oxford University Press, 1994), parts 2 and 3, has further material on archaic and Axial Age religions.

6

CHILDREN OF ABRAHAM

Judaism, Christianity and Islam

JUDAISM

The theistic model was developed in the Near East, among a nomadic tribal people who followed a God who, they thought, called them to discover a homeland of their own by the eastern Mediterranean Sea. This God, who was believed to have liberated them from slavery in Egypt and to have given them a law of justice and mercy, was a personal God known through mighty acts of deliverance in history, and issued an absolute command to seek justice in the world. Early Hebrew religion was not particularly concerned with life after death (unlike the Egyptians), or with escape from the material world into some spiritual realm. It may have begun with halting and ambiguous insights into a particular morally commanding and historically acting God, but it developed into a faith in the general providential ordering and moral purpose of history. For the God who gave laws for the Hebrew tribes and helped them establish a homeland came to be seen as the one and only creator of the whole universe, ordering history to fulfil a divine purpose.

The major prophets of Israel and Judah consolidated this tradition of the worship of one God of justice and mercy, which was in time to give rise to the Semitic faiths of Judaism, Christianity and Islam. Before the power of these traditions, the earlier pantheons of Egypt and Sumeria faded away, though they left traces of their existence in their successor faiths. The God of the prophets retained traces of his tribal ancestry. God was a jealous God, sometimes seeming to be concerned with the good of the children of Israel to the virtual exclusion of others. God's moral demands sometimes seem to us vengeful and harshly retributive, retaining many traces of a limitation of moral concern to humans, or even more restrictedly to males. Cosmic conflict was accounted for by the sternly retributive character of God, and by the fact that God is beyond assessment by any human moral standards. The cosmic moral purpose was seen as the manifestation of the glory of God, both in the beauty of creation and in the majesty of the divine anger. God requires human commitment to justice and mercy and complete obedience to the divine will, and the sovereign will of God is supreme and unquestionable.

The dominant model in this tradition is that of sovereign will. There is just one will that governs all things. It freely brings the cosmos into existence, and freely chooses that some creatures should be accepted into a special relationship with the divine. That relationship is conceived as basically personal, and it exists simply because that is what God, the supreme personal reality, wills.

There are of course many possible variations on this basic model. God might create a universe just so that it will express the divine beauty and immense power and wisdom (the 'glory' of God). God might create it so that there can be other creative and enjoying agents in existence. God might will a community in which love, co-operation and compassion can exist, and in which God might even share. God may determine all the acts of creatures, or may leave some of their acts undetermined, so that they have limited autonomy of choice. God may select some creatures for eternal relationship with the divine, or may decide that all creatures will have such relationship, or may leave to them the choice to enter into companionship with God or not. God may be of unlimited and absolute power, or may be limited in power, either by divine choice or by some necessity in the nature of things.

There are many possibilities of argument and disagreement. Jews have not been slow to exploit those possibilities. A well-known Jewish story tells of a Jewish man who was shipwrecked on a desert island. After many years of isolation he was rescued, and his rescuers observed two piles of stones at opposite ends of the beach. 'That is my synagogue, where I worship God,' he said, pointing to the pile on the right. 'What about the pile on the left?' he was asked. 'Ah,' he replied, 'that is the synagogue I don't go to.'

None of the great monotheistic traditions is a monolithic, universally agreed system. It can often be a problem to say just how many differences you are prepared to embrace in your community. But on the whole a Jew is a Jew by birth, custom, sensibility and practice, rather than because of holding a definite set of beliefs. The great medieval Jewish philosopher Maimonides set down thirteen principles of belief that are widely accepted, but though they have been in Jewish prayer books since the early sixteenth century, they have no authoritative status, and no Jew has to believe them.

Christians are much keener on having creeds and 'confessions of belief', with the consequence that many different Christian Churches have sprung up, especially in America, where it is considered perfectly proper to start a new church for almost any reason. For example, there are Baptists, Strict and Particular Baptists, Primitive Methodists and Wesleyan Methodists. Even where churches do not actually split, some groups are often strongly opposed to others within the same church. It seems impossible to get universal agreement on religious beliefs.

It is clear that there are many varieties of theism, and that even within one religious tradition there can be many diverse views. Nevertheless, ethical monotheism can be said to have its origin with the ancient Hebrews, and with their conviction that God had chosen a specific people, the children of Abraham, Isaac and Jacob, to enter into an especially intimate relationship – a covenant, construed sometimes as 'marriage'[84] – with God. Jews have retained a distinctive form of faith, which is conceived as given to the descendants of one man, and to those who ally themselves with those descendants. Its faith is not meant for all people, but sets this group apart from all others.

Remarkably, however exclusive and local this seems, ancient Judaism (or Hebrew religion, properly speaking) has been the most influential religion in the world. It has not just remained as a local cult, unlike most of the thousands of indigenous traditions, though they too are experiencing something of a revival in the modern world. Christianity, Islam and other more recent religious movements all acknowledge their debt to the Hebrew prophets. Yet Judaism has continued to exist, maintaining its own distinctive identity through persecutions and exiles, true to the law of the God of Abraham, Isaac and Jacob. It seeks no converts and has never seriously thought of world domination. It is happy to let others follow their own ways of faith. Yet of course it does make universal truth claims (often summarised as the Noahide Covenant) – that there is one God, one judgment and one basic moral law. Like many other particularist traditions, it will continue to exist as a distinctive socio-cultural form, and will resist absorption into any universal culture or faith.

The vast majority of Jews see the foundation of Israel as a secular state in 1948 as the restoration of the homeland that they lost under Roman occupation in 132 CE. The settlement of Israel at the cost of the dispossession of thousands of Palestinians is one of the most intractable political problems of the modern world. There are many different religious Jewish attitudes to this problem, but it is certainly too simple to say that the problem has a religious cause. The main cause is the *Shoah* and the promise of a homeland made by the British. The strong desire for a homeland is naturally closely bound up with religious sentiments, where they exist. But those sentiments vary from extreme territorial expansionism to a desire for simple coexistence with Palestinians. Again, religion is as various as its adherents. There is brutal, callous, intolerant religion and there is compassionate, kind and tolerant religion. It is for those who see Judaism as the service of a merciful God who wills love of enemies and justice for all people – key themes of the

Hebrew scriptures – to see that the faith expands and deepens concern for justice, concern for the oppressed and human flourishing.

The lesson of Judaism is that particularist religious traditions are not going to disappear, to make way for some universal global faith. For the foreseeable future, there will be differences between human beliefs, some of them very basic. There will always be conservative believers, who remain loyal to an original revelation – in the Jewish case, to the Torah revealed to Moses. There will be those loyal to the community of faith, but prepared to reinterpret and revise in accordance with what they feel to be new knowledge. And there will be those who acknowledge the revelation with gratitude, perhaps incorporating parts of it into their own beliefs, but remain outside the community of faith. For most humans, whatever their beliefs, Judaism can be a resource of spiritual insight, centred on the revelation of God as sovereign will to the prophets. For believing Jews, it is a revealed way of life that sets them apart for the reverence and love of a God of mercy and loving-kindness. There will always be unbalanced, spiteful and intolerant believers. If there were not, religion would not be necessary. The challenge for Jews is to make their religious tradition a real channel of moral power in the world, 'a light to the Gentiles'.[85]

CHRISTIANITY

The theistic model developed in a rather different way in Christianity, which began as a Jewish messianic movement, but after some preliminary skirmishes with the Roman Empire, got into the hands of the emperor Constantine, and was made into the official religion of what was, after all, a brutal militaristic empire. This was good for the spread of something, but was it the original gospel? Employed as a means of imposing uniformity ('orthodoxy') and suppressing dissent, the Christian Church changed from a largely pacifist millennial Jewish sect into an authoritarian imperial cult in just under five hundred years. The Roman Empire altered the character of Christian faith, but underneath the forms of socio-political dominance Christianity remained a primarily inward and spiritual faith.

The basic Christian belief is that Jesus was the Messiah, the figure for whom the Jewish prophets had long hoped, who would bring forgiveness of sins and reconciliation between ancient enemies, and usher in an age of justice and peace, establishing the rule of God on earth. Christians, however, give a new and radical interpretation to the idea of a Messiah (the 'chosen one' of God). Jesus does bring divine forgiveness and founds the Kingdom of God, Christians say, but he does so by suffering and dying on the cross, thus showing the unlimited love of God and the reality of the Kingdom as an inner rule of God's spirit in the hearts of those who turn to God. Jesus, according to orthodox Christian belief, was not just the servant of God. He was the earthly form of the eternal wisdom (the 'Word') of God. The whole universe was shaped on the pattern of that wisdom, and it will be brought to fulfilment within it. After his death, Jesus was raised to the presence of God, and so humanity has, in him, been permanently united to the divine nature. As the unique historical focal point of divine–human unity, Jesus is the true messianic king of all humanity, but this will only be fully revealed when history is completed in God.

So the Christian vision is that the creator God, the supreme sovereign will, does not just declare the divine will through revelation to the prophets. God actually unites humanity to the divine being, giving up the divine glory to share in human finitude and suffering, in order that humans can in turn be raised to share in the divine life. The sovereign will of God comes to be seen as a will to share in creaturely weakness and suffering, and unite the created cosmos, in a renewed form, to the divine being itself. The theistic model here unites the spiritual and the material more intimately, though the basic model remains that of the total dependence of the material cosmos upon the spiritual reality of God.

It is very easy to misunderstand or caricature the central Christian doctrine of the incarnation of the divine in human form. If Jesus was God, did he really have to learn to talk? Or did he know how to talk all the time, but did not tell his mother? There is a story – surely legendary – about the young Einstein, that he seemed a rather backward child, because he never said anything. Then suddenly one day, at the age of three, he said, 'This milk is too hot.' His astonished parents said, 'But you can talk! Why haven't you said anything to us before?' To which Einstein replied, 'Everything has been in order until now.' Was the baby Jesus like that?

There are legendary stories about Jesus, too, which involve him causing the death of unpopular schoolteachers and other things that, however desirable they may seem to young children, are morally dubious. The editors of the New Testament wisely left those stories out, though they can still be found in what are called the apocryphal (the word means 'hidden', but has the sense of 'dubious') gospels.

The way out of these difficulties is to accept the doctrine, defined at the Council of Chalcedon in 451 CE, that Jesus was fully human, not just God disguised as a human being. But his humanity was so united to the divinity of the eternal Word (or 'Son') of God that he <u>is</u> the Son of God in a full and proper human form. What does this do to his speaking abilities? Presumably he would have to learn to talk like any human baby, but he would never knowingly tell lies. He might have made mistakes, but they would not be due to laziness or inattention. Maybe it is best not to probe too far into what we can never know. But it does not seem absurd to say that God acted in a proper human nature, without ceasing to be God and without completely overwhelming that nature. To Christians, it even seems that this would be the fullest possible sort of revelation God could give of what the divine nature is like.

One thing all this entails is that the Christian faith is bound to emphasise the dignity of all human life – in which God has been pleased to dwell – and the unlimited love of God for every creature. So, even in the militaristic and imperialistic Roman Empire, Christian witness managed to stop infanticide, gladiatorial spectacles and indiscriminate torture. But it did become implicated in the defence of the Roman imperial system. The eastern half of the empire, Byzantium, was disliked by its subject peoples, and attempts to establish an official orthodoxy led to apparently endless quarrels about virtually unintelligible issues about what part of the Trinity emanated from what other part. Weakened by internal disputes and by war with Persia, the Byzantine Empire collapsed under the onslaught of Islam, which was welcomed as a liberator from imperial domination by thousands of subject people.

The western half of the empire collapsed under attacks of the Barbarian hordes, and the creation of Europe as a Christian civilisation out of its ruins took a thousand years. It has, however, been a history of almost continuous warfare, expressed gruesomely in the motto of the Spanish Knights of Santiago, 'Our swords are red with the blood of Islam.' St James, the apostle sent out by Jesus without sword or staff, and executed by Herod, came to be seen in medieval times as an avenging warrior in full battle armour mounted on a rearing stallion who was said to have personally killed 60,000 Muslim soldiers in one of the first battles for the Christian 'reconquest' of Spain from Islam. This is quite clearly a perversion of Christian faith, but the fact remains that by association with imperial conquests, even a peaceable religion can become an ally of violence.

Christianity was always a missionary faith, and spread throughout the world. But it was not until the European powers conquered the Americas, southern Africa and Australasia that Christianity established the dominant position in the world it now holds. So we have the strange spectacle of a Middle Eastern almost pacifist sect turning itself into the spiritual arm of European world-dominating colonial power. History thus confounds reason – or, some would say, it just shows the paradoxical and dialectical way in which reason works itself out.

It would be churlish not to mention the triumphs of European culture, inspired by this faith – the glorious cathedrals, magnificent paintings, soaring music and epic literature. It would be disingenuous not to point out that, underneath all this array of good and bad, there still lies the simple gospel of forgiveness through the self-giving love of God, who, as Athanasius put it, shared in human suffering, so that humanity can be raised to share in the divine life. And it would be myopic to ignore the fact that Christianity is no longer either a Middle Eastern or a European faith. It is growing most in Africa, South America and Asia, and so it is likely to become increasingly distanced from European culture in its future forms.

The lesson of Christianity is, often despite the best efforts of its adherents to undermine the lesson, that the supreme divine being has the character of unlimited, relational and reconciling love. Sovereign will becomes self-giving will, whose sovereignty is the persuasive power of love, whose self-disclosing revelation is a human life of healing and forgiveness, and whose promise is a sharing of fragmented creation in the divine life.

ISLAM

Islam presented the theistic model in a way that made a very sharp distinction between the material and the spiritual, the created world and the creator. From a Muslim viewpoint, the Christian contortions of doctrine concerning incarnation, Trinity and atonement, leading to interminable quarrels and mutual excommunications, can confuse the keenest mind. Its key doctrines, crudely put, that a man was God and that God is both three and one at the same time, can seem to threaten the transcendence and simplicity of the divine. So Islam insists on a complete contrast between the divine and all created reality.

Islam rejected the religion of incarnation in favour of a return to a simpler prophetic faith. Muhammad claimed to be a prophet and no more than a man. The Qur'an that, by tradition, was dictated to him by the archangel Gabriel was a simple and powerful message of the transcendent simplicity of God, the absolute superiority of God to all created beings, of the reality of divine judgement and the hope of Paradise.

For Islam, humans are not condemned to Hell because of 'original sin'. Each person is a free moral agent, and will be held responsible for his or her own actions on the Day of Judgement. God's judgement will be just but merciful, and divine forgiveness for the penitent is not conditional on any sacrifice, much less on the death of an innocent man – or, unthinkably for Muslims, on the suffering or death of God. There is no Church to teach authoritatively what is to be believed, no priests to control the dispensation of divine mercy, and no subtle disputation about the inner nature of God, which only learned theologians can resolve. God is sovereign will, and reveals a law, not, as in the case of Judaism, just for one people, but for all human beings. That law sets out a simple path, which will lead humans to eternal fellowship with God.

The lesson of Islam lies in its simplicity, its insistence on the supremacy and utter transcendence of God alone, its moral rigour that calls all persons to account for their conduct in this world, and its promise of Paradise for all who are penitent and seek to obey God's will.

Yet Islam, like Christianity, has been at times an imperialistic, intolerant and violent faith. Assassinations marked the line of succession to the Prophet. Within a hundred years Muslim warriors had conquered North Africa and Spain, and were later to threaten Europe from the east. The Ottoman Empire was one of the greatest empires the world has ever seen, larger and longer lasting than the Roman Empire. And – even though most Muslims, and virtually all traditional Muslims, would roundly condemn this – throughout the world today the call of *jihad*, understood by many to mean 'holy war', resounds in country after country calling people to kill in the name of God.

As so often in Christianity, in Islam too the call to spread God's law by the sword seems to be irresistible. The call to impose the law in all its purity on dissidents and infidels gives a seeming moral blessing to every impulse to hatred and tyranny that disfigures the human heart. Christians and Muslims hate one another as infidels, betrayers of God, even though each of them conscientiously claims to be completely faithful and submissive to God.

In the Muslim case, the original expansion of Islam was seen as a civilising mission to a benighted world, and Islamic warriors were seen by many as liberators from oppression by other empires, such as Byzantine or Persian. Islam founded universities and hospitals, was relatively tolerant to Christians and Jews (it was more tolerant to Jews than was Christian Spain, for example), translated the Greek classics, and created a great civilisation and culture while Christian Europe was undergoing what it calls the 'Dark Ages'. Europeans, the most successful imperialists in history, can ill afford to criticise the imperial ambitions of Islam as unequivocally evil, though all of us may feel uneasy now at an over-simple equation between religion and political power.

In the modern world, the great Islamic civilisation of the eighth and ninth centuries has long ago collapsed, and almost every Muslim country has only recently been liberated from European colonial rule. It is a tragedy of our age that many Muslims cannot easily coexist with non-Muslims, but the reality is that some Muslims turn to violence out of insecurity, rage and frustration at the way they feel themselves to be dominated and manipulated by Western powers. The basic problems are social and economic, and Muslims often feel that they speak for the poor and dispossessed of the world – in Palestine and in parts of former Yugoslavia, for instance – as opposed to Christianity, which speaks from the base of the greatest economic powers the world has ever seen.

The economic solution must lie in the establishment of a just world order, in which the rich of the West no longer live off the sweated labour of the poor of the economically undeveloped world, without which there will be no peace. Religion will continue to be bound to the desires and fears of those living in specific cultures, with all the ambiguity that involves. The only peaceful way forward for religion – and both Christianity and Islam say they aim at peace – lies in its recognition that God is a God of compassion and mercy, and that the course of history lies in the hands of God. Believers are meant to trust in the power of truth and love, in the power of God to bring about the divine purpose without the need to resort to unjust violence. If belief in divine providence means anything, it means that we do not need to resort to extreme measures to help God's purpose out.

Any authoritative traditional expounder of Islamic law will stress that the doctrine of *jihad*, holy war, is meant only for defence against unjust attack and the protection of the innocent – just as Christian 'just war' theory is. There is no great difference in theory between Christians and Muslims here. But both need to be very aware of the terrible capacity humans have for extending the range of justified violence beyond the limits set by divine law, and then justifying it by appeal to God. If force is necessary, it should never extirpate compassion and respect from the human mind. The application of justice must be cold and not passionate, though our concern for justice may be as passionate as can be. For we obey God best when we imitate 'the Compassionate and Merciful', and by that criterion we shall be judged on the Last Day. That is what the deepest form of Islamic faith declares.

The Semitic faiths have transformed the world, both for better and worse. They have been closely tied to great social, political and economic forces that have given to them a thousand differing forms, ranging from the execrable to the exalted. Underlying them is the fundamental idea that there is just one supreme spiritual reality, most adequately conceived as a supreme personal will, which sets a purpose for human existence which in turn determines what morality is. This personal will is experienced paradigmatically by the prophetic founders of these traditions, and it is experienced in less intense ways by their followers. It is possible for these faiths to live together, and even to be mutually reinforcing, but only if each agrees to renounce compulsion in matters of faith,[86] to accept that there will always be other forms of faith,[87] and tries to understand the spiritual traditions of the others with empathy and respect. No less than that is required by their common faith in a God who wills justice and mercy, a community of peace, and respect for all creation.

Find out more . . .

Oneworld publishes an excellent set of quite short readable books on world religions. Of special relevance to this chapter are:

Dan and Lavinia Cohn-Sherbok, *Judaism: A Short Introduction* (Oxford: Oneworld, 1999) and *Judaism: A Short History* (Oxford: Oneworld, 1999).
Keith Ward, *Christianity: A Short Introduction* (Oxford: Oneworld, 2000).
Frederick W. Norris, *Christianity: A Short Global History* (Oxford: Oneworld, 2002).
Abdulkader Tayob, *Islam: A Short Introduction* (Oxford: Oneworld, 1999).
William Montgomery Watt, *Islam: A Short History* (Oxford: Oneworld, 1999).

7

THE WAY TO
ENLIGHTENMENT

Buddhism, Hinduism, Confucianism and Taoism

DUALIST TRADITIONS

In the Indian subcontinent there were no major prophets who declared the law of God, the need for repentance and the promise of resurrection in Paradise. There were spiritual teachers, but they did not typically apprehend God as a commanding sovereign will. For many of them, the idea of one personal God was not found helpful in explaining the existence of suffering in the world. How could a good God create suffering? Seeing God as a personal being was also seen as unduly anthropomorphic, and a belief that this God sent down lists of absolute moral commands was too liable to give rise to intolerance of others, who might not be absolutely convinced of the rightness of those commands. Instead, a number of renouncing traditions developed, which adopted a basically dualist model of the relation of the spiritual and material worlds. The material world was considered to exist as uncreated, without beginning or end, and to provide the material environment in which human selves could exist, and in which they were trapped by attachment and desire to the wheel of suffering and rebirth. The goal of life is to achieve freedom from attachment, and live as a pure spiritual self, free of matter for ever. Mahavira, the great world-teacher of the Jains, and Patanjali, the teacher of Sankhya Yoga, both took such a basic view. Some early forms of Buddhism are rather similar. They also see the material world as an uncreated succession of atomistic parts. The human self is a construct or bundle of some of these parts, and has no independent substantial reality. Spiritual liberation again consists in achieving freedom from attachment. You will not then exist as a pure immaterial self. But there is an indescribable form of existence that is one with a supreme spiritual reality. This is not a separate personal being. It is rather a supreme spiritual state, a state of consciousness, wisdom, compassion and bliss. It does not create the world, and it does not stand over against human beings as something to be encountered or feared. Because it is sometimes spoken of as a 'non-dual' state, it might seem odd to describe these forms of Buddhism as dualist. But there is a sharp distinction between the bundles of particular properties that make up the experienced world and the limitless state of liberation, of *nirvana*. For some, but by no means all, forms of Buddhism these two forms of being are quite distinct, and neither is created by or ultimately dependent on the other. Such views are technically dualist.

In these traditions, instead of a prophet, the spiritual teacher is a liberated soul, one who has overcome greed, hatred and ignorance and achieved union with the supreme state of wisdom, compassion and bliss. That is the highest value, and it is attainable by human beings – as it was attained by Mahavira and Siddhartha Gautama, founder of Buddhism. The spiritual goal is thus seen as liberation from the material cosmos, entrance into *nirvana* or into a state of being liberated from passion and desire.

This dominant model is of liberated consciousness. Mahavira apparently conceived each liberated soul as a distinct consciousness of unlimited intelligence and knowledge, free of all attachments to material desire. Gautama Buddha seemed to speak rather of the dissolution of the individual self, though this teaching is complicated by the widespread belief that the Buddha, the Enlightened One, having attained *nirvana*, was omniscient and blissful. Underlying the many varieties of specific interpretation the basic model is well symbolised by the contemplative Buddha or the majestically standing and serene liberated soul of the Jains. There is no personal will ordaining all things. There is the personal journey of each individual person through many forms of experience, culminating in a state beyond attachment and desire, of liberated calm, mindfulness and luminescent awareness. And out of the overwhelming sense of compassion for the suffering of all beings there is a reverence for all life, which is much wider and more all-embracing than anything in the Semitic traditions.

Buddhism and Jainism remain small minorities in India. The Jains are content to remain a small community, but Buddhism has spread throughout the world. In India, the country of its origin, it was largely absorbed in the vast embrace of Hinduism, but it became firmly established in Sri Lanka, Thailand, China, Japan, Korea and South East Asia. In 379 CE it became for a time the state religion of China. It was once the official religion in Japan, and was dominant in Tibet and Thailand. It has lost influence there in modern times, having been especially vulnerable to attacks by anti-religious communism. But it has spread throughout the world, largely through groups of monks who teach meditation and mindfulness without insisting on allegiance to any set of beliefs.

There are of course many doctrines in Buddhism, and many different forms of practice, from the rigorous ascetic meditations of celibate Thai forest monks to the devotional chants of Japanese Jodo Shin Shu, married Buddhist priests. Yet throughout all these forms the dominant tone is one of serenity and detachment, and the main emphasis is not on intellectual beliefs, but on mental training in mindfulness and compassion.

The lesson of Buddhism is that there are methods of mental training that can lead to a life liberated from hatred, greed and ignorance, and to awareness of a transcendent state of compassion, non-attachment and wisdom. A traditional, and rather pessimistic, Buddhist opinion from the Theravada tradition is that it will take a very long time to reach that transcendent state – probably a few million lifetimes, in fact. By the time we get there, we will long ago have ceased to have any interest in the persons we are now, with all our peculiarities and likes and dislikes. We will, after all, have been millions of different people (and maybe a few animals) in the meanwhile. So if I ask, 'Will I achieve liberation?' the answer is 'No' – this personality is far from ready. But if I ask, 'Then is it the case that I will not achieve liberation?' the answer will also be 'No,' because all beings can achieve liberation. Becoming suspicious, I might ask, 'So you say that I will both achieve liberation and not achieve it?' to which the answer is 'No' – that would be self-contradictory. In desperation, I try one last time: 'Will I neither achieve liberation nor not achieve it?' But by now it is no surprise that the answer is 'No.' However, since the answer to all these questions is also 'Yes,' we probably need a new word. Perhaps 'Yo' would do, and it would be the answer to almost all Buddhist questions. But what a well-schooled Buddhist might rather say is: 'If somebody offers you a medicine which will release you from suffering, don't waste time asking for a course in pharmacology before you accept it.'

Buddhism is an eminently practical faith, in which practice takes priority over theory. Yet, as with the Semitic traditions, there is a set of canonical sacred texts, which are treated as authoritative. They are not revealed by God through prophets, but they are records of the teaching of the supremely Enlightened One. Buddhists have been much more successful than theistic believers in advocating tolerance and compassion for all living things. There have, nevertheless, been militaristic forms of Buddhism, such as the bands of warrior monks who participated in medieval Japanese dynastic conflicts, and underwrote the Samurai code. What Buddhists do not usually have (and many probably do not want) is a lively sense of personal relationship with God, and a hope for the future redemption or transformation of the world. For this reason, Buddhism is sometimes seen as rather negative or 'world-denying' by Semitic believers. But a faith that claims to offer a path to supreme bliss and universal compassion is hardly negative, and Buddhists resent that description.

This may suggest that an ideal might be found if the theistic emphasis on devotion, personal relationship and practical love for others, and the potential goodness of the material world, could be combined with a Buddhist stress on serenity, mindfulness and compassion. This is an ideal that has been attempted within many of the huge variety of traditions that constitute Hinduism.

IDEALIST TRADITIONS

Though renouncing movements have always been strong in India, the dominant Indian traditions worship many gods, and interpret them as personalisations of one ultimate reality, *Brahman*, of which all things are parts. *Brahman* is the Self of All, a reality described as *sat–cit–ananda*, consciousness, intelligence and bliss. It is the sole ultimate reality, and includes all the diversity of the cosmos as part of itself. The Upanishads, the sacred texts in which this doctrine is expressed, are said to be 'heard', revealed to seers by the gods, and even to be eternal archetypes on which the creation of worlds is patterned. As in the Semitic traditions, there is appeal to revelation, which inspired individuals receive from the spiritual realm, and orthodox Hindus will accept the 'heard' scriptures as inerrant and definitive.

The spiritual is construed as one mind-like being, self-existent and of supreme value, of which all the gods of the Indian traditions are parts or expressions. But the Supreme Self is not set over against the cosmos as something different. It is the underlying reality of the universe itself, which is spiritual in nature.

There are two major interpretations of this general view, with many sub-variants, most of which exist somewhere in India. One is the interpretation of Sankara, most generally accepted by Shaivites, devotees of Shiva. The whole material universe is seen as an illusion or ephemeral appearance of an underlying reality, which is not material at all. We think we are finite individuals embodied in matter. But in fact we are suffering from an illusion, just as when we think we are lying on a beach in the

Bahamas, and it turns out to be a dream. The trouble with the illusion we are in is that it brings suffering and pain with it. It is more like a nightmare. If we can wake up, we will find that we are free from suffering, and in a realm of infinite bliss and knowledge. We will be released from our sense of separate individuality, which cuts us off from other people and traps us in attachments to things. We will cease to exist as separate selves, and find that we are really identical with the Supreme Self, which is the only true reality. The religious quest is to come to experiential knowledge of oneness with the Supreme, and awareness of the illusory nature of one's individual identity and the material environment in which one seems to exist.

The other major interpretation is that of Ramanuja, generally adopted by Vaishnavas, devotees of Vishnu – often under the form of his worldly manifestation, Krishna. The world is not an illusion. We really are separate selves, but we are still usually deluded into thinking that we are essentially the specific personalities and bodies we happen to have in this life. We are actually purely spiritual souls, and as such we are tiny but distinct parts of the Supreme Self. We are the body of the Lord, just as the cells of our bodies are parts of us. The cosmos emanates from the Supreme as a very small part of its self-expression or self-realisation. So material bodies are not just illusions. They are ways of expressing or realising our true spiritual natures. But we are mostly ignorant of the fact that our true nature is spiritual, and that the material world is the body, the self-expression, of the Supreme Lord. Because of that ignorance, we identify ourselves with particular bodies, and get attached to things, which cause suffering to us. Liberation consists in realising our true spiritual nature as parts of *Brahman*. For this view, matter has a more positive role to play in realising the possibilities of Spirit (just as a piece of music is a material performance which realises the spiritual intentions of the composer, assuming she has some). The cosmos is the play (*lila*) of the Lord, and the goal of the universe is, in one version, to become fully conscious of its intimate relation to the Lord, and to become the gladly obedient instrument of the Lord's self-expression. Ramanuja's view might more properly be called theistic, as he does see the universe as created by *Isvara*, the supreme Lord. He does nevertheless hold that there is only one spiritual reality of which all material things are parts, so he might be called an 'idealistic theist', which sounds quite a nice thing to be.

The fundamental model in these views is of a Supreme Self of intelligence and bliss. The material cosmos either conceals that Self (that is the 'illusion' view) or expresses part of its nature (the 'expression' view). The spiritual goal is to become aware of your unity with that Self, either in the strictest sense of oneness, of absolute non-duality, or as being a part of it.

The Self may be seen as playing out its own internal potencies without beginning or end, through infinite universes. Or it may be seen as generating free souls, which then undergo the karmic consequences of their free creaturely choices, which usually entail suffering, until they are liberated from their attachment to desire and wilful self-deceit. The cosmos itself is the expression of illusion or ignorance, a realm of desire and bondage. But it is also the expression of the inherent potentialities of the Supreme, and so can be a realm of love and devotion. The moral purpose is the renunciation of desire, and the increase of personal devotion, which can bring final freedom from suffering, either by achieved supra-individual union with the Supreme or by loving devotion to the Supreme as part of its emanated reality.

The lesson of Hinduism is that at the deepest level the human soul is one with the Divine Soul, that human life is a spiritual journey towards that realisation, and that the way to such realisation lies in freedom from egoistic desires and in devotion to the Supreme Lord, who perfectly expresses in finite form (or in many finite forms) the Divine Self which most of us express imperfectly.

As a social reality, Hinduism is not, of course, free of the troubles that beset most religious systems. Relations between different sects can sometimes be marked by violence, and Hindu nationalism tries to identify being Indian with keeping Hindu traditions, thus excluding Muslims and Christians, for example, as 'foreigners'. Until recent times, when there has been an Indian diaspora around the world, Hinduism remained to a large extent ethnic, firmly rooted in the sacred land of India (and Nepal). In its desire to see all forms of faith as diverse expressions of the One Real, it accepted the self-immolation of widows, animal sacrifice and all sorts of tantric rituals within its fold. At a popular level, Hinduism can seem to exhibit a reactionary adherence to tradition, advocating practices such as astrology and magical incantations which are far from the sublime teachings of elite teachers like Sankara and Ramanuja. The doctrine that the divine incarnates many times can lead to extreme devotion to many rather implausible candidates. Also, the crucial doctrine of reincarnation has sometimes had the unfortunate consequence of making the poor and handicapped responsible for their own condition – they are poor because they did something in a previous life to deserve it. Hinduism in the caste system enshrined a doctrine of extreme human inequality, based on a doctrine of this sort. So all is not purity and light.

In saying this, however, I am only pointing out that at the level of popular and historically largely illiterate religion the Indian traditions of both Buddhism and Hinduism can become regimes of blind adherence to tradition, rigid hierarchy (allegedly based on degrees of religious insight) and magical practices to obtain wealth and fertility. It would be wholly mistaken to ignore the main Hindu tradition of spirituality, which has a sophisticated and spiritually demanding understanding of one supreme spiritual reality, conceived as ultimate in reality and value.

MONISTIC TRADITIONS

In China Confucius and Lao-Tzu founded East Asian traditions that are concerned with the harmony of nature and the discernment of the 'Way of Heaven (*Tian*)' in social and political life. These traditions sometimes degenerated, in the Taoist case, into quasi-magical practices for achieving health and longevity, and in Confucianism became associated with extremely conservative political regimes, not easily capable of change. The emphases of these traditions are different, Taoism being more concerned with conforming to the flowing rhythms of the natural world, and Confucianism being much more concerned with social and political propriety and order. But in both, conflict in human life results from an imbalance of natural forces, and the religious purpose is to restore and maintain that balance, enabling the Way of Heaven to be realised on earth.

When Buddhism moved into China, a distinctive set of Mahayana schools gave a radical reinterpretation of the Buddhist way, which harmonises with traditional Chinese outlooks, with reverence for nature and for the ancestors. Ancestor worship at first seems strange to those in the Semitic traditions, for whom worship is reserved for God. But cults of the saints, the honoured dead, exist in most religious traditions, and to revere the ancestors is to make a personal connection with the powers and virtues that have been realised in past human lives. The honoured dead are mediators between the spiritual and the physical worlds, either by presence or by memory. The graves of the dead embody the ideals of their society. The dead are near to the gods, and so are channels of spiritual power. The ancestors regard us still, and our honour to them kindles our own hope that their lives have not been in vain, that the future will be what they wished and more.

To revere the ancestors is to revere human values and the possibility of their realisation in human lives. It is not, as it may seem, an unhealthy concern with death, but a way of affirming hope for life. And in general, East Asian Buddhism is not at all a world-denying faith. It becomes an affirmation of human possibilities in lives transformed by spiritual insight.

For the great Buddhist sage Nagarjuna, '*samsara* is *nirvana*', the world of suffering and rebirth is identical with the world of bliss and freedom from sorrow. *Nirvana* is not another realm beyond this. It is this worldly realm seen with the enlightened eye. Buddhism in this form teaches that insight into the Way is true Enlightenment. Spiritual reality is not seen as apart from the world, or as a personal being. It is not even a hidden Supreme Self of all the world. It is the Way of the world, a way of balance and harmony, of calm and dispassionateness. It is thus in what may seem a strange development for a renunciant faith, this-worldly and social, calling all to a life of compassionate action and holding out for all the hope of true Enlightenment now or in other Buddha worlds. The fundamental model here is of the Balanced Way. The spiritual goal is to walk the narrow path between the opposites of *yin* and *yang* that make up the world, and so to realise the inner nature (the Buddha nature) of reality within the life of politics and society.

In Japan, which Buddhism reached in about 538 CE, a similar set of themes came to exercise a dominant influence. The indigenous Shinto, which was largely based on reverence for spirits of the natural world and for ancestors, combined with Chinese forms of Buddhism to generate a number of Japanese Buddhist schools, which share a similar world-affirming character. In Japanese Pure Land Buddhism, the religion even embraces a rich stream of personal devotion, and a desire for personal salvation through the grace of a compassionate bodhisattva (one who defers personal enlightenment out of compassion to help all sentient beings) in a 'Pure Buddha Land'.

The lesson of East Asian spirituality is that the spiritual way is a way of living in the world which is in harmony with the fundamental potentialities of nature, so that the spiritual is not another realm after death or one attained only by ascetic denial, but is the truly apprehended nature of the social and material world, when mindfulness and clarity is attained. However, the dominant tone of this spirituality has been conservative and quietist, and so though it is this-worldly it has come into conflict with modern forces which look not for a conformity to the inner laws of nature but for a more progressive or even revolutionary transformation of material reality into something different and better.

Chinese religion suffered a catastrophic attack by Maoist communism in the twentieth century, because it was seen as hierarchical, tied to an obsolete past, superstitious and allied with an obsolete value-system. Japanese religion suffered, not a violent attack, but a devastating ideological onslaught from Western capitalism, which was deeply opposed to the rather quiescent Buddhist values of non-possessiveness, non-competitiveness, reverence for the natural world and indifference to material goods. Korea had the misfortune of suffering both attacks at once, from communism in the north and capitalism in the south.

Thus the power of traditional religion has been greatly weakened in the developed nations of East Asia, and it remains to be seen whether and in what way the East Asian religious traditions can accommodate themselves to the rapid forces of social and economic change that are apparently rendering many traditional values obsolete. Perhaps here again the future will lie with some reinterpretation of traditional religions that can mitigate the worst excesses of communism and capitalism while adapting to a general ethic of material progress and development.

There is to some extent a reaction against forms of communism and capitalism that seek to subdue the material world and use it as purely instrumental to human well-being, and against views which see the human condition as being wholly alleviated by revolutionary social change and the realisation of basically materialistic goals. There is a return to a desire for harmony with and reverence for the natural world, and a return to goals of human action that are more inward and self-transforming. East Asian religious traditions may be revitalised, and not destroyed, by their contact with secular and materialist philosophies, if they can adapt traditionalist attitudes to a more dynamic and egalitarian culture. There is no reason why this should not happen, for the basic Buddhist philosophy that all things are interconnected, transient and in dynamic flow, and that all things can and should manifest the Buddha nature (the *dharma-kaya* or Enlightened Mind), is in principle compatible with new technologies and more democratic forms of social organisation.

THE GREEK HERITAGE

The Fertile Crescent, India and East Asia all gave rise to great canonical traditions, with a set of definitive sacred texts, and authoritative founders whose teachings were taken as binding on their followers. The concepts of one personal creator God, of one Supreme Self of which all things are part, of the liberated state of wisdom, compassion and bliss and of the balanced way of mindfulness became the foundational ideas of vast empires and of a thousand local cultures. But the fourth leading cultural complex of the Axial Age, the Egyptian/Greek/Roman complex that underlies the classical culture of Europe, had a different destiny. The religious life of that culture died, swamped by its near competitor, the one creator God of the Middle East. The Greek gods no longer exist, as real objects of devotion and worship. Yet the Greeks left something that was destined to transform the Middle Eastern God in a fundamental way.

The Greek inheritance is not strictly speaking religion but philosophy, a philosophy in search of a faith that can touch both the non-literate masses and the poets and philosophers of the elite literary tradition. Plato and Aristotle both constructed impressive philosophical systems that related human life to sophisticated ideas of Transcendence, but they failed to make any connection with the religious life of ancient Greece. It was as though they were waiting for a different form of religious life within which their ideas could find a meaningful role. That form of life was destined to be Christianity, which was itself transformed by its contact with the Greek philosophical world.

Plato's philosophical picture traced conflict to the inability of the material world fully to embody the perfection of the Good. The moral purpose of the cosmos, Plato held in his dialogue Timaeus, is partly to express in as perfect a way as possible the many forms of goodness which are partial reflections of the Good, and partly to achieve liberation from matter, which can never fully embody goodness, and return to the realm of the purely Ideal. Plato's philosophy is in some respects rather close to the Buddhist model, with its ambivalent possibilities of a positive evaluation of the material as a participation in the spiritual, or of a negative evaluation of the material as the restriction and imprisonment of the spiritual. Aristotle's philosophy was more materialistic, and discounted the possibility of liberation from the material. He still saw matter, however, as basically purposive, and as making possible a life of virtue, a way of embodying Goodness in the material and social order.

The Greek model of Spirit is the Good, not a personal being, not a cause of the world, but an archetype of its possibilities and an ideal for its striving. Strangely, it was within Christianity, and very largely through Augustine, that this model passed into later European thought, where the Logos, the eternal Christ, became the archetype of all things and the lure of perfection towards which they move. A different strand of Platonism, combined with much of the thought of Aristotle, influenced later humanistic currents of thought, prefigured in Stoicism and recovered in sixteenth-century Renaissance humanism, which find the cultivation of the virtues to be the most important task of humanity, which relegate personal gods to the realm of superstition or popular practice, and which find goodness to be its own reward, to be pursued simply for its own sake. The three major Semitic faiths have all been deeply influenced in their traditional forms by the Greek idea of the Good, and the combination of Plato, Aristotle and the prophets of Israel and Islam has produced a powerful intellectual system, the internal tensions of which continually drive it on to new re-statements of faith.

CONCEPTIONS OF ABSOLUTE VALUE

I have suggested that, of the six logically possible models of transcendence, only four – dualism, monism, theism and idealism – have been seriously explored by the religious traditions of post-Axial times. Each model became associated with a particular cultural complex, and they developed standard, canonical patterns for interpreting experiences of transcendence within those complexes. The theistic model took root among the Hebrews of the ancient Near East, and evolved in three different ways in Judaism, Christianity and Islam. For Jews, the Transcendent was conceived as one supreme personal God who has a moral purpose for history, and acts to bring it about, choosing the people of Israel for a special vocation in doing so. For Christians, God was much more intimately involved with the material or created world, entering into it in incarnation and elevating it to share in the divine life (the 'body of Christ'). For Muslims, the essential distinctness of creator and creation was again stressed, and emphasis was placed on one universal law for all people, and on the hope for a new life after death (the resurrection of the dead) for God's creatures. The history of religions was complicated by the involvement of Christianity and Islam in great military empires, which were often in competition with each other. This made these models, despite their basic similarity, harden into opposed ideological systems with little understanding of one another. But it is important to note that the connection of these faiths with imperialistic systems was always a contingent one, and that it perhaps belongs to a period of world history which has already come to an end, though its death-throes seem rather prolonged.

The idealist model found a home in the Indian subcontinent, and developed a number of different forms. For some, matter is virtually an illusion, or an unreal appearance. The world of space-time is a realm of suffering, and the religious goal is release from it. For others, matter has a much more positive role as the 'play' or self-expression of ultimate Spirit, *Brahman*.

The dualist model formed a set of traditions both in India and in East Asia, in renouncing movements that seek a separation of the spiritual from the material, and pursue liberation by abandoning all material goals.

The monist model took root most securely in East Asian societies, being found in forms of Buddhism, Confucianism and Taoism which seek a 'balanced way' of mindfulness and inner freedom, of dutiful life or oneness with nature, in which spirit and matter can achieve a delicate and enriching harmony.

It would be wrong to confine these models to the geographical homelands of the Semitic, Indian and East Asian religious traditions. But the models did become associated with the cultural history of these areas, and the way they developed reflects that history as well as the more abstract intellectual concern to achieve a rational integrated worldview, and the accumulation of traditions of prayer, meditation and experience that were prompted by the basic models.

It would be wrong to reduce religious traditions either to their socio-political cultural contexts, the philosophical worldviews that became characteristic of them or the specific types of experience they evoked. All these factors are important. Cultural lifestyles, philosophical systems and distinctive kinds of experience all give shape to religious traditions. But the fundamental claim that all these religions make is that they are ways of relating to a real, objective, transcendent reality – something other and more than a society, a philosophical system or a set of human experiences.

All these religious traditions express an almost universal human concern with a supernatural reality. These are obviously very different images of the Transcendent Real, but it is fairly easy to account for the differences. Some people think that personhood is the highest, most valuable form of existence. So God must be a supremely personal being, even a supreme person. Others, however, regard persons as essentially limited, being finite, dependent on others in so many ways, and subject to many moods and feelings. For them it will be unrealistic to think of just one supreme person as the highest value. One will need to have many persons, with different characters and abilities, a diverse community, even if under the rule of one 'high God'. Others again will think that the supreme value must transcend personhood altogether, and be found in an impersonal state which possesses intelligence and bliss, into which finite beings can enter or with which they can merge, but which in itself is beyond all finite limitations, including the limitations essential to personhood. Or it may be thought that the Supreme Value is not beyond the finite world, but is its innermost nature, which enlightened vision is able to apprehend.

The differences are differences in ways of imaging absolute value. Since what humans regard as values are strongly influenced by their own personal temperaments, cultures and histories, it is not at all surprising that there are different images of what an absolute value might be. But the passage from seeing religion as an attempt to relate to supernatural powers in order to attain human good or escape human harm to seeing religion as pursuing the good life by participation in one supreme objective value – the saltation of the Axial Age – does mark a decisive change in understanding. It requires serious reflection on what is of ultimate value for human life, and an attempt to bring ancient human practices and rituals under some sort of systematic understanding of reality.

These traditions all see human life as finding its true fulfilment in appropriate relation to a transcendent spiritual reality or state. That relation involves an overcoming of selfish attachments and a physical and mental discipline that will establish the relation securely in human lives. As they develop, traditions adopt a set of canonical texts, traceable back to founders who are their source or inspiration. Moses writes down the statutes and commandments that he hears from God. Jesus' life and teaching, and the impact of his risen presence, is definitively recorded in the gospels and the letters of the New Testament, which are inspired by the divine Spirit. Muhammad recites in the Qur'an the message he receives from God. Gautama teaches the way to the enlightenment he experienced, and it is authoritatively recorded in the Sutras of his community. The anonymous gurus of India recite the Upanishads as they hear them from the gods, or the gods themselves may take human form and teach their disciples. The followers of Confucius and Lao-Tzu pass on a body of definitive texts, which enshrine their teachings about the way of living in harmony with the cosmos. Authoritative teachers and canonical texts define the great traditions. Each tradition makes a claim to inerrancy and finality. These are teachings from the gods themselves, or from minds which have penetrated the ultimate secrets of spiritual reality. They are revelations of ultimate truth.

A factor of great importance is that the 'great religions' were not just purely intellectual interpretations of a reality of supreme value and power. They came to be associated with socio-economic complexes, and to form influential systems of 'orthodoxy', which then often opposed other complexes as 'false' or 'inadequate' in various ways. Judaism, Christianity, Islam, Hinduism, Buddhism and Confucianism have all become badges of cultural and imperial identity, and that has helped to give them a confrontational and polemical character.

Recorded human history is a series of wars, conflicts, betrayals, infidelities and hatreds. It is not to be expected that any human activity will be free from that chain of greed, hatred and ignorance. Perhaps in music and mathematics the purity of sound or number offers temporary release from the tyranny of passion. Yet the drums of war, the petty jealousies and antagonisms of musicians, the abstract equations which make nuclear bombs possible and the employment of pure science in the service of ever more terrifyingly destructive weapons remind us that even the purest activities remain earthed in the human striving for power and dominance.

So it is and must be with religion. At moments it may strive to touch eternity, to talk of peace and compassion, to apprehend a realm of Spirit, which is pure and passionless. But precisely because it speaks of that which is of greatest value to human beings, that upon which their lives are ultimately centred, it must become involved with what people actually value and pursue – and that is, however much we seek to conceal the fact, wealth, property and power.

Thus even the great monastic communities of western Europe, such as Cluny Abbey, founded on renunciation of the world and denial of the flesh, quickly became owners of vast estates and wielders of enormous political power. They no longer protested against the world. They *were* the world, in all its pageantry and power, and they validated the dreams of empire, which they consecrated as Crusades to destroy the infidel.

That is why people should not look to religion for salvation or for a solution to the ills of the world. Failure to see the possibilities for corruption and destruction in religion is a failure of spiritual perception of the first order. Few people fail to see the destructive possibilities of other people's religions, but they can be remarkably blind to their own. While Auguste Comte, Ludwig Feuerbach and Karl Marx saw the oppressiveness or ignorance of the religions they knew, they completely failed to foresee the oppressiveness of communism or state socialism, an atheist programme, the crusade of humanism, which exterminated heretics to an extent the Inquisition had never dared to attempt.

When all is said and done, it is no reason for renouncing politics that it is corrupt and corrupting. It is no reason for renouncing religion that it is involved in the political and cultural conflicts of all human societies. These considerations, however, do give a powerful reason for seeing all political and religious systems as ambiguous, as needing constant self-criticism and as in constant need of reform.

In a world like this, the claim (even if justified) to possess the most perfect political or religious system, beyond criticism and irreformable, is apt to lead to the most irreformable tyranny. In a world like this, there is only a chance of avoiding the worst excesses of greed, hatred and ignorance if we are forced to do so by the critical opposition of others. That is a form of opposition, not by violence and suppression of opinion, but by commitment to debate and discussion, and the assured freedom to express opinions.

This is a hard lesson to learn, actually to encourage opposition to one's own deepest beliefs, and it will perhaps never be learned by those who think they already have the truth with absolute certainty, and that dissent means either disloyalty or personal wickedness, so that dissent is already a choice of evil. It was rarely learned by the great traditions in the first centuries of their existence. In their ideal form, they ask for the over-coming of egoistic desire in order to achieve a vision of or a unity with a reality of supreme value. In their actual existence, they have often tended to repress dissent and enforce conformity to the unchanging standards of a past age. From such ambiguity there is perhaps no escape. But it would be an advance at least to see and admit that ambiguity is ineliminably present even in social forms and institutions that seek to embody the highest of human ideals.

Find out more...

Walpola Sri Rahula, *What the Buddha Taught* ([1959] Oxford: Oneworld, 1997/ NewYork: Grove Press, 1986) is an excellent introduction to Buddhism.

Peter Harvey, *An Introduction to Buddhism* (Cambridge: Cambridge University Press, 1990) provides a helpful view of the history and teachings of Buddhism.

Klaus Klostermaier, *Hinduism: A Short Introduction* (Oxford: Oneworld, 2000) provides a general introduction to Hinduism.

More detailed material can be found in Friedhelm Hardy (ed.), *The Religions of Asia* (London: Routledge, 1988).

Patrick Burke's *The Major Religions* (Oxford: Basil Blackwell, 1996) is particularly good on Chinese religions, and has good bibliographies.

PART III

AFTER ENLIGHTENMENT

8

THE SECOND REVOLUTION

From Evidence to Experience

The religious revolution of the Axial Age, while real enough, was still often restricted in moral outlook. It tended to give rise to exclusive, authoritarian and paternalistic traditions, which viewed other traditions either with indifference or with contempt. Largely ignorant of or indifferent to other traditions, each one claimed sole possession of absolute truth. That truth was in its essential elements unrevisable and had to be accepted on authority. Naturally, therefore, a class of interpreters of the tradition grew up, in whose hands the guardianship of the tradition lay. Their task was to preserve the tradition in its original purity, and to resist revisions that might undermine it. Religion became in one sense essentially conservative, protecting an original set of truths given in the past against change. The religious institutions thereby created were to dominate the world for two thousand years.

That authority, however, was destined to be put in question by irresistible forces of change. Those forces most clearly came to the fore in Europe. When Christianity passed into the wider Mediterranean world it used the concepts of Greek philosophical thought (concepts of 'nature', 'person', 'substance' and 'essence') to formulate its main doctrines of incarnation and the trinitarian being of God, and in the West it adopted the language and many of the structures of the Roman Empire as the faith developed into the established religion of the empire.

The culture that helped to mould early Christianity was partly that of the great, but dying, civilisations of Greece and Rome. Though Christianity often tried to distance itself from classical pagan thought, Plato and Aristotle remained models and ideals of rationality for all those scholars who were concerned with the systematic exposition of Christian doctrine in the early Middle Ages. In John's gospel, Jesus was presented as the incarnate *Logos*, or intelligible wisdom of God. Since the whole universe was said to be patterned on him, there was always inherent in the Christian worldview a belief that the universe was an intelligible work of a rational creator. Moreover, humans were said to be made in the image of God, and Jesus was the perfected form of that image. So human persons were seen as rational creatures, the highest form of material creation, capable in principle of understanding and even of participating in the work of creation.

The idea of creation as a rational structure, and of humans as rational beings capable of understanding that structure and of reflecting in their rational activity something of the nature of God, laid the ground for a form of Christian humanism which gave reason a rightful authority, not solely dependent upon revelation, and which made human persons objects of respect in their own right.

The first great flowering in Europe of confidence in reason and respect for humanity as possessing inherent dignity came in the eleventh to thirteenth centuries, and is well represented by the works of Anselm and Peter Abelard, finding its summation in the theological compendia of Thomas Aquinas. His work was indebted to the earlier scholars of Islam, who had translated the Greek classics into Arabic, and made the works of Aristotle available as models of systematic and critical thought. But in Islam attention turned away from scientific investigation of the world to concentrating on submission to divine law. The divine will, perhaps because it was not seen as expressed in *Logos*, remained inscrutable, to be accepted without question, not to be critically examined. Humans, not being conceived as created in the image of God, were in no sense sharers in the divine nature, and could be wholly subordinated to the demands of the divine power. In the Christian world, however, God's will was in the end rational, and could be understood – so questioning in order to discover the underlying reason of things was justified. And since persons are meant to share in the divine nature, they are to be respected as children of God and not treated as mere means even to the realisation of the divine purpose.

THE PROTESTANT REFORMATION AND EVIDENTIALISM

So the stage was set in twelfth-century Christian Europe for the encouragement of critical reasoning and for the setting out of the God-given rights of human persons. But it was in the sixteenth century that the unity of Christendom itself was shattered by an explosive acceleration of these tendencies. The Protestant reformers used critical reason to throw doubt on the claims of the Catholic Church to interpret scripture. They claimed the right of all persons to interpret scripture conscientiously for themselves, and thereby undermined the traditional appeal to the teaching authority of the Church. As a necessary consequence, they established the right to dissent and to the free expression of belief, without which they could not themselves exist.

The Reformers insisted strongly on the final authority of scripture, and the subordination of reason to the revealed truths of scripture. But it was too late. Having established the right of all to interpret scripture in the light of personal conscience, they could not prevent a close examination of scripture, which led to a questioning of its consistency and inerrancy. Having established the right of conscientious dissent, they could not prevent free expression of the belief that traditional interpretations of scripture were to be subject to the demands of critical reason.

Reason need not in this context be thought of as some sovereign faculty that somehow gives direct insight into the inner nature of things (though of course it belongs to the *Logos* tradition that it may indeed be such). It is simply the attentive reading of scripture that leads to the discovery of discrepancies, however small, in the gospel narratives, and then to natural questions about who wrote the gospels, when and for whom, and what their cultural limitations might have been. This could have happened in Islam, but it did not, perhaps because the Qur'an was originally recited by one person, and thus does not have the complexities of different authorship and of different accounts of the same events from different viewpoints. Many scholars would say that problems do lie in the Qur'an about the sources of its material, but this did not become a topic of intellectual debate as it did in Christianity, largely because historical questions did not loom so large for a faith which accepts its sacred text as directly dictated by God as for a faith such as Christianity, which makes central historical claims about the life, death and resurrection of a person who lived long ago. Once critical reason was let loose, the historical nature of Christianity almost inevitably led to the development of a critical historical methodology which did not develop in the same way in Muslim societies.

The reformers, whether they meant to or not, encouraged the growth of a spirit of free critical enquiry which was to lead to the questioning of the authority of the Bible itself. This spirit also helped to encourage a new attitude to the investigation of the physical world of nature. The investigation of the natural world had been hampered by overreliance on the authority of Aristotle, and a purely rational approach to nature that preferred *a priori* speculation to observation. The reformers took leave to criticise Aristotle as well as the Church, since they saw that much of the Church's teaching, as they received it, was taken from Aristotelian or Platonic streams of thought. They thus felt free to question the received Aristotelian science, and investigation of the natural world could proceed without being hampered by having to conform to what the ancient Greek philosopher said.

The hypotheses of Copernicus (in 1543 he wrote *On the Revolution of the Heavenly Spheres*) and Galileo (in the seventeenth century) entailed just such a rejection of Aristotelian science. The well-known dispute between Galileo and the Catholic Church was not primarily a matter of reason versus revelation. It was rather sense-based close observation versus the supremely rational philosopher Aristotle – in other words, observation versus pure reason! The Church chose to be on the side of pure reason, backed up of course by scripture, which was itself supremely rational. It was close critical observation and detailed empirical analysis that undermined both Aristotle and the Bible as sources of truths about the physical universe, which were not derived from observation. The intuitive rationalism of Christian tradition, which saw human reason as illuminated by divine reason, was replaced by the critical rationalism of the new humanism, which saw human reasoning as a matter of close observation and critical questioning of all alleged evidence. It is not that the reformers had this explicitly in mind. It was rather that their rejection of Church authority encouraged free critical questioning of all accepted authoritative sources, and this attitude spread to the natural sciences as well as to theology.

Something else was required for the birth of natural science in its modern sense. That is the acceptance of the experimental method, the supposition that close observation of nature could reveal general principles in accordance with which it operated and which might enable its operations to be predicted. This supposition naturally springs from a belief that there is one rational author of nature, and that the human mind is able to trace the rational principles of created nature because of the human mind's basic affinity with the divine mind.

But to get the experimental method going, since it involves the experimental manipulation of nature, one has to rid the natural world of any sense of sacred inviolability. Though the *Logos* tradition clearly articulated the belief that nature is the intelligible creation of a rational God, it also tended to see creation as participating in the divine nature in some sense, and as dimly exhibiting the perfect ideas and exemplars in the divine mind. As long as people concentrated on trying to define these perfect ideas – defining the 'true natures' of things – and accepted that nature must be left unchanged as God's intended creation, modern science did not get started. What was needed was the clear separation of nature from God, and the search for mechanical principles of nature's operation, rather than traces of divine essences.

The Protestant Reformation contributed to this change of approach by clearing away as superstition all thoughts of spirits, demons or sacred elements of nature. God alone was sovereign, and nature was the instrument of divine purpose. Sacramentalism in its most general sense, according to which many natural elements could be effective signs and symbols of the divine, was downgraded.

Of course I am not suggesting that the Reformation was responsible for the rise of modern science. My purpose is rather to suggest that the Reformation had the effect of encouraging within religion itself both critical enquiry and freedom of the dissenting conscience. This in turn encouraged the spread of critical enquiry more generally in society. And that was certainly one of the preconditions of the growth both of modern science and the critical attitudes that are characteristic of the European Enlightenment.

Such an incorporation of criticism and dissent within a religious tradition was bound to lead to major problems, especially for a tradition that had required acceptance of truths on authority as part of true faith. As the scientific attitude began to be generally accepted, religious beliefs were bound to be questioned as to the evidence for their authority.

It is the growth of critical method that leads to scepticism about the revelation of unobservable truths. If those are truths about a supernatural world, the challenge is to ask on what evidence they are based. If they are truths about ancient history, and especially about miraculous events in ancient history, the challenge is again to ask what evidence there is for their occurrence. Intuitive rationalism is the natural ally of religion, at least insofar as religion is taken to be rational. The empirical method, however, picks away at all *a priori* claims, subjecting them to the requirement of testability and repeatability, until they begin to fade away.

The seventeenth and eighteenth centuries in Europe are often called the 'Age of Reason'. But more characteristic of them was the rapid growth of the empirical method, with its demand that every factual assertion should be based on sense-observation, and that belief should be proportioned to evidence. It might better be called 'the Age of Evidentialism'. Sir Francis Bacon summed it up well in his *Novum Organum* of 1620: 'We may have hopes of great results from an alliance so far unconcluded, between the experimental and rational methods.' The rationalism of the Greek and Christian traditions was to be allied with the evidentialism of the 'new philosophy' to produce a more fruitful understanding of the world.

There can be no doubt that a more fruitful understanding was provided by the empirical method. Even those who profess to doubt the objectivity of scientific knowledge propagate their views by computers and mobile phones, and fly around the world in advanced technological machines to deliver their lectures. Sometimes, however, the idea of personal experience as a whole was entirely subsumed under the idea of publicly accessible, repeatable and testable evidence. Whereas it seems plausible to require that evidence must put factual claims beyond reasonable doubt, that is not true of many personal experiences. There can be vivid and transforming personal experiences of immense significance which are not accessible to others, and which can change a person's whole view of the world without providing anything like universal certainty.

Those who insist upon the sole sufficiency of scientific method are forced to ignore the most important testimony available to human persons, the testimony of personal experience that can only be known by introspection. All feelings, evaluations and interpretations are set aside as purely subjective and unreliable, while all reliable knowledge must conform to the paradigms of empirical science – it must be objective, value-free and established by dispassionate observation. The scientific worldview, at least when taken to its extreme, can threaten to depersonalise and desacralise nature, leaving it as a machine to be observed and manipulated, rather than being an object of respect and compassion as a valued creation of God. Eventually, humans themselves will come to seem parts of the machine, and belief in freedom and rational enquiry will begin to be undermined.

The restriction of experience to what can count as evidence virtually rules religion out of court. Though some philosophers, such as John Locke, tried to argue that religious belief is based on good evidence, the evidence of design in nature, of miracles and fulfilled prophecies, it soon seemed to most people that this was rather poor evidence. Few if any miracles of biblical proportions have been tested under scientific conditions. Many prophecies look suspiciously as if they have been manipulated to fit the facts. Before long, Darwin was to propose a simple but brutal explanation for the mechanism of evolutionary change, which appeared to render the argument from design redundant.

EVIDENCE AND EXPERIENCE

Religious belief is not fundamentally a matter of evidence. Religion may be based on experience, but that is very different from saying that it is based on evidence. The crucial differences can be spelled out in ten ways.

First, evidence is a matter of public record. It must be publicly accessible, obtainable by anyone in the right conditions of observation. Much human experience, however, is not publicly accessible. I may experience many things which I do not tell anyone about, and in that case they often have no way of knowing what I am experiencing. This is particularly obvious in the case of religious experiences, where I have to ask people if I am to have any idea of what they have experienced. Then I have to rely on their reports, since there is no public access to their experience.

Second, all scientific observations must be repeatable. I must be able to perform the experiment you performed, to check your results. But personal experiences are unrepeatable in principle. Every time I listen to Beethoven's ninth symphony, even to a particular chord within it, I hear it in quite a different way. What has gone immediately before, and what

I expect to come after, enter into the experience of hearing itself, giving it a unique context, which makes it impossible to repeat exactly. This is why it is useless to seek exact correlations between brain-states (which, as physical, are in principle repeatable) and personal experiences of a reasonably sophisticated sort, such as hearing music (whose intrinsic character differs on every occasion). Every personal experience has a character of uniqueness, deriving from the complex and ever-changing web of experiences of which it is a part, which makes it absolutely unrepeatable, however hard one tries to repeat it.

Third, in scientific investigation we seek underlying general laws, which will explain how an event occurred, given a certain set of initial conditions. But in matters of personal experience we do not seek to understand them by uncovering general laws, which cause them to arise. Rather, we seek to understand them by interpreting them in terms of their significance in the life of the experiencing agent. We do not seek law-like explanation, but patterns of significance, of motivation, intention and desire, which might enable us to interpret them as meaningful in the life of a person. Historians and novelists seek understanding of how persons see things, what they aim at, or what motivates them. They do not seek to set out laws in accordance with which persons invariably act, in similar circumstances. A very hard-headed scientist may insist that such personal interpretations can be reduced to law-like explanations in the end. But no one has ever come near doing so, and every attempt in the social sciences to do so has failed lamentably. The fact is that understanding physical processes (where general laws explain very well) and understanding persons and their experiences (where we are seeking ways of seeing the world within which actions make sense to the agent) are different sorts of explanatory activity. That points to a crucial difference between what counts as scientific evidence and the many forms of personal experience with which the natural sciences simply do not deal.

Fourth, in the sciences we deal with 'knowledge-that', with propositions that can be precisely and clearly formulated. But in matters of personal experience, and particularly of the experiences of other persons, what is needed is 'knowledge-with', or empathy. 'Knowing-with' is a matter of my seeing how you feel or see the world, and it requires sympathy and sensitivity. We can know-that something is the case without feeling anything at all. But we can only know-with another person if one has some sharing of feeling with them, some ability to know what it is like to be in the state they are in. And that often cannot be put into words, into knowing-that propositions at all.

Fifth, scientific knowledge is dispassionate and aims at total objectivity, in the sense of saying something that could be said by anyone in any state. But personal knowledge is importantly reactive. What we know of another person is a function of our own personality. Some degree of love and trust are required before we can understand another person at all. As knowledge of them grows, we learn what our own capacities and dispositions permit us to learn. Typically, therefore, different people understand another person slightly differently. That is why group dynamics are so interesting, as each person in the group sees each other person in a slightly different way. It becomes apparent to everyone else that what each person says about another expresses his or her own reactions and personality. There are, of course, some things that are just correct or incorrect about other people. But in the end our judgement of them reflects our own sensitivity and their response to us. Personal knowledge can seek to discount prejudice and stereotyping. But it can never eliminate a reactive relation to another person. Nor should it do so, because only by entering into such a relation of appreciation and judgement can we know other persons adequately.

Sixth, the sciences advance by measurement. Variables have to be filled in with specific values, and those values must lie on a common quantitative scale. But experiences are immeasurable. There is no quantitative scale of happiness, or of any other personal experience. There *is* more or less. We know when we are more or less happy. But the pleasure of hearing Beethoven cannot be measured against the pleasure of hearing Mozart. And there is no measure by which we can agree the precise values of specific human experiences. To that extent, quantitative science cannot get a grip on human experiences. This is another important way in which evidence (the data of science) is different from experience (the data of consciousness).

Seventh, the sciences insist upon the possibility of experimental control. If you cannot experiment, varying boundary conditions to see what happens, science cannot get started. Personal experiences cannot be experimentally controlled. You cannot take an experience, isolate it, divide it into its component parts, and then vary some of those parts, keeping the others constant. Experiences are holistic, not atomistic. The parts take their quality and texture from the whole. Whereas you can isolate a gas in a container and vary the pressure, you cannot isolate one component of any complex personal experience. Introspective psychology virtually came to an end when it was realised that it could do little more than obtain reports of what was felt after some fairly crude adjustments of visual or sensory data. What can be obtained are some fairly general reports of the subjective effects of such adjustments. They may indeed be interesting and even surprising, but they get nowhere near the precision and specificity which is required for a physical experiment. In short, it is possible to study experiences in a general way, and to do so may be extremely useful. But it is not possible to study them under experimentally controlled conditions, because so many of the data are not isolatable in any satisfactory way.

Eighth, the natural sciences are normally predictive. They enable us to make precise predictions about what will happen in stateable situations, other things being equal. We cannot predict human experiences, except in a general way – and even then, we must admit that we may well turn out to be wrong. Economists are notorious for making predictions that do not come true. There is always a reason – people wanted something else, or were simply irrational. The fact is that attempts to predict complex human situations are at best general and probabilistic. Humans always have the capacity to surprise and to be creative. Who can predict the next scientific invention? Well of course no one can, or it would already have been invented. We like people to be generally predictable, but not always and not exactly, or they would be too boring. Novelists know this very well. Some scientists have yet to recognise it as an irreducible fact about experience.

Ninth, it is important for the sciences that their data should be precisely describable, not just vaguely so. There are many experiences that can hardly be described at all. They seem to be cognitive, to give knowledge or at least some sort of apprehension. But all attempts to describe what is apprehended fall lamentably short. This is especially important for experiences describable as religious. There is felt to be an object, other than human or physical, of such experiences. But it is usually felt essential that it be beyond adequate description. In experience, but not in science, there is knowledge without adequate description. That is enough to show that the sciences, and the sorts of data they count as evidence, do not by any means cover the whole of what is apprehended in experience. Both in one's own mind, in knowledge of other persons, and in claimed apprehension of some religious object, experience goes well beyond what can be counted as evidence.

Tenth, it is often held that anything that is evidence must convince all competent observers beyond reasonable doubt. As the humanist writer W.K. Clifford said, 'It is wrong always, everywhere, and for anyone, to believe anything upon insufficient evidence'.[88] The rational person must proportion belief to the evidence available, and only believe as strongly as the evidence will allow. This is almost totally inapplicable in the case of personal experiences. I may have a completely overwhelming experience that I cannot describe to anyone else, and which they may doubt I have had. I may not know what to do with it, or how to categorise it. If I am rational, I will have to try to give it some interpretation which fits into my general worldview, even if that requires a good deal of adjustment. But the effect on me, and the strength of my belief, may rationally go well beyond what would convince anyone else beyond reasonable doubt.

In religion, a discernment of a challenging or supremely attractive value may draw from me a total commitment to pursue that value in my life. That is not a matter of evidence. It is a matter, as Kierkegaard said so well, of passionate commitment made in objective uncertainty.[89] The commitment is not arbitrary. It is made in response to a discernment that overwhelms me, perhaps re-orients my worldview, and changes my life. To ask whether I have enough evidence to put the matter beyond reasonable doubt is to ask the wrong category of question. It is to turn religious insight, commitment and empowerment into quasi-scientific observation, evidence and dispassionate belief. If I do that something has gone terribly wrong. Of course religious beliefs will fail the evidential test. But enough should have been said by now to suggest that the evidential test does not apply to some of the most important areas of human experience.

The scientific worldview is one of the triumphs of the human spirit, and its gains have been immeasurable. But it errs if it claims to cover the whole of human knowledge and experience, and if it reduces physical nature to little more than a mechanism without objective value or purpose. It is fair to point out that modern science seems to have largely overthrown the mechanistic model that was characteristic of early modern science. In quantum mechanics and field theory the clear boundaries that may seem to have been drawn between personal experience and objective evidence blur or even collapse. Yet the mechanistic model dominated Newtonian science. It is deeply ironic that this model, conceived by Boyle and Newton as a tracing out of the elegant laws of a supremely rational God, should have led to growing scepticism concerning the Christian revelation. But it was so.

Christian revelation is based upon the record of miraculous acts of God, most notably the resurrection of Jesus from the dead. Newton himself believed in miraculous interventions in nature by God. What was to undermine belief in miracles for many people was that the nature disclosed by Newtonian science seemed to show a seamless web of causality in accordance with general laws, into which miracles would intrude as arbitrary and irrational supernatural interferences. Miracles began to seem improbable because of lack of evidence for them obtainable under controlled conditions, because of new, more rigorous standards of the investigation of natural processes, and because of a new understanding of the laws by which natural events occur.

By the time of David Hume, the traditional idea of a miracle as a sign of the presence or purpose of God, occurring in a context which transcends the normal regularities of physical nature, had been replaced by the idea of a miracle as an interference in the elegant laws of nature by a supernatural spirit, for which there is little scientifically controlled evidence. Within the mechanistic worldview miracles begin to seem irrational and unnecessary. But if they are renounced, traditional Christian revelation will need to be radically rethought. Again this was not primarily a matter of reason versus faith, for it is quite rational to expect a personal God to show signs of divine presence and power which are not explicable by general physical laws alone. What has happened is that evidentialism, the demand for overwhelming empirical evidence for all factual claims, displaces trust in the witness to personal experience of a transcendent reality, claimed to be known in and through extraordinary physical events. After the sixteenth century, religion had to rethink its claims in the light of the experimental method, which was so successful in science. It had to justify its claims in the light of a fully critical reason. That is a task so difficult that there are those who say it cannot be done.

Find out more . . .

John Locke's *The Reasonableness of Christianity* [1695] (in many collections) is a clear statement of a seventeenth-century attempt to render faith and evidentialism compatible.

Mark Richardson and Wesley Wildman (eds), *Religion and Science* (London: Routledge, 1996) contains many helpful essays on the relation of science and religion. Part I, on the history of the debate in early modern Europe, is most relevant.

Mary Midgley, *Science and Poetry* (London: Routledge, 2001) discusses scientific and non-scientific knowledge.

Roger Forster and Paul Marston, *Reason, Science and Faith* (Crowborough: Monarch, 1999) is of interest in providing clear, readable discussions of the main issues in science and religion from a conservative Christian viewpoint.

9

THE DREAMS OF REASON
Revelation and Imagination

It was the rationalist philosophers, especially Descartes, Spinoza and Leibniz, who have given 'the Age of Reason' its name. They argued that there are truths innate in the human mind, which give insight into the hidden structure of reality, and are not based on sense-experience. In that sense, they are attempting to retrieve the Christian (or, in Spinoza's case, the Jewish) tradition of the universe as expressing the divine *Logos* (Philo of Alexandria had incorporated that into Jewish tradition), and of the human mind as participating in or reflecting the divine Mind, in which all ideas or essences primarily exist.

However, they were affected by evidentialism. Their method was very different from that of Anselm, who was one of the most purely rationalist philosophers of all time. Anselm attempted to prove the existence and nature of God from first principles of reason. Yet he said that he 'believed in order to understand', and for him reasoning was an activity of the mind, illuminated by the divine Mind, and always guided by the teaching authority of the Church.

The rationalist philosophers had lost this faith that the Church had privileged access to the divine Mind. Even when they were Catholics, like Descartes, they were aware that the teaching authority of the Church had been seriously challenged by the Galileo controversy of 1633 (Descartes' *Discours* was published in 1637). They were aware that the Bible contained no systematic teaching about the nature of the physical world, nor was it systematic even about the nature of God. They were aware that much Church teaching was based on an unquestioning acceptance of Aristotle, and that Aristotelian (or worse, Platonic) physics had in fact held up the investigation of the physical causes of things for centuries.

So they were ready for a new start. And that start was evidentialist as much as it was rationalist. Descartes' method was fourfold: 'never to accept anything as true when I did not recognise it clearly to be so'; to divide every problem into simple parts; to proceed from the simple to the complex; and to include as complete a range of data as possible.[90] The method was critical, analytical, atomistic and synoptic. This method is not in fact rationalistic, in the sense of appealing to universal truths known by reason alone. It is a clear exposition of the empirical method, which was to revolutionise the practice of science. It hopes to build up knowledge cumulatively, piece by piece, always adducing evidence for its claims and appealing to the agreement of all competent observers.

Even the famous Cartesian principle of fundamental doubt is evidentialist, since – after toying with the idea of a malignant demon and discovering in his own mind a self-evident idea of God (this is one of the few pieces of *a priori* rationalism in his works) – Descartes assumed that the evidence of the senses could indeed be trusted.

When Descartes writes that by his method he 'was assured of always using my reason, if not perfectly, at least to the best of my power', he is not appealing to some universal infallible faculty of the mind. He is simply saying that the most reasonable and reliable way we have of gaining knowledge is to observe very carefully, and so far as is possible without prior beliefs as to what we will find; to break things down into their simple components; to explain the complex in terms of the simple;

and to make sure we cover all the relevant evidence. Reason, for Descartes as much as for David Hume, is the servant of observation. It has a few *a priori* principles, but they are little more than elementary rules of thought, which enable it to proceed effectively. Without observation little concrete knowledge can be obtained.

But what of the great rationalist systems, such as that of Leibniz, for instance, which proves that reality consists of monads, sentient atoms, arrayed in sequential and hierarchical order? The fact is that these systems are visions of an ultimately intelligible reality underlying the apparent chaos disclosed by sense-observation. They are prompted by the same factors that led to the rise of systematic theology ('theology' was a term first used by Peter Abelard in the eleventh century for a systematic exposition of Christian doctrine), a desire for system and order. In Islam, Ibn Rushd had juxtaposed Aristotelian philosophy with revealed truth, and, though this is disputed, was widely taken to have advocated a doctrine of 'double truth', with no contact between the two. But eleventh-century Christianity aimed at a more ambitious synthesis (which is probably what Ibn Rushd really wanted). The truths of the faith would complete the truths of reason, and the faith itself would be seen to be wholly rational.

This was prompted by a vision of universal consistency, coherence, integration, elegance and structure, which flowed from the *Logos* itself, and was mediated by inspired Church teaching. However, when that Church teaching was challenged, a number of different visions of intelligible unity opened up. There had always been Jews and atheists in Europe, and they were now as free as Christians to attempt a systematic vision of reality. In any rational system of thought, much depends upon the primary axioms and upon the sorts of data that the system allows to be included. The intuitive reason of an atheist will not be identical to the intuitive reason of a Christian. One includes God as an axiom and apprehensions of the supernatural as data, where the other does not include either. It is not surprising, then, that none of the basic self-evident truths of the philosophers seemed to agree with each other.

Nevertheless, all was not chaos. Reasoning is an activity of mind, which requires accurate awareness, the discernment of order, elegance of formulation and coherence of the simplest possible general theories with the full variety of observed facts. The ideal is that of mathematical thinking, in which all is derived by small deductive steps from axioms, which are in turn justified by their agreement with the full range of known particular conclusions. A very small change in the axioms or in the range of values to be included – in the definition of 'substance', or in the acceptability of appeals to subjective consciousness or to spiritual experiences, for example – will lead to different systems.

It is important to notice that mathematics is a highly imaginative and creative discipline. It is not just a matter of calculation – machines can do that better. It is a matter of insight, of creative re-formulation and patterning, of aesthetic sensibility. A good mathematician is not a human computer, but a poet of the mind. Reason is an intuitive, synoptic, integrative faculty of grasping things as a whole and intuiting their inner connection and coherence. The reasonable person is not someone who only believes what he or she can deduce or directly infer. Such a person would be a plodding pedant. The reasonable person is one who can see deep relationships, relate many disparate factors in one creative insight, and make judgements in complex situations which release one from old perceptions and enable one to go forward in a new and unanticipated way. The person of balance, good judgement and judicious criticism is the reasonable person. Judgements are paradigmatically personal, and involve imagination and insight. So reason is not a mechanical deductive faculty, which sorts everything out into clear-cut categories and allocates them to their proper place in a completely understood system. Such a mechanical faculty is what the German philosophers after Kant called 'understanding' (*Verstand*), not reason (*Vernunft*).

Reason transcends understanding, as the attempt to grasp things as a whole, to see beyond the categories of understanding into the hidden continuities and convergences of things. Reason is closest to what we might call creative imagination. Since it is intuitive, it naturally expresses the personality of the reasoner as well as the universal rules of reasoning by which it operates.

Different rationalist visions of the universe may be seen as imaginative visions using different sets of axioms and including different sorts of data, but agreeing that there is a rational way of thinking, which accepts careful (and wherever possible repeated) observation; generalisable principles of argument (not making an exception in one's own case); an ideal of the greatest possible elegance and systematic order (in the awareness that there may be limits to elegance and order); avoidance of self-contradiction; comprehensiveness; coherence with all well-established knowledge; and fruitfulness for further investigation (either by predicting testable consequences or by suggesting analogies for understanding wider ranges of phenomena). It aims at setting out a well-ordered system in which some truths can be seen to follow from others, and the primary truths lead to conclusions corroborated in experience. It strives for imaginative depth – an ordering of data in an elegant way, from a perspective that unites many data in an orderly way, so that diverse data illuminate one another. It aims for inclusiveness – including the established insights of the past, and correcting them in a wider frame.

Width of experience, judgement honed by dialectical discussion, appreciation of diverse views, skill in arranging data in an elegant, fruitful way – these involve personal skills of intellect and imagination and feeling, working on data available to one in a cumulative tradition. In sum, the rationalist seeks a rational and imaginative system – not a constraining rigid framework, but a basis for organic, developing, fruitful growth. There is not at all a great gulf, but rather a gradual and natural progression, between rationalism and Romanticism, and it is the Romantic imagination which chiefly characterises European culture even from the seventeenth century – after all, the age of Monteverdi, Rembrandt and John Donne – not a crabbed and confined pseudo-universal reason. This sort of rationalism does not have to be religious, but there is no reason why it should not be, and as a matter of historical fact most rationalists have been religious in the broad sense of seeing objective reason as supremely expressed in spiritual reality.

The 'Age of Reason' is thus not at all opposed to religion as such. Nor is it opposed to imagination and feeling, to experience in its widest sense. Data of revelation could well be included in the axioms of a rational system. But sometimes the new rationalism combined with new evidentialism to insist that all alleged truths should be based on the sort of evidence the natural sciences required. When such canons of evidence were applied to the historical records of the Bible and combined with the worldview of Newtonian science, serious doubts were raised about their reliability as an inerrant factual record.

So by the eighteenth century the belief that the Bible was an inerrant authority was as widely disbelieved as was the belief that the Church was such an authority. There were plenty of people who accepted an inerrant teaching authority in religion, though it was becoming clear to everyone that the number of such alleged authorities had increased enormously since the sixteenth century. To have one inerrant authority may seem bad enough, but to have a choice between ten or more competitors was just too bewildering. For many, the belief in a text that contained a set of propositions guaranteed to be true, about matters inaccessible to normal human methods of investigation, evaporated.

The propositions of the Church had been questioned by the reformers. Now the propositions of the Bible were questioned by the historians, whose very quest to recover an authentic past from the Bible appeared to undermine many previously accepted assumptions. So in eighteenth-century Europe there was a crisis of religious authority. For many, the crisis could only be resolved by a new understanding of what counts as evidence and of what authority in religion can justifiably be.

THE APPEAL TO EXPERIENCE

It was the Prussian theologian Friedrich Schleiermacher who first explicitly proposed an understanding of revelation as not consisting of a set of true propositions to be accepted on authority. What he did was to challenge the empiricists' restriction of experience to sense-observation. There are, he held, other sorts of perceptions ('intuitions', *Anschauungen*), which give knowledge of objective reality. Religious faith is based upon a distinctive sort of non-sensory apprehension, what he called an 'intuition of the infinite', or of a reality upon which we are absolutely dependent.

Revelation can be seen as the self-disclosure of objective spiritual reality, which we apprehend by non-sensory perception. This sort of revelation is not likely to be inerrant or even very clear, since we can be aware of a reality that we cannot describe very accurately, and which appears to us as it does largely because of the limitations of our faculty of perception. When we come to describe such a revelation, our description may be limited and tentative, though the experience itself may be vivid and life changing.

This opens the way to seeing the Bible as a record of personal experiences which, in the case of Christianity, can be traced back to the foundational experiences of Jesus, who knew God, Schleiermacher thought, in a uniquely vivid and unbroken way. Schleiermacher himself did not accept that miraculous events occurred – attributing the records of them to exaggeration and legend – but it is clearly possible that there could be experiences of miracles (like the resurrection), which are also important revelatory events. They, too, would not necessarily be recorded in inerrant propositions, though they would be objective events (not just states of mind), which manifest the presence and activity of God. As extraordinary events, they would be open in principle to public inspection. But as manifestations of God, their character would depend on the beliefs and receptivity of the experients. If the apostles saw the risen Christ, their testimony that they had seen this would be powerful. But any speculations they might make on the basis of such experiences – such as the date of the end of the world – could well include some false inferences. This enables one to give authority to the New Testament as a reliable testimony to both public experiences (the resurrection of Jesus) and private experiences (the transforming influence of the Spirit) of great religious significance, while allowing that the detailed records of and inferences from such experiences are not inerrant.

On such an account of revelation, religious authority would lie in especially vivid or authentic experiences of great religious teachers or prophets, and would be passed on within a religious community as experiences that are evoked by their lives or teachings. The demand for evidence would be met by pointing to experiences of the spiritual both in the lives of believers and paradigmatically in the life of the founding teacher of the tradition.

Within Christianity at least this account is plausible, since Jesus did not leave any body of writings or dictated divine teachings. The faith is based on memories of his life, but especially of his death and resurrection and the experience of the Holy Spirit after those extraordinary events. The personal experience of Jesus, with its intense awareness of God, witnessed to by the gospels, the experiences of the apostles at Pentecost and the visions of the resurrected Jesus are primary data of faith. It is not that propositions are unimportant, but it does seem that it is experiences and not dictated words that form the primary content of Christian faith.

Such an account will not work so well for religions (such as some forms of Christianity and virtually all forms of Islam) that maintain that their scriptures are dictated by God. But even in Islam it may be held that it was the Prophet's overwhelming experiences of God as commanding and merciful that underlay his sense of 'hearing' the suras of the Qur'an. Their main spiritual message is clear and vivid, though the particular stories in which that message is conveyed may derive from many sources, both Talmud and New Testament, and be drawn from the unconscious reservoir of ideas in the mind of the inspired Prophet.

It is the experience of God, a shadow of the Prophet's own experience, which is evoked by the poetic recital of the Qur'an, and which gives life to Islam. A liberal Muslim could hold that the Qur'an does communicate a sense of God and carry inspired teaching about divine sovereignty, judgement and mercy, without holding that it is free from factual error (for instance, about events in the childhood of Jesus that most Christians would take to be legendary).

Most Muslims today might not think this an acceptable view of divine revelation. They feel committed to a propositional, inerrant, view of revelation – for how can God communicate untruths? But the experiential view does not say that God communicates lies. It says that the self-disclosure of God to Muhammad inspired in him a beautiful and powerful poetic discourse, whose contents were drawn from the stock of ideas and images available to him in his culture, and which conveyed the spiritual truth of the presence of a holy God, while naturally including elements formed from the Prophet's own beliefs and understanding. One might hope that even if such a 'liberal' understanding is unacceptable to believing Muslims, at least it can be taken as a respectful and appreciative view of Islam from a liberal Christian viewpoint. A Christian need have no reservation in taking the Qur'an as a revelation of God in this sense, and even if Muslims must disagree with that view of revelation, they may see that it does not downgrade Islam as in principle inferior to Christianity.

The key to understanding the move to an experiential understanding of revelation is to accept that God does not simply put sentences into human minds. Rather, God makes the divine presence known in a powerful way to inspired human minds, which then respond to that disclosure by forming the ideas and feelings and hopes they have in new ways. The inspiration of God, we might say, does not replace human thinking. It guides and directs it, perhaps ensuring that some central understandings are put in place, but leaving human imagination and freedom of thought a great amount of play. This gives an understanding of religious authority that permits critical analysis of evidence and argument, even when they occur in canonical scripture, while accepting the reliability of the testimony of the founding teachers of a religious tradition.

It also encourages a view of religions as developing cumulative traditions, building upon an originative disclosure, but extended by continuing experiences of the spiritual interpreted by the concepts of the tradition, and by continuing reflection which seeks wider factual and moral insights as the tradition moves into new situations and general knowledge of the world extends. So revelation, reason, experience and tradition will not be quite different sources of religious thought. Revelation provides originative and normative experience; reason seeks an integrating vision of reality within which such experience can find an intelligible place; personal experience confirms revelatory experience to a lesser degree, while extending it to new contexts; and tradition preserves the memory of a cumulative chain of spiritual experiences which, it is to be hoped, leads to ever more comprehensive and inclusive perspectives.

EXPERIENCE AND LANGUAGE

This reflects in a slightly different way the influential distinctions made by George Lindbeck in *The Nature of Doctrine*, between propositional, experiential and cultural/linguistic views of doctrine.[91] He is, I think, entirely right in distinguishing propositional views – that God communicates propositions to human minds – from experiential views – that God discloses the divine presence to human minds, though not usually in words. But he criticises the experiential view, because he thinks it means that we have experiences before we have words, and then use words to describe them. This, he thinks, is the reverse of the real situation, where the sorts of words we have determine the sorts of experience we can have. For instance, Catholics may see visions of the Virgin Mary, but Hindus almost never do. Muslims may see visions of Muhammad, but Christians do not. Doctrines, formulated in words, come first, and then experiences may come later and confirm them.

So Lindbeck prefers what he calls the cultural/linguistic view. This sees language preceding experiences and our descriptions of them, and as embedded in distinctive forms of life and ways of acting. Thus the rituals of religion, with the language associated with them, are activities

I learn, which make possible for me specific forms of interaction with a postulated spiritual realm.

Lindbeck is importantly right in saying that language is a social practice, not a mere copying or exact description of clear and distinct private mental events. But personal experience often does call for new attempts at linguistic description and expression, and can drastically modify existing forms of linguistic expression. I may experience the spiritual realm for myself, and my visions and apprehensions may generate new ways of speaking, new images and metaphors, which may in turn be incorporated into modifications of ritual practice. Language is important to ritual, but experience is also important to language, as the individual's integration of new experience into learned categories of interpretation leads to new and innovative linguistic forms.

Linguistic tradition is vitally important in religion. But experience is an equally important factor in enabling us to understand diverse traditions, and to revise or advance our own tradition in creative ways. It is thus possible to run together the experiential and cultural–linguistic dimensions in such a way that new and vivid experiences prompt the linguistic tradition to move in new directions, while the existing interpretative tradition governs to some extent the way in which the religious object is experienced.

If this is done, the subjective and idiosyncratic nature of many personal experiences can be ironed out by testing them against a cumulative tradition of reflection and practice, while the tradition can be given new life and vitality by experiences that build upon and develop earlier paradigms. We can also avoid any tendency to think that there is no such thing as a rational – as opposed to an irrational – religious outlook. It is true that we will never have an absolutely neutral and unbiased viewpoint in religion. We may concede that diverse views seem rational to different rational agents, because our experience and knowledge is limited. But working within one cumulative tradition, we can learn to discern what is central and what is peripheral, how the tradition has developed and how it now needs to develop to include new knowledge and experience. In all traditions, self-contradictory beliefs, or beliefs which are radically inconsistent with other knowledge, or inferences made which are logically invalid, disqualify such views from rational acceptability. Each religious view must seek a rational basis, in the sense that it must take its place within a coherent and plausible view of the world. The fact that different worldviews seem plausible to different people does not undermine the attempt to seek such a rational basis for yourself.

EXPERIENCE AND AUTHORITY

This is not a matter of subordinating revelation to reason. Rather, by comparison and analysis of alleged instances of revelation, influenced by whatever spiritual experiences we have and by the knowledge of the world which we think is well established, we are gaining an idea of what could count as authentic revelation, and of what the limits of revealed authority will be. So an experiential view of revelation need not say that faith is just a matter of subjectively encountering God as a personal reality. It may add that there are propositions that are properly acceptable on authority. That authority will be based on acceptance that the teacher has a more intense and authentic experience, which is evidence of superior spiritual understanding. Whether that is strictly inerrant, however, especially in matters not directly related to the apprehension of God, is another question. To the extent that we do not think God actually dictates truths to the teacher, or to the extent we believe that even superior spiritual experience is of a reality beyond full human comprehension and infinitely rich and complex, we will be inclined to stress the metaphorical and provisional character even of authoritative propositions. That does not mean they are false. It does mean that they may be very hard to interpret, and will invite further reflection and expansion at a later date. Such reflection gives rise to cumulative linguistic traditions, within which there is a continuing effort to seek more expansive and reasonable formulations of the reality which gives rise to the basic experiential insight of the tradition. In this way, reason, revelation, experience and tradition all co-operate in the development of a mature religious outlook.

On an experiential view, religious traditions, using the language of myth and symbol, relate highly imaginative stories that carry spiritual truths within them. They do not so much relate literal truths as tell imaginative stories which allude to truths or evoke spiritual experiences in an often cryptic way. If we see religious revelation as a matter of a paradigm imaginative response to divine self-disclosure and of a cumulative tradition incorporating and reflecting on many lesser personal experiences, we will be less liable to think that God has spoken inerrantly to one group of people, but left all others almost completely in the dark.

What sometimes alarms religious believers is that in Europe some of the most influential writers deny that any claim to spiritual experience can survive the evidential test. Restricted evidentialism, as has been seen, holds that allowable evidence is confined to what is observable by the senses, publicly and repeatably. The proper response is, I think, not to reject appeals to experience altogether. On what other basis could revelation be received by humans? It is to insist that there are important human experiences in which the mind is in direct contact with spiritual realities.

It is clear that such experiences will vary according to the spiritual maturity of the observer and the conceptual framework that enables the observer to interpret them more or less adequately. There will be wise, holy and reflective experients, as well as silly, selfish and impulsive ones. Spiritual teachers of genius will gain insights that can transform our vision of things. They may not be infallible, but they will show a depth of insight not available to most of us.

So an experiential account of revelation will allow for prophets and sages who can extend our experience, deepen our insights and reorient our actions in relation to the spiritual reality they apprehend. We will have to say, however, that many teachers are mistaken in some of their teachings, if only for the reason that they contradict each other, and so cannot all be correct. We can follow a particular teacher, but many – probably most – teachers must be thought to be mistaken in some particulars. That will not really be surprising, if revelation is taken to be, not the reception of inerrant truths, but the apprehension of a deeply mysterious and perhaps infinitely complex spiritual reality.

Schleiermacher was not quite sure what to make of the diversity of religions in the world. In his early work *Speeches on Religion* (1799), he applauds the variety of religions, and states that, since God is infinite, it will need many religions to gain any adequate idea of the divine nature. But in his later work *The Christian Faith*, he seems certain that Christianity (especially Prussian Protestantism) is the supreme religion, and is destined to take over the world.

This vacillation is easy to understand. Insofar as we concentrate upon human experience and response, there seems little reason to prefer one form of experience to others, and good reason to suppose that the greater the variety of experiences the more adequate our grasp of the spiritual is likely to be. After screening out experiences associated with delusional beliefs about our own personality and the objective environment, a range of experiences remains between which there seems little to choose in terms of intensity and seeming authenticity.

But if we concentrate on traditions of interpretation, on visions of the ultimate rationality of the world, incompatible truth-claims soon come to the surface, and hard choices have to be made. Either there is a loving personal God or there is not. Either Jesus is the unique incarnation of God or he is not. Yet all beliefs about God are extremely hard to spell out exactly, and our understanding of them is likely to be very inadequate. So the truth is hard to discover and even harder to formulate. In such a situation, disagreement can be a good means to spur us on to seek a truth as yet not fully formulated. With such a provisionalist and experientialist attitude, we can both hold to the ideal of one absolute truth and celebrate the diversity of limited human attempts to find it. That is an attitude that both religion and the natural sciences can share.

Find out more . . .

Friedrich Schleiermacher, *On Religion: Speeches to its Cultured Despisers*, trans. Richard Crouter (Cambridge: Cambridge University Press, 1988) is the book that first argued that experience is the real basis of religion.

Rudolf Otto, *The Idea of the Holy*, trans. John Harvey ([1917] Harmondsworth: Penguin, 1959), defines the basic religious sense as a sense for the 'numinous'. Though many would feel his view is too restrictive, this is a classic statement of an experiential view.

George Lindbeck, *The Nature of Doctrine* (London: SPCK, 1984), contrasts propositional, experiential and 'cultural–linguistic' views of religious belief, criticising a purely experiential view.

John Hick, *The Fifth Dimension* (Oxford: Oneworld, 1999), gives an experiential view of religion on a global scale. This is a development from the view he stated in a Christian context in *Faith and Knowledge* (London: Macmillan, 1957).

10

MATTERS OF MORALITY

From Autonomy to Theonomy

REASON AND MORALITY

I have traced the way in which, in European Christianity, the critical and experimental method of the natural and historical sciences came to have a major influence on how religious faith was viewed. On the one hand, a restricted evidentialism was born which disallowed any appeal to spiritual realities at all. But on the other hand, a new emphasis on experience as a source of revelation produced a form of critical faith, which is able to accept ancient traditions as in large part metaphorical and symbolic expressions of that personal relation to transcendent reality that is taken to be the heart of religion.

Religion is, however, not just a matter of experience. It is essentially concerned with ways of living and acting, with commitment to a specific conception of the good and to a way of life that is empowered by participation in that good. Religion is essentially practical.

Just as reason came to exercise a critical role in matters of factual belief, so it came to exercise a similar role with regard to morality. This in turn had a major impact on religion. There was nothing new in connecting Christian morality with reason. *Logos* theology, finding creation to be inherently rational, was after all a central part of Christian faith. Surprising though it may seem, in the Christian tradition morality has always been a matter of rational reflection, not unquestioning obedience to scriptural texts. But this reflection was governed by three major factors: acceptance of the doctrine of the creation of all things by God, which gave the order of nature a divine sanction; acceptance of the doctrine of incarnation, which gives human nature a unique dignity; and acceptance that the teaching of Jesus and perhaps the teaching authority of the Church corrects and guides human reason when it may be led astray by passion and desire (for instance in the case of divorce or improper sexual relationships, or in an over-high evaluation of purely sensual goods).

The ethical teaching of the great medieval theologian Thomas Aquinas, influenced to a great extent by Aristotle, founds moral reflection upon a rational discernment of those natural inclinations that are placed in human nature by God. Christian virtue, he says, consists in fulfilling the inclinations of human nature, and in completing those inclinations by orienting them towards their final end, the knowledge and love of God. Reason discerns God as the foundation of the rational order of the cosmos, and discerns the proper ordering of human passions towards their final end. Revelation completes natural human morality and sometimes corrects a mis-ordering of human inclinations. But it does not contradict reason. On the contrary, it confirms the rational structure of created human nature.

The Aristotelian worldview became an early casualty of the new experimental method in the natural sciences. Its assumption that all things have an inherent *telos*, an end to which they strive, was rejected. In addition, human inclinations tended to be seen by Protestant reformers as depraved, corrupted by original sin, and as unreliable guides to God's purposes. So reason could no longer look to nature to see what its purposes are, or to human inclinations to see how one ought to act.

Of course, what the reformers wanted was that people should look to the Bible to see how to act. Unfortunately, the critical reason that they had liberated from Church domination looked critically at the Bible and found it more morally confusing than helpful. Apart from apparently justifying genocide (in the invasion of Canaan by the Israelites), slavery and private vengeance, it said very little about the major moral problems of early modern Europe, about the proper use of capital or about universal human rights. These problems could be mitigated where there existed a tradition of interpretation to show how ancient laws might be abrogated by later insights, and underlying principles could be mined from the texts and applied in new ways to present circumstances. But take away that tradition, let all interpret the texts for themselves, and there is plenty of room for conflict between a literal reading of ancient laws and the moral perceptions that by the eighteenth century were giving rise to demands for liberty, equality and fraternity in France and America.

But things were even worse than this for those who hoped to read moral rules directly from the Bible. Once you look at the gospels closely, it becomes apparent that inherent in the teaching of Jesus from the first was a preparedness to put accepted rules in question, where they seem harmful to human dignity and flourishing. This is what Jesus did in his teaching on Torah, always stressing that healing, forgiveness and reconciliation are more important than keeping rules for their own sake.[92] Christian morality is based on the teaching of Jesus, but that teaching precisely questions all traditional rules to see whether they tend to human flourishing or not.

St Paul similarly writes that all the laws of Torah are summed up in the principle of loving your neighbour as yourself.[93] And he repeatedly insists that 'the written code kills, but the Spirit gives life'.[94] So it looks as though it is central to a Christian view of revealed morality to look at it critically and ask how it can best be interpreted in a way which leads to human fulfilment and flourishing – which may even require a renunciation of a law's literal sense (note how Jesus' teaching on the law of 'an eye for an eye' renders the law completely inapplicable, without actually saying that it is wrong[95]).

Critical questioning of the Bible by Christians meant that morality could not easily be founded on a simple appeal to biblical authority. Yet this in itself did not threaten to undermine Christian morality. For it brought into the foreground the basic Christian criterion by which moral rules could be assessed: do the traditional rules make for human flourishing, for love of one's neighbour as one loves oneself – or not?

Nonetheless, critical attitudes did challenge elements of traditional Christian teaching about morality. Paul at one point said that women should submit to their husbands.[96] Is that an absolute rule for Christians? If one took it as a propositional revelation direct from God, the answer might be 'yes' (though even then, the text may be abrogated by other Pauline teachings about the equality of all in Christ, or by deeper reflection on general Christian insights about the dignity of human personhood). But if we take Paul's letters critically, adopting a more experiential interpretation of revelation, we can see them as expressions of his own response to his experience of God in Christ. We are free to see this as a culturally limited response that needs amendment in the light of wider cultural experience and greater awareness of the radical nature of the gospel call for equal respect for all humans. We can then be much more ready to radically amend or even reject specific moral rules in the New Testament if they can be seen to belong to a temporary local context, and if, applied literally in different contexts, they contradict the basic moral principle 'do what makes for human flourishing'.

The problem is that this moral principle does not seem to be particularly religious. That raises the crucial question, what is morality based on? It should no doubt be connected with reason, but critical reason cannot, it seems, obtain its basic rules from Church tradition, from inspection of actual human desires (which are often egoistic and are no longer seen as implanted by God), or from a simple reading of biblical texts. Nor can it obtain moral rules from nature, especially when the evolutionary view develops that nature is 'red in tooth and claw', so that natural processes too need to be subordinated to considerations of human flourishing.

It looks as though reason may have to be given up – and some eighteenth-century moralists did just that, attempting to replace it by appeal to the sentiments, especially of benevolence or sympathy. Immanuel

Kant came up with the most influential suggestion, that reason does not obtain its rules from anywhere; it just makes up its basic rules for itself. Morality is, as Kant put it, not heteronomous, taking its moral principles from elsewhere. It is autonomous, prescribing its principles for itself.

KANT AND THE PRINCIPLE OF AUTONOMY

For Kant, the principle of autonomy is that every will is a law to itself, a self-legislating member of a community of co-legislating agents. This he thought was a purely formal principle governing the actions of any rational being, and given the existence of desires, it would of itself provide the content of a rational morality. My moral principles are the principles I could will everyone to act in accordance with. I can work that out just by reflection on what principles of this universalisable sort everyone could agree to. For example, I can only tell a lie if I can will that everyone could agree to telling lies. But I would not be prepared to accept such a situation. Therefore it is immoral to lie.

Morality is once again a product of reason, but not of intuitive reason, which discerns the good and the beautiful as a supremely rational object of rightly ordered desire. It is a product of purely formal reason, whose role is to pick out those principles of action upon which all rational agents could agree. It requires no reference to a supreme Good or to any disclosure of what true goodness is. It is what Charles Taylor, in a powerful book on the development of modern thought, calls 'procedural Reason',[97] taking its ends or goals from human nature as it actually is, and seeking to make them conform to a general abstract formal principle. Kantian autonomy seems to divorce morality from religion completely, and it is not surprising that Kant rejected any revealed morality in favour of a purely self-legislated moral law. But his view of morality was much more dependent on religion than it may seem to be.

When Kant spoke of autonomy he was not suggesting that everyone could decide for him- or herself what ought to be done. That is a drastically demythologised version of Kant. He was referring to the capacity of the rational will to be a legislator of law. He meant that practical reason (*Vernunft*, not *Verstand*) could discern the basic obligation of human nature to realise the happiness of others and the goals of creativity, culture and knowledge in oneself.[98]

There are rational goals of human activity, and there is an absolute obligation to realise those goals for all without exception. Reason, he thought, subjects all human desires and purposes to the test of whether they can be realised in ways that do not subordinate some agents unfairly to others. All rational agents would agree that persons are rational agents who should realise their natures in all possible compatible ways in a non-egoistic community of wills.

A condition of the possibility of moral action, Kant thought, is that we regard ourselves as knowing, free agents capable of enjoying many activities and experiences. Without such a conception, the idea of goodness – of what is worthy of choice – fails to make sense. For we need knowledge of what can be chosen, freedom to choose it and inclination to give a reason for choice. So any moral agent must logically agree that knowledge, freedom and happiness are goods, things worthy of choice by any rational sentient agent. Since it is rational to wish for as much good as possible, any purely rational being wills a maximal extension of knowledge (of what can be chosen), of freedom (power to choose) and of happiness (fulfilment of desired purposes), compatibly with a similar extension for all others in the moral community.

What is distinctive about Kant's approach to morality is that he tried not to found moral principles on some intuition of moral truths, on the contingent existence of feelings such as sympathy or on the revealed commands of God. He wanted to found morality on the demands of reason alone. Reason will itself decree that only some desires and goals can be willed equally for all. But to do that, reason has to be seen as supremely impartial, primarily concerned with the greatest possible extension of the cognitive and volitional powers of rational sentient agents, and as unconditionally commanding.

That may seem to be a wholly secular view. Alasdair MacIntyre, however, has argued that what he calls 'the Enlightenment Project' of providing an independent rational justification for morality must fail when morality is disconnected from a generally teleological view of human nature.[99] There can be no agreement on why one should act morally if a teleological view of human nature is rejected. Kant's project fails along with those of David Hume and Søren Kierkegaard, since there is no longer any agreement on what basic human nature is, and how it is to be realised.

I think MacIntyre is right in suggesting that justifications of right action depend on views of human nature, though he understresses the extent to which views of human nature have been contested throughout human history. There has never been an agreed view of what human nature is, and in that sense there has never been a universally agreed morality. Kant was right in thinking that some basic moral goods, such as happiness, knowledge and freedom, can be universally agreed. But he was wrong in thinking that any general justification can be given for regarding these goods as categorical obligations to maximise them in a completely impartial way. Any such justification will depend on some view of human nature that makes it reasonable to have a total commitment to the pursuit of moral goods for their own sake. So MacIntyre is right in thinking that a specific sort of absolute, impartial, self-realising morality depends upon a teleological view of human nature, which is implicitly theistic. But Kant is right in claiming that there are some basic attributes that any rational agent would agree in calling good, because they are conditions for considering oneself a moral agent. Moreover, if we were to think of goodness as being objectively instantiated, goodness would have to be considered a maximal case of those basic goods. It would have to be conceived at least as maximally knowing, creatively free and supremely happy. We could thereby generate a moral conception of God, even if we did not think such a being exists. What would fail in a wholly secular context would be the attempt to justify believing that a supremely good God exists, or to justify a policy of acting to maximise such goods ourselves.

It would be useless to say that these were self-evidently moral demands to realise impartially our cognitive and volitional powers. For is there any room in a secular view for unconditional commands of any sort? Is it reasonable to be absolutely impartial in a world in which each competes against others for scarce goods? And why should we aim to realise our cognitive and volitional capacities if we do not want to do so? Kant is thinking of reason (*Vernunft*) as something that commands that we realise as many distinctively personal capacities as we can, in a moral community. But that is just what a God would will who creates rational sentient agents – persons – in order that they should fulfil their purpose by realising their fullest potentialities of creativity and understanding in co-operation with others. Such a God does not issue arbitrary commands, expecting blind obedience to them. Such a God wants created persons to shape their own natures by learning to understand appreciatively and act creatively in co-operation with others, by imitating in an appropriate way the perfections of the divine nature.

For Kant, the heteronomous self receives its orders from others, and so remains in a state of moral infancy. The autonomous self learns to create and enjoy and share with others its own freely chosen values. As it grows in moral maturity, it does not become more isolated and alone – that would be false autonomy and egoism. It becomes more sensitive to the needs of others, more able to co-operate with them in the pursuit of many rationally choosable states and activities, more strongly bound to the moral law of creating the maximum possible values in which all can share. That is because my autonomous rational will, in its essence, when it is not deluded by inordinate desires, is a will to the realisation of goodness. It completely overrules all egoistic and short-sighted principles.

In Kant's hands, the principle of autonomy decrees that every rational sentient agent must consider itself to be a free source of conscious and creative goal-seeking activity, in a community of similar agents. The fundamental principles of morality will become clear, he thought, when we discover what goals such autonomous agents could positively intend for themselves and others in such a community. There are many possible objections to the feasibility of this project, though this is not the proper place to consider them.[100] Kant was not saying,

'Do your own thing, whatever it is' (the principle of radical autonomy). He was saying, 'Pursue goals that you could intend everyone to pursue, which will extend the cognitive and creative capacities of persons as much as possible' (we could call that the principle of personalist autonomy). Thus he says, 'In all the actions which affect himself a man should so conduct himself that every exercise of his powers is compatible with the fullest employment of them.'[101] We cannot will anything that would impair our ability for the fullest realisation of our personal powers. Kantian morality is a morality of self-realisation, of personal flourishing, in a community of agents for whom all must have equal respect.

It is not surprising that Kant saw the rational will as the voice of God, not as an external commanding person, but as an inner and absolute obligation to the realisation of goodness. Kant, in his posthumous unpublished work, actually identified practical reason with God,[102] and he had long held that religion is 'the recognition of all duties as divine commands'.[103] If we ask why we should obey reason, Kant's answer is that this is what realises our transcendence over the phenomenal, the supremacy of the spiritual to the material. In committing ourselves to moral action, we commit ourselves to the rule of reason over nature, and to the primacy of the immaterial over the material.

KANT AND RELIGION

Kant is after all by no means an atheist. Humanity has dignity, for Kant, precisely because humans, in virtue of their possession of reason, are members of the transcendent realm. As members of that realm, they may and even must hope for that coincidence of happiness with virtue that only a God can ensure. Kant's autonomous morality is far from being non-religious. It is just a peculiarly strangulated sort of religion, which seems to fear experience of God, but really needs the idea of God to make sense of the primacy it gives to reason.

Kant's rejection of revelation in morality was a rejection of propositional revelation, of acceptance of moral rules just because they are to be found in some holy text. He also shied away from religious experience, but he admitted that there was such a thing as moral experience, the sense of awe before the majesty of the moral law. His famous saying, 'Two things fill the mind with ever new and increasing amazement and reverent awe ... the starry heaven above me, and the moral law within me' makes the point forcefully. The sense of the commandingness of the moral law is a form of experience that those who lack any sense of transcendence must fail to have.

Kant's inability to find any specific disclosure of the character of God in the person of Jesus, or to allow for any experience of grace or of the Spirit, places him outside the Christian tradition. But his 'autonomous morality' strongly affirmed the transcendent reality of reason and its supreme sway over human life. It allowed for awe before absolute obligation and reverence for humanity as a being transcending the phenomenal, for an objective purpose of personal self-realisation, and also for the hope of future happiness-in-accordance-with-virtue. These are the echoes of a Christian vision of humans as participants in the Divine Reason, as those who apprehend an objective moral goal of personal flourishing in community.

Kant's espousal of an autonomous morality is easily misinterpreted as the thought that morality can be founded on human nature and reason alone, without any reference to spiritual reality. Radical autonomy, very different from Kant's, is the view that I can decide for myself what to do, without reference to anything other than my own free choice. Such a view eventually undermines the supremacy of reason and the dignity of human nature that Kant was concerned to preserve.

If we drop God, the perfectly rational creator, out of the Kantian argument, we are left with a purely hypothetical ideal of a community of perfectly rational agents, all agreeing with one another. But what we have on earth are many communities of agents who prefer their kin to others, who are in competition for scarce resources with most other people and species, and who desire the happiness of those they love more than the happiness of people they do not know. The hypothetical community of purely rational agents may live in heaven. But they are never likely to live on earth, and the resolute atheist needs a much more realistic morality, which starts from actual human desires and the will to power in an intrinsically competitive world, not an imagined absolute obligation to follow a hypothetical and probably unrealisable ideal.

Such an absolute obligation to the hypothetical and unrealisable prioritises the ideal over the actual, and ultimately relies upon the idea that underlying the natural processes of the observed universe there is a moral order which exercises rightful authority. Moreover, for Kant that moral order is manifested in space and time as the dynamic power of reason (*Vernunft*), which realises its infinite goals through the self-sacrificing acts of human persons. This sort of religion posits no external object of worship or source of moral authority. It places the supreme object of reverence within, in the activity of reason. Its principles are generated by personal reflection on the proper goals for a community of rational agents, but once generated they have absolute authority. Kant's religion is in the end an inner religion of self-realising Spirit – a religion that Hegel was to develop in his notion of *Geist* or Absolute Spirit.

The notion of an external personal God is only ambiguously present in the Kantian religion of reason, but the notion of a transcendent spiritual, moral reality, which manifests itself in rational agency, is quite clear. Human subordination to an absolute moral command, human inability to do what is right, faith in an unseen power to remedy that inability, and to assure us of future happiness-in-accordance-with-virtue – these are the marks of Kantian religion. They are not secular. In Kant, the Enlightenment changed the character of religion, stressing the immanent, rational and self-realising nature of Spirit, not the commands of an external God. But it did not replace religion by a supposedly universal and purely secular basis for rational morality.

What strikes most religious believers as peculiar about Kantian religion is its declaration that knowledge of God is impossible, that God is only a postulate of moral faith, and that revelation from God has no place at all in moral life. Its positive affirmation that moral truth does not depend upon revelation from God, and that ancient scriptural texts should not be exempt from moral questioning, are permanent contributions to critical religion.

The Enlightenment established that moral perception has an independence from, and even in one aspect a certain priority over, religious apprehension. All are capable of apprehending the elementary moral truths of justice, impartiality, benevolence and honesty. Those who have, or claim to have, religious apprehensions of spiritual reality are required to test those apprehensions by whether they match up to the highest moral perceptions we have. Even the idea of God itself, the idea of a being 'than which no greater can be conceived', is shaped in the light of our ideas of what values and goals are greatest, or most rationally choosable.

There remains a place for revelation, for disclosures of the transcendent, which are in the canonical traditions felt to be apprehensions of that which is supremely good. Such apprehensions may need to be tested against our existing notions of goodness. But they may well move us beyond existing notions into new perceptions of the depth or range of moral obligation, or of the character of the truly good life. If there is a supremely good and beautiful, it will attract by its own power insofar as one discerns it truly. Our desires will be changed by attending to it. What a revelation of transcendence offers is not blind obedience but instructed discernment, not radically arbitrary choice but attentively cultivated and freely given love. For all his greatness, Kant failed to see that, and to that extent he failed to see what was really involved in a religious morality. But he was right in stressing that all claims to revelation must be tested by their capacity to extend our perception of and commitment to the greatest achievable flourishing of creativity, sensitivity, compassion and co-operation. The moral task of critical religion is to enrich the widest flourishing of personal life.

LIBERAL MORALITY

The Enlightenment had begun in the Christian *Logos* tradition, which led to a vision of nature as the intelligible handiwork of a rational God, and to a vision of humanity as sharing in the Divine Reason. In its combination of rational thought and careful appeal to evidence, it led in the seventeenth-century development of scientific thought to a new vision of the universe as a vast emergent totality which no ancient scripture had, or could have, envisaged. It led in the eighteenth-century revolutionary formulation of the 'rights of man' to an insistence that principles of human conduct should be rationally justifiable by reference to their contribution to human flourishing. And it led in the nineteenth century to the full development of a critical approach to history and to the historical claims made in revealed scriptures. In science, in morality and in history, traditional claims about the nature of the physical universe, about principles of human conduct and about events in ancient times were put in question.

This questioning could and did lead to a crisis of religious authority. Historical criticism would lead to the rejection of all revealed truth as a product of superstition and legend. An insistence on the use of scientific evidence would lead to the rejection of religion as primitive and false science. And the requirement that all principles for action must be justified solely by reference to human desires would lead to the rejection of traditional religious morality as a set of unjustifiable taboos and prejudices.

The rejection of religion was seen by many as a clearing away of superstition and obscurantism. But then in a quite unexpected way critical reason came to be turned against itself. In a world in which there is no God and no structural intelligibility, why should reason be important? How can the ephemeral contents of human brains, thrown up as accidental products of evolutionary processes, pretend to understand absolute truths? Reason itself comes to be seen as an evolutionary survival strategy, subordinate to the drive to reproduction and the will to power. It is in that way that critical reason undermines its own authority. The European Enlightenment produced a crisis, not only in religion, but in the understanding of human beings as rational agents with unique moral value and dignity.

It is important, if the positive insights of the Enlightenment are to be retained, that reason should retain a rightful authority. But that implies that the cosmos must be seen as sustaining and manifesting intelligibility. The religious affirmation of a spiritual, rational basis to reality is the most compelling grounding for such a view. The crucial question for critical religion is therefore whether the affirmation of spiritual reality can be made in a fully rational way, without reliance on anti-scientific, unhistorical or morally authoritarian principles.

The actual religious response to the widespread criticism of religion in Europe was twofold. One response rejected liberalism and modern thought, and insisted that the Bible was historically accurate and morally binding, to be accepted on authority as true, because God preserved it from error. The other response was to revise views of revelation, accepting the presence of legend, factual error and morally limited perceptions in the biblical records, but upholding the Bible's authority as a witness to genuine experiences of objective spiritual reality, developing through reflection on and revision of a cumulative tradition of belief and practice.

If humans experience the divine in ways commensurate with their cultures and temperaments, the discernment of Spirit as morally commanding will not issue inerrant and unrevisable moral rules. It will develop deepening insights into human nature and its proper fulfilment, and the efficacy of specific social and personal principles for realising such fulfilment. Imaginative response, reflective interpretation and a continual rethinking of the cumulative tradition will all play their part in moral decision making. Traditions of revelation will develop by rational reflection, as insights into what reason requires change in accordance with further knowledge of the natural world, and with new experiences of the divine.

Such an understanding characterises what may be called 'critical religion'. It largely originated in Germany in the eighteenth and nineteenth centuries. Different writers emphasised different forms of critical religion. Kant found in Christianity a metaphorical or pictorial expression of moral truths that could be more clearly formulated by human reason. Hegel also saw Christian dogmas as pictorial expressions, but of metaphysical truths about the nature of reality which philosophy could formulate more clearly. Schleiermacher interpreted the pictures as expressions and evocations of feelings or intuitions of the infinite, and picked that out as the distinctive feature of religion, as opposed to ethics and philosophy.

They all agreed that traditional religion presented pictures or symbols, not literal truths. But were they pictures of moral, metaphysical or experiential truths? The general judgement of German liberal theologians such as Troeltsch, Harnack and Ritschl was that the speculative rationalism of the Greeks had on the whole been a bad influence on Christianity, and that an emphasis on personal experience or 'mysticism' led to a chaos of subjective fantasies, an endless series of irrational Romantic day-dreams. In these judgements they agreed with the traditionalists, but the liberals could not go back to an acceptance of inerrant propositional revelation. They focused on what they took to be the original moral teaching of Jesus: his call to repentance; his hope for a 'kingdom of God', a just society; and his simple teaching of the universal fatherhood of God. Christianity was simple ethical monotheism, and its original teaching (shorn of the complications of Trinity, incarnation and atonement) was to obey God's will for justice and mercy, and hope for a future realisation of God's moral purpose for creation.

This is not, as some have held, a reduction of religion to secular morality. Kant's moralism, I have suggested, was not just a matter of human rational decision. It was founded on belief in the transcendent reality of reason, on the dignity of human nature, and on the hope for liberation from evil and a realisation of moral purpose somewhere and somehow. The liberal theologians who followed him, and were so much influenced by him, also founded their moral views on the transcendent reality of God, on the possibility of forgiveness and hope for the kingdom of God. Theirs was a simpler theology, but not a vacuous one.

Sometimes liberalism has been interpreted as a rather naive optimism about human rationality and progress – in opposition, for instance, to a pessimistic Christian belief, held by some, that human nature is enmeshed in evil and headed for the doom of the world in a catastrophic Armageddon. However, faith in reason is a consequence of faith in a wise creator of all things, and faith in humanity is a consequence of faith in the realisation of God's purpose. If those transcendent beliefs are given up, then the liberal programme may indeed seem shallow and unduly optimistic. But if there is a wise and loving creator with a purpose for the universe, then in some sense there must be a realisation of a good purpose, whether or not it is in the future and on this planet.

Traditional beliefs have often stressed the presence of evil and divine judgement and retribution. In doing so, they have been influenced by beliefs that the world will soon come to an end and that infidels have knowingly rejected God. Greater knowledge of the vast extent of the universe, of the evolutionary development of humans and of the possibility of improving the environment and human health by technological change has modified all such beliefs.

The world may come to an end, and technology may end it. But if that happens it will be a failure of God's purpose, not the fulfilment of a divine plan. If it is possible to improve social conditions – and the American and French Revolutions of the eighteenth century suggested that it is – we should certainly do everything in our power to do so, and we should do everything we can to prevent a planetary catastrophe. Humans are not fully rational, and progress is not automatic. The liberal programme is not deluded about the human condition. But it affirms that rationally justifiable policies and material and social welfare should be pursued as strongly as possible. If that is humanism, it is a humanism that is licensed by a religious experience of transcendent reality as wise and compassionate, and as having a good purpose for creation. That purpose essentially involves a concern for human welfare. It underpins what the Christian theologian Paul Tillich called 'theonomy', for which universal human flourishing is a moral demand rooted in an objective and commanding reality whose purpose will ultimately be realised. Theonomy, said Tillich, is 'culture under the impact of Spiritual Presence'.[104] In a theonomous morality, the humanist ideal of self-realisation in community is directed by commitment to a Spiritual Reality which gives that ideal commanding force and promises that finally it will be realised.

FROM LIBERALISM TO LIBERATION

For many in the modern world, 'liberalism' has become a negative term, suggesting a strongly laissez-faire attitude which encourages an irresponsible personal freedom of action and expression, and whose most natural political ally is what is seen as the exploitative and ego-driven capitalism of the West.

This is a total misunderstanding of the Kantian view that the moral goal is the equal freedom and flourishing of all, not the unfettered flourishing of some at the expense of others. But it is true that the European Enlightenment was the product of an elite culture based on surplus wealth for a small proportion of the population. Democratic participation was limited to wealthy property-owning males, and non-European cultures were seen as primitive and in need of education by the West.

It took a very long time before a truly global perspective led the cultured elites to see members of every race and both genders throughout the whole world as full members of one human moral community. It has taken the disastrous wars of the twentieth century to remind Europe of its own barbaric and power-hungry heart. It has taken the threat of the destruction of the earth to focus the attention of the developed world on the starving millions of the non-Western world. It has taken the rapid development of molecular biology, evolutionary theory and ecology in post-Newtonian science to prompt awareness of the interconnectedness of all things in the natural world, and the necessity of concern for all living things.

A concern for the liberation of the poor, the suffering and the oppressed was always implicit in the liberal agenda of equal concern for all. But when stress was placed on the cultural advancement of European leisure-elites, the vast majority of the earth's creatures were regarded as contributory means to what was truly a magnificent but very exclusive culture. A change of focus was needed, so that the liberation of the oppressed could be clearly seen as a priority for moral and religious action.

Sometimes religion was seen as a barrier to the liberation of the poor into a life of material freedom and full participation in society. Marxist-Leninism set out to destroy religion, seen as the justification for hierarchical social structures and the provision of deferred (after-life) satisfactions for the poor. But in fact the major religions had always seen justice as a primary concern of faith. What was required was the realisation that justice had to be instantiated in social structures, not in some heavenly realm, and that liberation was unreal if it did not involve real freedom from want, disease and socially caused suffering. What was required was not the death of liberalism, but an acceptance that liberalism was not for the few, that it was unreal without liberation from all that made individual self-realisation an empty ideal for the vast majority.

The move towards liberation began to be made with the social reformers of eighteenth- and nineteenth-century Europe. One of the first areas in which it became apparent was in the field of penal reform. The consideration of what a concern for human welfare requires led to a much less retributive attitude to human wrongdoing and to a much greater concern for all beings capable of suffering, human or not. The 1789 Declaration of the Rights of Man placed a moral boundary around individual human life, which even God could not invade without good reason. Each individual, it was said, had a right to freedom, to life, and to the fruits of his (or her) labour. Such rights, however, could be forfeited by immoral acts, and at that time it was usually assumed that retribution was a basic moral law, 'an eye for an eye'.

As people began to think of individual rights and of individual welfare, it began to seem no longer obvious that rights could simply be forfeited by wrongdoing. When Jeremy Bentham advocated the greatest happiness of the greatest number as the basis of morality, the moral basis of retribution was put in question. Those who cause great harm should no doubt receive some penalty. But is it really for their welfare that they should be punished for ever in Hell, or even that they should be made to give an eye for an eye?

Once people came to place the welfare of the individual first, it came to seem obvious that reformation was preferable to strict retribution, and that the doctrine that God is love is hard to square with purely retributive justice even without hope of reformation. The Christian tradition contains both harshly negative strands of endless punishment for sin and more positive strands of loving concern for individual welfare. Most Christians had just lived with the paradox. Challenged by the humanistic morality of the eighteenth century, and liberated from a literalism which forces one to accept unpalatable truths on authority, Christians began simply to drop the idea of eternal hellfire, and insist instead on the unlimited love of God for the ultimate well-being of every individual creature. The abolition of slavery was followed by the abolition of capital punishment in many Christian territories. Gender equality and concern for other sentient animals is still being sought in the twenty first century. But at least concerns for the flourishing of all beings and for liberation from want have now been placed on the moral agenda of most religious traditions.

Liberation morality, which is the fuller realisation of what was always implicit in liberalism, challenges every practice that does not have regard for the well-being of every creature. Because it thereby challenges many traditional practices, it is sometimes said that liberalism undermines all moral beliefs. On the contrary, liberalism has very strong moral beliefs in the dignity, freedom and equality of persons. It will oppose any belief that undermines these fundamental values, whether that belief is religious (denying freedom of worship), political (denying the right of dissent) or moral (denying equality before the law). It will oppose preference on grounds of race, sex or wealth. It will oppose any expression of freedom that impedes the freedom of others in avoidable ways. A liberal society is one in which freedom, equality and dignity are respected and protected. These are not, however, just secular values. There is a religious justification for such a society in the existence of a spiritual being of supreme freedom and worth, who wills that all finite persons should equally be images of that freedom and dignity.

Liberalism in religion means the rejection of arbitrary rules, accepted solely on authority, that restrict freedom and equality. But it also means a total commitment to principles which support and encourage the fulfilment of all finite persons and the fullest extension of their creative freedom so far as that is possible compatibly with a similar fulfilment of others – that is the Kantian principle of autonomy – personalist, not radical, autonomy. The specifically religious dimension is a total commitment to love of, empowerment by and participation in the Supreme Good, which is construed in terms of supreme creative freedom, affective knowledge and unrestricted love. It is that commitment that transforms autonomy into theonomy.

There is a clear difference in attitude between the extremes of traditionalism and liberalism. The former sees God as supreme sovereign and the divine will as channelled down through a layered social hierarchy, and as subordinating individual freedom to its uncompromising and unchangeable demands, in the face of which humans have no inherent rights. The latter sees God as loving creator, and the divine will as encouraging the social participation of all, as calling for the exercise of creative freedom, and as setting a moral barrier around each person, which no one, not even God, should transgress. In Europe the move from the former to the latter was prompted by the growth of scientific attitudes which saw this world as the arena in which fulfilment could and should be sought, of moral attitudes which discerned possibilities for radical social change, and of historical attitudes which bred scepticism about the superior wisdom and rationality of ancient practices and traditions.

Authority need not be wholly overthrown, though it sometimes was. Authority has many strands, such as the defining experiences of outstanding religious teachers (the prophets or sages), the imaginative genius of the poets and artists of a tradition, the insights of the morally sensitive and the visions of the philosophers of faith. None of these might be infallible, but there are defining moments in which decisive insights become established which seem irrevocable.

The German liberals, in their concern to stress moral action as the heart of religion, were perhaps too suspicious of 'mysticism' and rationalism. Spiritual experience is the basis of religious belief, and such belief needs to be integrated as far as possible with other well-established knowledge to provide a coherent and plausible worldview. The real change in views of religion that occurred in early modern Europe was not to dissociate religious from factual beliefs (though that was the programme of the radical Enlightenment), but to dissociate religious faith from an authoritarian set of beliefs and principles, and from the institutions and cultures that sustained and were sustained by that authority.

Religious faith could instead be rooted in experiences of transcendence, expressed and evoked by images and symbols, derived from an irrecoverable history by mythic narrative, tested against the moral criterion of human flourishing and the greatest possible flourishing of all beings, and against the rational criterion of consistency and consonance with a constantly developing human knowledge.

Find out more . . .

There are many editions of Kant's works in English. The most important ones for this chapter are:

Groundwork of the Metaphysic of Morals, trans. L.W. Beck (New York: Library of Liberal Arts, 1959). This is a difficult, but small book, and essential reading for Kant's moral philosophy.

Also *Religion Within the Bounds of Reason Alone*, trans. T.M. Greene and H.H. Hudson (New York: Harper, 1960) which contains many surprises for those who only know the 'Critiques of Reason'.

Keith Ward, *The Development of Kant's View of Ethics* (Oxford: Basil Blackwell, 1972), provides my interpretation of Kant on morality and religion.

Alasdair MacIntyre, *After Virtue* (London: Duckworth, 1981), is a book on modern moral philosophy that challenges many secular ideas.

There are a number of good modern books on liberal religion and its problems. One is:

J'annine Jobling and Ian Markham, *Theological Liberalism* (London: SPCK, 2000).

PART IV

CONVERGENT SPIRITUALITY

11

MANY PATHS, ONE GOAL?

The Continuing Impact of the
Enlightenment on World Religions

Nineteenth-century Christian liberals thought that Christianity (usually German Protestant Christianity) was the most adequate form of human religion, precisely because it alone, because of the peculiarities of European history, had faced up to the radical challenge to traditional authority posed by the evidentialism and critical rationality of science. It had formulated a version of Christianity that was consonant with science and with a proper moral autonomy. It was equipped and ready to become the one global faith of the future.

In this they were almost certainly wrong. Judaism, which most of them regarded as a virtually dead religion, still had remarkable vitality and has recovered a sense of its unique identity in the modern world. Judaism, however, shares in the general cultural history of Europe. It has faced the Enlightenment in much the same way as Christianity has, and it has emerged with canonical (Orthodox), critical (Reform and Liberal) and secularised streams of thought and practice showing few signs of decay. Like Christianity, it has fragmented into various forms. But it is virtually certain that it will endure as a self-consciously distinct religious tradition as long as this world endures. It has not been superseded, and will not be superseded by Christianity, and that is a fact liberal Christians have to accept.

ISLAM

Both Christianity and Judaism have been shaped by their existence within the European Enlightenment, where critical attitudes to religion have been most marked. Many forms of Jewish and Christian faith have a distinctly modern feel, even if unbelievers and more traditional believers alike think that they should not. But are other religious traditions, which have not encountered the European Enlightenment in the same way, susceptible to a similar change? I think the answer is certainly yes, and that they have already been strongly affected, but in rather different ways.

What the Christian liberals almost certainly did not know was that a thousand years before them a rather similar set of moves had taken place in Islam, a religion that many of them dismissed as primitive and legalistic, as traditionalist par excellence.

It is often said that Islam, unlike Christianity and Judaism, has not had to come to terms with the European Enlightenment, and with the criticism of religion that involved. That is true, but in its early years Islam did come into contact with Greek philosophical thought in a major way. As it took over the Byzantine Empire, it inherited the Greek philosophical tradition, especially as interpreted by neo-Platonists such as Plotinus, and important seats of learning were established where neo-Platonism took firm hold. Many works were translated into Arabic, and it was largely from that source that they were later translated into Latin in thirteenth-century Europe.

As the works of Aristotle were commented upon by Ibn Sina, known in the West by the Latinised name Avicenna (980–1037) and Ibn Rushd, known in the West as Averroes (1126–98), a strong philosophical tradition developed, which was intended by its authors to complement the Qur'anic revelation. Ibn Rushd, for example, argued that the universe exists without beginning or end, and by necessity. It emanates continually and without ceasing from God. Personal immortality was unlikely, since Aristotle's doctrine of the soul seemed to allow at most for the disembodied existence of one supreme Active Intellect, not of many individual minds. Further, the highest truths were accessible by reflection and intellectual intuition, open only to philosophers. The truths of revelation were imaginative myths or pictures, which expressed these profound truths in ways accessible to less speculative individuals. The Prophet was not telling lies, but he was expressing in metaphors and symbols what could be known by philosophers in its truer and higher form.

Greek rationalism was alive and well in the Islamic world many years before it started to have an impact on European Christianity. It produced some of the same tensions: was creation really compatible with the eternity of the universe? Is the law really a symbol of higher truths? Is bodily resurrection not part of revealed faith, even if the philosophers doubt its possibility? There were many eminent Muslim liberals in the tenth to thirteenth centuries CE, teaching that revelation is supremely rational, and therefore that its main function is to point to the inner rationality of all things, a rationality expressed in myths and images – which are appropriate but not literally true – for many of the faithful.

If liberal rationalism was present in Islam, so was liberal experientialism. Sufis such as Rumi (1207–73), al-Arabi (1165–1240) and al-Farabi (875–950) taught that the heart of Islam was experience of God. All religions, they said, are united around this central core, and revelation is primarily a way of expressing the way to achieve such unitive experience in accessible form. God is so intimately present in every part of the world that the world becomes virtually the self-expression of the Divine. All creation is patterned on the universal man, the *Logos* or archetype of all things in the eternal being, which each human self should embody in its own unique way. The goal of religious life is to achieve a state in which the sense of one's own individual self fades away in blissful consciousness of divine unity.

Islam did not need the Enlightenment to formulate an experientialist view of revelation. Early in its history its philosophers (the Mu'tazila) saw the prophets as humans whose minds were illuminated by the divine light, and who in consequence perceived the inner rationality of the world to a high degree – in the case of Muhammad, to the highest human degree.

Of course the Qur'an consists of propositions. But these are largely poetic, imaginative and symbolic, their cryptic and penetrating force challenging interpreters to come to creative decisions in new situations, and putting in question all conventional norms. The stories of the patriarchs need not be literal histories. Their religious meaning is more likely to lie in the allegorical lessons they have to teach about development in the spiritual life. If the *shari'a*, the Islamic law, is to be a living and creative tradition, and not a dead inflexible code, its strength will lie in the precedents it gives for new decisions, made in the light of total obedience to God. The goal of living by the law is that it should lead to the ultimate experience of *fana*, of the fading of the sense of self in the light of the presence of the One Ultimate Reality.

These elements of rationalism and mysticism are still present in Islam, though they are not its predominant forms in the modern world. There are always fateful choices to be made in the life of religion. One of them is between embracing creative, speculative and moral thinking, and rejecting it in favour of strict adherence to an allegedly original tradition in all its purity. For the most part Islam chose the latter course. The Ash'arites, the anti-philosophers, taught that it was blasphemy to see revelation as a lower form of philosophy, that Aristotle was a pagan who had nothing to teach Muslim revelation, and that Greek philosophy had to be decisively superseded by Islam. Al-Ghazali was one of the most influential writers, and he argued that the 'philosophical' positions were incoherent in themselves and inconsistent with revealed truth. Islam turned away from speculative philosophy, and the Christian theologians of the Enlightenment were hardly aware that it existed.

Al-Ghazali had, however, made Sufism respectable within Islam, and wrote that 'to be a Sufi means to abide continuously in God and to live at peace with men'. Philosophy might be suspect, but experience remained centrally important, and it is probably Sufi teaching of the possibility of direct mystical experience of God that accounts for much of the historical spread of Islam throughout the world. Interpretations of *shari'a*, too, may vary widely. There is no overwhelming reason why the traditions of the Prophet's life should remain binding in their circumstantial detail, and the injunctions of the Qur'an are capable of extremely divergent interpretations, including some that could be called 'liberal' – advocating human freedom, equality and responsibility, and largely confining the application of a distinctive Islamic law to the area of religious practice and family life.

The violent and ultra-conservative elements of Islam that catch the headlines in the modern world are products of the same historical, social and economic forces which have dethroned Christianity from being the controlling force of European life. Critical scientific secularism, in its embodiment in the relativistic, amoral, technologically dehumanising and even world-threatening West, is seen by some Muslims as a vindication of their rejection of rationalist philosophy, and as something to be opposed, possibly even with violence.

Muslim nations are still reacting against what they see as recent colonial exploitation by Europe, puzzled by the failure of Islam to continue its spectacular successes in the first Muslim century (in the seventh and eighth centuries CE) and torn between supporting various nationalist movements and seeking a pan-Muslim and anti-nationalist global community of Islam. So the Enlightenment comes to many Muslims as something alien and exploitative, threatening the distinctiveness of their culture and supportive of the economic domination of the world by the Western nations.

Nevertheless, there has in recent years been a Muslim diaspora, and Muslims are to be found in almost every country in the world, very often as minorities who must live alongside majorities of other faiths. This is a new situation for Islam, which has traditionally aimed at political domination in the countries where it is present, even while often being relatively tolerant of other faiths. Encounter with an economically dominant West, the growth of a Muslim diaspora and awareness that acceptance of global diversity is a condition for human survival in an increasingly interconnected world – all of which reveal Islam as just one distinctive set of traditions among others – is forcing Islam to reassess its traditional picture of itself as the final perfect revelation for all humanity.

In one way this should be easy. Islam has rarely been exclusive in the way that Christianity has been, since it holds that every age and people has its prophets sent from God, and that God judges all people by their conduct. It is nevertheless hard for Muslims truly to accept freedom of practice in religion and full equality for all morally acceptable faiths – just as it was hard for the Roman Catholic Church to do so before the second Vatican Council. For that, you would have to accept that your own revelation is not so clear and convincing that all people of good faith will accept it, that it is important that people should embrace faith freely, and that God can be revealed and apprehended in different ways, even if some of those ways are relatively limited. Such beliefs are already to be found within Islam, and they only await the right economic and social circumstances to be brought to the forefront and consciously espoused as important religious principles.

Questions of textual and historical criticism have generally not arisen in Islam as they have in Christianity. As and when they do, resources exist in the tradition for reinterpreting Prophetic inspiration as context-dependent and partly dependent on materials already present in the mind of the Prophet, to be reshaped by the inspiring power of God. Many Muslims will continue to feel that the text of the Qur'an is sacrosanct, not susceptible to critical historical analysis. But there remains ample room for interpretation of the complex meanings of the text, of the relation of different verses of the Qur'an to one another, and of the text's applicability in changing circumstances. In these senses, even if the term 'liberal' is rejected, largely because of its association with Western anti-religious movements, there is plenty of scope within orthodox Islam for critical religious thinking.

The real area of concern for Muslims, as for Jews, is not so much doctrinal orthodoxy as obedience to revealed divine law. In this respect, there will always be orthodox groups that regard the Qur'anic laws as non-revisable, and to be taken literally. But the main Islamic tradition is one of continuing legal interpretation, in which deeper principles are elicited from particular Qur'anic injunctions and the traditions of the Prophet (the *hadith*), and given new applications in new circumstances. Traditional Islam tends to regard past legal decisions as binding, giving rise to a rather conservative attitude to moral questions in a rapidly changing world. But it is clearly possible to take a more creative view of legal interpretation, which stresses much more the need for extending old attitudes in the light of new scientific knowledge of human nature.

Humans are, after all, regarded in Islam as vicegerents of God, as the stewards and custodians of the natural world, and as bound together in communities of justice and compassion. So the basic principles of ethical interpretation should be based on what, under the direction of God, makes for human well-being. This is not radical ethical autonomy, a matter of fulfilling whatever desires one may happen to have. It is a matter of fulfilling the purpose for which God has created humans. On a Muslim doctrine of creation, that purpose is to realise the capacities present in both general and individual human nature, and thereby bring God's creative intentions to fruition. To do this freely and creatively is to espouse the principle of personalist autonomy. There is plenty of room in Islam for interpreting the law in such a way as to increase respect for the dignity and God-created value of all persons.

Thus three main principles of the Enlightenment – the political principle of freedom of religion, the critical principle of free enquiry and the moral principle of the value and dignity of human persons – were already present in tenth-century Islam, even if limited in various ways. A truly global Islam is able to renounce any programme of dominating the world, accept that God's rule of justice and peace will always be seen in diverse ways by different people, and strive to exemplify the true *jihad* of persuading humans to submit freely to the commands of a God who wills that all should realise and enjoy the good things God has created.

That may be an ideal rather than an observable reality, but it is one which is not alien to Islam, and which is already seen by many as the inner kernel of the Prophet's teaching.

INDIAN TRADITIONS

Judaism, Christianity and Islam share a common heritage in the prophets of ancient Hebrew faith and in the philosophers of ancient Greece. It may be felt that Indian religions are quite different in character. However, though they do not have prophets, they have inspired religious teachers who claim to have a special relationship with *Brahman*, the one ultimate reality underlying the realm of appearances. They have scriptures, most notably the Vedas and Upanishads, which are said to be inspired by the gods, usually verbally. And they have a rich philosophical tradition of reflection on the ultimate nature of reality, which has many points of contact with the European tradition. So they are more like the Semitic religions than may at first appear.

There is general acceptance in India that there are many paths to knowledge of the One Ultimate Real. There is no centralised and universally accepted religious authority, but there are a number of teaching lineages, to one of which believers usually belong. Thousands of local deities are all embraced as aspects of one spiritual reality of which all individual things and the universe itself are parts. The three most widespread traditions are those that worship Shiva, god of destruction and renunciation; Vishnu, the preserver (especially as manifest in avatars, most notably Krishna); and the Goddess (often as Kali or Durga), who is both beneficent and threatening. The differences between them reflect different perceptions of *Brahman*, the one Real with which all things are ultimately identical.

Indian religious practice is conventionally divided into the way of knowledge (meditation leading to an experience of unity), the way of devotion to a god and the way of works (either ritual or moral practice). There is a broad agreement that the goal of religious practice is *moksa*, or release from the sufferings of life which are caused by possessiveness and grasping desire, and entrance into a state, conceived in various specific ways, but consisting most importantly of knowledge, bliss and freedom from rebirth.

All these traditions exist under the name of Hinduism, a religion which has not usually tried to spread throughout the world, but which has aimed to be the all-including religion of India. Its strategy has usually been to absorb the main elements of other traditions within its own complex structure, but nevertheless to insist on the priority of its scriptural texts and acceptance of its main customs and practices (most obviously the caste system and the Brahmanical priesthood) and an acceptance of the propriety of worshipping the deities of the Indian pantheon. This has caused problems with religious traditions, such as Christianity, Islam and Buddhism, which refuse to integrate with Hinduism. While clearly not capable of embracing all religious groups, Hinduism has retained its hold on the hearts and minds of the vast majority of Indian people. In the twentieth century, as an Indian diaspora has spread throughout the world, a number of Hindu movements have taken root in Europe and America, to the extent that it can now truly be called a world religion.

Throughout its history, Hinduism has undergone a number of important changes. An early one can be detected in the difference between the polytheistic, world-affirming hymns of the Vedas and the more non-dualist faith, recommending desire for release from the world, which is found in many Upanishads. The tension of aiming at a joyful individual existence in this or some future world, and aiming to lose all sense of individuality in the Real, has remained in Hinduism ever since, and different teaching lineages take different approaches to it.

Encounters with the ascetic tradition of early Buddhism occasioned further changes, and the ninth-century teacher Sankara is generally credited with having incorporated some major Buddhist teachings into Hinduism, which envisaged the deities as aspects of one Reality that was ultimately beyond human conceptualisation – *nirguna Brahman*,

Brahman without qualities. This suggests a doctrine of 'double truth', a level of pictures and images for those who cannot ascend to the final truth, and a level of highly sophisticated non-dualism for the learned. Such a doctrine is capable of playing the role within Hinduism that critical liberalism played in European Christian thought – that is, subordinating the myths and stories of the scriptures to a deeper truth underlying them.

The Muslim invasions into northern India from the eighth century, culminating in the establishment of the Mughal Empire in 1526, caused Hindus to respond with a reaffirmation of indigenous traditions. In that reaffirmation there was perhaps a stronger stress on the basically monotheistic nature of much Hinduism. The deities were often represented, like the saints of Christianity, as vehicles of particular aspects of spiritual power. Underlying them was the one ultimate reality, *Brahman*, which could easily be given a theistic colouring by stressing its manifestation as a personal Lord, whether Vishnu, Shiva or Kali. Justification for this could readily be found in the scriptures, which do clearly speak of all things as parts of a Supreme Self. This view is very similar to some Sufi teachings about all things being immediately dependent upon the will of God, and so a deep unity between Islam and Hinduism was revealed, most evident in the reign of Akbar (1556–1605). Unfortunately, political struggles proved stronger than the teachings of religious scholars, and later more repressive Muslim rulers provoked Indian resistance, giving rise to a hostility between aniconic Islam and image-worshipping Hinduism which later led to the division of the subcontinent into India, Pakistan and Bangladesh.

In the nineteenth and early twentieth centuries India was subject to European colonisation, especially by the British. Again, this was sometimes seen simply as a clash of cultures, a war between colonialists and the indigenous population. But there was also a fascinating interplay of thought between European philosophical idealism of the Hegelian school and classical Indian thought. Committed on scriptural grounds to the identity of *Brahman* and the cosmos, the absolute idealism of

Hegel, which saw the whole of history as a self-expression of Absolute Spirit, was very attractive to Indian scholars.

Hegel himself saw Indian religion as largely a mass of superstitions, and in any case idealism did not remain in favour in Europe for very long. So the connection between the two traditions was not generally perceived. But many Indians were educated in European schools and universities, and a Hegelian approach proved fruitful in the renaissance of Hinduism that took place towards the end of the British Raj in India. This is evident in the recovery of self-confidence in an indigenous idealist (or non-dualist) Indian philosophy, and it is also evident in a new emphasis on religious experience that became characteristic of Indian religious thought at this time.

Classical Indian religion accepts the literal authority of the *sruti*, the scriptures 'heard' by ancient seers and spoken by the gods. But after the nineteenth century a new form of Hinduism rose to prominence, which based its appeal upon the experience of liberation that was known and taught by the great gurus. Schleiermacher had tried to base Christian doctrines on the experience of 'absolute dependence', known in its fullest degree by Jesus. So many religious teachers in India (such as Sri Aurobindo and Radhakrishnan, President of India) saw Hinduism as primarily experiential, and as justified by the experience of liberation which could be achieved by the practice of non-attachment and by meditation.

There are, of course, doctrines and scriptures in Hinduism, and many Hindus would take them literally. But others, like Vivekananda, the apostle to the West of the Ramakrishna Mission, regard liberated experience as the essential element, and see doctrines and scriptures primarily as helpful means to such personal knowledge. As Hinduism spreads in the Western world, it often claims not to be a religion (an authoritarian institution with a set of mandatory rites), but to be a form of spiritual education (so for instance the Indian religious group the Brahma Kumaris run a 'World Spiritual University').

Hinduism can bypass questions of historical authenticity by insisting on the primacy of present spiritual experience, and by relegating matters of traditional custom and belief to the level of 'skilful means'. In India, Hinduism can still be used as a nationalistic and chauvinistic test of 'true Indianness', and a way of excluding 'foreign' elements (such as Muslims and Christians). But as it enters into the global community, Hinduism becomes largely a practical path to liberating personal experience, able to accept a multitude of deities and religious practices as subsidiary aids to enlightenment.

The irony is that, just as Christian missionaries in nineteenth-century India could see Hinduism as a set of superstitions and reactionary practices, so the Hindu diaspora is now able to represent traditional Christianity as a set of unduly exclusive beliefs, based on shaky historical evidence, and unable to see the value of the many paths to God that exist in the world. Christianity, as many Hindus see it, still seems to be trapped in unresolvable arguments about abstract doctrines, and has failed to concentrate on the meditational techniques that lead to a truly liberated life, and which are the real heart of religion.

It is easy for each religion to see the negative points in the other. But the fact is that both Christianity and Hinduism – and more broadly the Semitic and Indian religious traditions – have by very different paths drawn nearer to a common understanding. Both have traditions within which a plurality of interpretations is acceptable – or at least exist, if not accepted by all the others! Both have important strands for which the narratives or stories which are found in scripture can be accepted as at least partly legendary, and subsidiary to the goal of spiritual enlightenment. Both agree that there is one spiritual source of all things, perfect in wisdom, intelligence and bliss, present in all things, knowledge of which is the primary religious aim. Both accept that the spiritual path is a way of overcoming attachment to selfish desires and finding true human fulfilment. Both, at their best, affirm reverence for persons, and for all living beings. So in the global community that is inevitably emerging on this planet, there is a convergence – not on doctrines, but in spirituality, in ways of spiritual practice, meditation and prayer, which lead from ignorance to knowledge, from selfishness to love of the Supreme Self, from darkness to light.

The Indian religious traditions have not worked through an Enlightenment of the European sort. But they have entered into a new global role in which conformity to ethnic customs and ancient beliefs takes a secondary place to the encouraging of a personal search for spiritual experience and freedom from greed, hatred and ignorance. If the moralism of the Semitic traditions and the inwardness of the Indian traditions could meet, the possibility of a real spiritual convergence which could include all the spiritual inheritance of humanity would be closer to realisation. That is one of the most positive hopes for the future of the human species.

EAST ASIAN TRADITIONS

The Semitic tradition is theistic, and Indian traditions, despite the notable presence of dualism and idealism, are dominated by theistic elements, but it may be thought that the East Asian traditions – such as Mahayana Buddhism, Taoism, Confucianism and Shinto – are much harder to include in a convergent spirituality for the future. This is far from being the case, however. The East Asian traditions offer an ethically centred and broadly humanist spirituality that is a positive complement to theistic traditions, which may sometimes seem too little concerned with human welfare. East Asian traditions are very diverse, but they often have a central concern with harmony with the natural world and with wider social communities.

Many East Asian traditions function without being formalised into institutions with rigid public hierarchies and exclusive rules of membership. In Japan Shinto, for example, has since the Second World War been divorced from national rites of emperor worship, and exists as a set of temple ceremonies and personal rituals to honour the ancestors and the *kami*, the spiritual presences of springs, trees and mountains. It is a relatively unsystematised set of rites for maintaining contact with the spiritual realm, as manifested in personal and natural images, and it can be a means of trying to obtaining good fortune or a way of establishing a sense of harmony and unity with the human and cosmic community of being.

Concern with a positive and harmonious relationship with nature is also characteristic of Buddhism in East Asia, where it has taken on a number of special forms, which no longer try to remain true to the allegedly original historical sayings of the Buddha. They often rely on revelations that buddhas and bodhisattvas (beings who defer final enlightenment in order to help those still bound by the wheel of rebirth) in spiritual realms give to individuals of much later generations – as with the Lotus Sutra, perhaps the most popular East Asian scripture, which was revealed long after the historical Buddha's death.

It is characteristic of Mahayana Buddhist schools that there are countless compassionate bodhisattvas, or enlightened beings, who devote themselves to helping all beings to attain *nirvana*. Everyone will become a buddha eventually. All life is to be reverenced and treated with compassion. *Nirvana* is often said to be, not some other, non-sensory state, but this very world of change and time, seen as a glorious stream of appearances that are to be enjoyed without clinging. *Nirvana* and *samsara* are, it may be said, the same, and enlightenment is to experience this during this earthly existence. For *nirvana* is the 'blowing out' or extinguishing of attachment and grasping desire, and *samsara* is the endless chain of co-dependent appearances. To experience that chain without attachment is to extinguish passion and enter into the bliss of enlightenment, without moving from where one is.

There are many forms of East Asian Buddhism, which range from the 'just-sitting' meditation of Ch'an or Zen to the deeply devotional chanting of the Jodo Shin Shu school. Some schools teach that one must attain *nirvana* by resolute striving, and by one's own power, while others teach that the grace of compassionate bodhisattvas is enough to free one from sorrow for ever.

What is characteristic of such forms of Buddhism is that they do not have a theoretical belief in one creator God. They stress the need to practise moral obedience, meditation and compassionate insight. They teach freedom from greed, hatred and ignorance, and the possibility of attaining a state of mindfulness, selflessness, universal compassion, wisdom and benevolence. They do not see the cosmos as parts of one cosmic Self, as Hindus do, though they may worship many deities out of honour and respect. But neither are they just humanists, since the state of *nirvana* is not just the state of some human mind. It is a transcendent spiritual reality, though one which may be envisaged as wholly immanent in the cosmos, and certainly not a personal being or self-contained substance beyond the cosmos.

Most forms of Buddhism are very tolerant of diverse religious practices, and Shinto, Confucianism and Taoism can coexist easily with various forms of Buddhism. What is distinctive of Buddhism is monastic practice, and where the monastic rule is upheld, many forms of belief are permitted as skilful means for individuals at various stages of their spiritual path.

We might see a dominant tone of East Asian spirituality as being the search for a harmonious and enlightened life within the world, seen as having a spiritual basis beyond and of greater value than the purely sensory realm, but which is rarely reified as a transcendent personal being. That is the Chinese 'Way of Heaven', the Tao.

There is a sense in which such forms of spirituality have never had to face the questions of the critical historian or moralist. For it is part of the tradition to interpret histories and stories as of little ultimate account, to be accepted insofar as they are conducive to enlightenment. Similarly, there are no divine commands that are supposed to be obeyed even if they seem to contradict common sense. Morality is a matter of conduciveness to compassion and enlightenment, and moral conduct follows from right seeing and thinking, not from obedience to some revealed code.

Nevertheless, modernity has clashed with East Asian religious traditions in a spectacular way. European-generated notions of radical change and technological progress have impacted on Asia in two quite different but explosive ways. One is through the impact of communism – another heir of Hegel, by way of Marx and Mao – which calls for a complete restructuring of society and of all hierarchical traditions. From a communist point of view, most Asian religions seem backward and immobile. Communists would say that religions do not envisage the possibility of material improvement, tend to look to the past for inspiration, and encourage ritual practices that impede a true view of the material basis of human life. They would say that Confucians support very hierarchical and family-centred views; Taoists seem largely concerned with useless rituals rather than with changing the material basis of society; and Buddhists are obsessed with the idea of rebirth, and thus see no need to change present social structures. These charges may be very unfair, but sympathetic understanding is often an early casualty of culture clashes. There has certainly been a clash of cultures within Asia, as communist ideas of equality, class warfare and revolutionary change have fought, often with extreme violence, against traditional religions.

The other impact of the European Enlightenment has been very different. It is the impact of free-market capitalism, which again gives a primary importance to the material (economic) basis of society, but stresses individual freedom rather than equality, and economic competition rather than violent overthrow of the rich. It has proved difficult to hold onto ideas of world renunciation, harmony with nature or the maintenance of traditional social rites of superiority and subordination in face of the relentless drive of capitalism to make money, shape nature to productive ends and let economic competition bring the most enterprising to the fore, whatever their background.

The traditional Asian religions have adjusted to these challenges in various ways. Socially engaged Buddhism accepts the challenge to work for better economic conditions for all, and is able to see that as a new form of its ancient commitment to universal compassion. Traditional Chinese and Japanese rituals are repackaged as ways to achieve mental and physical health. Chinese medicine does have techniques, such as acupuncture, which may surprise Western medicine but which are efficacious. And perhaps there is much to be said for social conventions and for the harmony and balance that can challenge the emptiness of a concern with material success.

The globalisation of religion again becomes a new feature of religious life, as these reformulated traditions spread throughout the world, contributing, not sets of doctrines so much as practices for achieving mental and physical health, and finding a true balance with nature and the environment. If there is to be a truly convergent spirituality in the modern world, it must include traditions which are not primarily concerned with worship of a supreme being, but whose concern is with inner mindfulness and harmony with the natural forces of the cosmos – which are for them more than natural (material), but not projected onto a personalised supreme being. This too is part of the spiritual heritage of humanity, and it could be a necessary counteractive to an overemphasis on acceptance of one set of propositional doctrines or on an obedience ethic that fails to ask seriously about the welfare of all beings in this complex and interdependent world.

Find out more ...

In three accessible volumes, *The Heritage of Sufism*, ed. Leonard Lewisohn (Oxford: Oneworld, 1999) provides valuable insights into the mystical heart of Islam.

Sarvapalli Radhakrishnan, *The Hindu View of Life* (London: Allen & Unwin, 1927), and *An Idealist View of Life* (London: Allen & Unwin, 1932), present an attractive revision of traditional Indian religious thought.

Paul Williams, *Mahayana Buddhism* (London: Routledge, 1989), is an authoritative account of East Asian Buddhist thought.

Geshe Kelsang Gyatso, *Joyful Path of Good Fortune* (London: Tharpa Publications, 1990), is quite different, a Tibetan monk's practical guide to meditation, based on the Mahayana scriptures, *The Stages of the Path*.

12

INDRA'S NET

The Spectrum of Spiritual Truth

I have sketched the global history of religions in four main phases. Representatives of all these phases continue to exist, and will probably do so for the foreseeable future. I characterised the first phase as the 'local'. That is a phase in which local myths and rituals develop and are passed on through largely oral tradition. Religious experts cultivate relationships with supernatural powers, both for good and evil, and the spiritual realm is conceived as diverse and complex. There is little relation with science and little attempt to achieve an integrated worldview. There is little concern with the religions of other human groups, and such a tradition is often used as the support of a local and distinctive way of life, which is to be preserved against any attempts to merge it into a wider cultural milieu. Indigenous religions have revived in many parts of the world, partly as a reaction against the forces of globalisation, which threaten to eradicate or marginalise local cultures. They often survive within the great world religions as local cults or permitted forms of religious practice. So in Hinduism and Catholicism we can find devotions to local saints or gods, and the use of astrological and magical practices. The appeal to many local spirit powers or to ancestors to avoid evil and obtain good is characteristic of this form of religion, and it expresses a deep tendency in the human psyche to seek alliance with a multi-faceted supernatural realm.

The second phase of global religious life I have called the 'canonical'. In it there takes place at least to some extent the rationalisation and moralisation of ancient traditions. In the early human river-valley civilisations the spirit powers were systematised and their adherents began to claim universal truth for them. Moral codes were set out, ratified by the authority of the gods, but making some claim to express objective and universal values. In its most developed forms this gave rise to a view of religious faith as the overcoming of egoism by devotion to one supreme spiritual reality, whether that was thought of as personal or impersonal, transcendent or immanent. The Hebrew prophets preached obedience to one supreme sovereign will of justice and mercy. Indian gurus taught renunciation of the individual self and union with the supreme cosmic Self. Enlightened sages spoke of liberation from desire by entrance into a realm of pure intelligence and bliss, sometimes seen as beyond and distinct from the sensory world, and sometimes seen as the hidden inner essence of the world. Greek philosophers spoke of the quest for a vision of the Good beyond the transient forms of appearance.

These paths were diverse, but they all posit one reality of supreme value, having the attributes of compassion, wisdom and bliss, in conscious relation to which human lives can find their proper fulfilment. Being products of imperial elites, they tended to be closely associated with imperial and elite cultures, and their claims to universal truth sometimes allowed the growth of intolerance and repression of competing views. The religious views tended to be expressed in sacred texts, which were given absolute and final authority, and the 'orthodox' were often sharply distinguished from the 'heretics', who were discriminated against in various ways.

In the modern world such forms of traditional orthodoxy are very strong. Christianity and Islam especially find themselves competing for universal acceptance by all people as a revealed, final and absolute truth. Hinduism and Buddhism are less evangelistic, but they too tend to lay down standards of orthodoxy for whole cultures, to which all members of those cultures should submit. The paradox of this phase of religious life is that it clearly teaches the submission of self to a reality of supreme moral value, and yet it tends to oppose and caricature views that differ from its own.

For some orthodox believers, scriptural texts will be interpreted as literally as possible, and moral rules will conform as closely as possible to those laid down in scripture. This will often lead to clashes with critical historical reflection, with much scientific knowledge and with any appeal to moral autonomy. There is no necessity for such clashes to lead to violence or intolerance, however, since even the most literalist views usually call for compassion and understanding as central elements of their way of life. Such literalism can be found in every religious tradition, and it is naturally allied with conservative social and political attitudes, insofar as conservatism also wishes to preserve past traditions with as little change as possible.

There will also, however, be non-literalist forms of orthodoxy. For them, too, it will be important to affirm the final and unrevisable authority of the scriptural texts. But they will have a feeling for the metaphorical or allegorical and esoteric meanings of the texts, and will therefore stress the necessity of interpretation and of the authority of tradition, in discerning what the texts mean in differing circumstances. The meaning of particular texts will be seen to depend upon an interpretation of the total text, which may be illuminated by new cultural developments, enabling one to see it in new ways. In the case of moral rules, attempts will be made to discern the underlying principles beneath particular moral rulings in very different contexts. In other words, there will be a place for developing knowledge and interpretation, though the text will retain a decisive normative status as a basis for interpretations. This stress on metaphor, interpretation, context and developing perspective has always been implicit within the major religious traditions. Traditional Islam, for example, takes such a view, and though it takes the Qur'an to be the literal word of God, it is by no means always interpreted literalistically. Perhaps, after all, God is not as literal-minded as humans sometimes are.

The third phase of global religion is the 'critical'. It moves beyond the understanding of orthodoxy as an unchangeable norm, set at some specific time in the past, for all future belief and practice. Orthodoxy attempted to develop a rational and systematic worldview and a consistent and codified set of moral principles, but they were based on a given and unquestionable revelation. In the European Enlightenment, reason was unleashed from revelation, and began to insist on the right and duty of critical examination of all truth-claims, from whatever source.

Critical faith presses the question of the historical authenticity of ancient traditions. It presses the question of the epistemological basis of traditional religious claims to truth. And it presses the question of whether traditional religious moral codes do in fact make for human flourishing and fulfilment – and indeed for the well-being of all life, as they usually claim.

Such criticism may lead people beyond the bounds of religious faith altogether, if ancient traditions turn out to be founded on legend, if we can find no reliable grounds of claiming truth in religion, and if religious morality turns out to repress many human lives, and condone violence and intolerance.

Perhaps for this reason, orthodox believers have often condemned what they call 'liberal' forms of religion as giving in to the forces of secularism, and as giving up the fundamental tenets of revealed faith. But critical views have entered religion to a great extent, especially in the developed world, in Europe and America, and they are likely to remain strong in all cultures that take scientific knowledge and critical enquiry seriously. Precisely because they are influenced by the European Enlightenment they are sometimes seen as new forms of cultural imperialism, and as attempts to impose democratic capitalist views on other cultures. But in fact, insofar as faiths are truly critical, they will also criticise and examine any such connections with capitalist elitism, and attempt more expansive views of the sort of faith that is appropriate for the modern world.

For critical faith, the methods of historical scholarship and moral insights that have developed largely because of the humanist influences of the Enlightenment will be fully applied to religious texts and traditions. The key doctrines of the tradition may be kept, and tradition and revelation may be highly valued, but there will also be a stress on freedom of scholarship and of personal interpretation, which will permit a much greater degree of pluralism within religious traditions. Friedrich Schleiermacher is the Christian theologian who best represents such a view. He certainly held that he belonged to the orthodox Protestant faith, even though that faith was quite properly subject to change over the centuries. There is no problem with being a critical Jew, since you can profess allegiance to the biblical tradition, to its teachings of justice and mercy, of worship of one God and of hope for a community of peace without accepting that God literally handed Moses tablets of stone. Other traditions, too, can be critical, and indeed most canonical traditions in the modern world have been able to absorb a great deal of critical thought. However, all traditions could still display a much greater humility about many of their own traditional alleged certainties, and a much greater respect for the traditions of others than has been historically apparent.

A more radical religious option is to reject orthodoxy in principle. A view can only be termed 'orthodox' if it is declared to be so by some authoritative body, which has the power to declare what is true or acceptable. It is possible to reject any institution or text that claims such a power, and to affirm that no one can infallibly decree what is true in advance of investigation and new experience. To reject orthodoxy is to reject the right of any institution or person or text to declare what correct belief is, irrevisably and without error. It is not to reject all authority, when that authority is accepted as developing, subject to particular errors, and always to some extent provisional in its pronouncements. This could be termed strong religious liberalism – the view that each person is free to decide the truth for him- or herself, and of course to form or join in free association with whoever agrees. A strong religious liberal may come to quite conservative views, and be happy to be a full member of a mainstream religious tradition (if permitted to be so). But the strong liberal's acceptance of tradition and authority will always be critical and revisionist to varying extents, though such an attitude may be held to be compatible with allegiance to the basic insights of a given tradition (that is the position of some of those who are often called 'liberals' in Christianity and Judaism).

Sometimes such a person's interpretation of faith will give priority to moral or speculative considerations, with particular traditions seen as ways of expressing such considerations. So within Christianity there are strands that stress the importance of moral obligation or of liberation from injustice, and strands that stress the desirability of constructing a coherent and plausible worldview. But none of these strands need deny the fundamental revelation of the nature of God given in the person of Jesus, the ultimate norm of Christian faith. Rather, what is stressed is the diverse and personal nature of our interpretation of the revelation given in and through Jesus, and the need for any interpretation, including our own, to face up to the strongest critical analysis and the possibility of revision in the light of new knowledge.

It is easy to see how, within Islam, Hinduism and Buddhism, such forms of strong liberalism exist, as diverse groups interpret their traditions in new ways, sometimes splitting off to form new subgroups. One of the ironies of religion is that on occasion strong liberals strongly deny that they are liberals at all. Often they claim to be going back to some more ancient or authentic form of faith. Their liberalism is seen, however, in the freedom they claim to form their own interpretative tradition, and reject the authority of a wider institution. So we get the paradox that strong liberals can see themselves, and even seem to others to be, extreme conservatives. What that shows is that we have forgotten the meaning of the term conservative – 'conserving of tradition' – and we give it another meaning, namely, 'what I take it upon myself to think this text or teaching really means'. So it sometimes happens that small very conservative religious sects are in fact much more strongly liberal than 'liberals' (critical thinkers) who live within a religious tradition, and are concerned both to preserve it and to interpret it in the light of new knowledge and moral insights. All that shows is that delusion is as common in religion as it is elsewhere in human life.

The fourth phase of religious life, which arises from an extension of the critical phase, may be termed the 'global' phase. In this phase, all religions are consciously seen as parts of one global phenomenon of human religiosity. The intellectual elitism of the liberal tradition, which advocates the superiority of one tradition over all others precisely because it has become critical and experiential, is replaced by the acknowledgement that all human cultures have something to add to the spectrum of spiritual truths, and what they say must be heard.

A person who takes such a view can say that the many traditions naturally arise from diverse histories, cultures and personalities. There may be many diverse metaphors for the supreme spiritual reality, and many provisional or partial descriptions that may express part but not all of the truth about such matters. Perhaps the truth lies as yet undiscovered, and all existing traditions are differing, and equally incomplete, attempts to move towards it. John Hick has proposed what he calls 'the pluralistic hypothesis', that 'the great post-axial faiths constitute different ways of experiencing, conceiving and living in relation to an ultimate divine Reality, which transcends all our varied visions of it'.[105] If we see many traditions as partial descriptions of such a complex spiritual reality, that is a form of pluralism.

John Hick's own preferred version of pluralism is that many traditions provide more or less equally authentic ways of approaching a spiritual Real, which remains beyond all of them and is ultimately unknowable. What I am suggesting is not quite identical to that, though it is certainly indebted to Hick's pioneering work in this field. One problem with Hick's view is that the pluralistic hypothesis would not be accepted even by all 'the great post-axial faiths'. Some forms of Buddhism would deny that there is one ultimate divine Reality. There is only, they might say, the perpetual flow. Other faiths would deny that 'the Real' transcends their vision of it. Some Christians, for example, would say that God really is essentially a Trinity of Father, Son and

Spirit. There might be more to God than we know, but what we know captures the essential nature of God, and does so accurately.

The pluralistic hypothesis is thus not an agreed belief among the great religious traditions. It must be an interpretation of those traditions from a specific viewpoint that they do not all share. The pluralist has to say that there really is a divine Reality, and Buddhists do experience it, though they misinterpret it. If the divine Real is beyond all our descriptions, Christians who say that God is essentially a Trinity are mistaken – they mistake an image for the reality. In other words, the pluralist is making definite claims to truth. It follows immediately that not all religious beliefs can be equally true. According to Hick, both religions that say there is no divine Reality and religions that say they know exactly what it is are less adequately true than pluralistic religions, which admit a divine Real, but deny there is accurate knowledge of it as it is in itself.

What we might call 'hard pluralism', John Hick's own view that the great religions present more or less equally true knowledge of the Real, is self-refuting. That is because it affirms that its own view of the Real is more correct than any views that oppose it (and many religious views do oppose it). Therefore some religious views are more correct than others. QED.

Pluralism as such, however, as Hick officially states it, is not self-refuting. It only says that many religions offer genuine ways of relating to the same spiritual reality. It does not say that they all recognise this reality in its true nature, or that they are all more or less equally true, or that the Real-in-itself is completely unknowable.

I am suggesting that the ultimate spiritual Reality is not wholly unknowable, but is genuinely known in various partial ways in diverse religious traditions. Some religious beliefs may be mistaken, and some may be more adequate than others. For instance, views that acknowledge their partiality and limits will in fact be more adequate than views that claim that they have a complete grasp of the truth.

It is possible that one existent tradition has expressed the central basic truths of religion in a way that is wholly adequate, or at least more adequate than any known alternatives. The view that only one tradition expresses such a basic truth is sometimes called 'exclusivism'. It says that only one tradition has the truth about spiritual reality, and it probably adds that only if you accept that truth will you be saved, or liberated. Only if you believe Jesus is your saviour, or only if you believe the Qur'an is God's word, or only if you believe that the sense of self is an illusion, will you be saved or liberated.

In the long run this is probably quite right. There can be only one truth about spiritual reality, and if salvation is right relationship to that reality, you cannot be saved unless you know what reality truly is – unless you know the truth about it. But can we be sure that only one religion has that truth? Or that any religion has it?

It may seem rather odd to say that no religion has the truth about spiritual reality. But it might not be a question of all or nothing. We could say that no religion has the whole truth – perhaps the whole truth is beyond our mental capacities, or has not yet been formulated. In physics we might say that we do not have the whole truth about the universe. But we still have lots of truths, partial though they may be. So it might be in religion. There might be lots of partial truths, spread about between many religions, but nobody has the whole truth. This would be a form of 'pluralism'. Many religions would contain partial truths about ultimate Spirit, but none would have the whole truth. Each of these religions would offer a path to salvation, but the final goal of salvation would be beyond anything we can imagine. It will not be quite like anything we envisage in any present religion, though many religions may offer paths that will eventually lead to it (after death, presumably).

The idea that religious truths are partial truths is very appealing, precisely because it seems rather arrogant to say that we have the whole truth about an ultimate spiritual reality, when so many sincere, intelligent people disagree so much about it. On the other hand, it would be very odd to say, 'This is what I believe about Spiritual reality, but of course it is not true.' We have to think that our own beliefs are at least nearer the truth than the beliefs of people who disagree with us. So it would seem very odd to say, 'I believe there is a loving personal God. Some Buddhists believe that is an infantile delusion. And of course their belief is just as good as mine.' Sometimes we just have to commit ourselves. Either God is a delusion or not. We cannot have it both ways – even partially.

So there is a place for an intermediate view, one that is sometimes called 'inclusivism' – one tradition has a more adequate grasp of the central truths about spiritual reality than others. But other traditions do contain important spiritual truths – and enough spiritual truths to set people on the path towards ultimate salvation. Everyone will be saved (if they are) by accepting the truths found in this one tradition, eventually. But meanwhile, through no fault of their own, they follow ways in which there are less adequate formulations of truth, and therefore relatively incomplete paths to salvation. So, for example, a Buddhist could say that Muslims should obey the law of God. But, for Buddhists, there actually is no God, so surely Muslims must be mistaken. But, by following the law of God, Muslims will nevertheless learn to be compassionate and mindful, even if (according to a Buddhist view) in limited ways, and so will prepare themselves for achieving a higher (Buddhist) path in a future life. Buddhism may be true, but it would not be right, given their beliefs and cultures, for all Muslims to become Buddhists – not in this life, anyway.

Inclusivism is thus one form of pluralism, which accepts that there can be many ways of relating to one spiritual reality, some of them more adequate in one respect and others more adequate in other respects. But one of those ways might contain a most adequate conception of what ultimate spiritual reality and ultimate salvation will be like. That will in no way devalue the experiences and beliefs of those in other religions, but it will maintain the full seriousness of claims to truth in religion.

Wherever truth is claimed, disagreement is logically possible. So disagreements are ineliminable from religion. A characteristic of imperial religion is that it seeks to eliminate disagreement by any means necessary. But that attempt was always doomed to failure. Nothing becomes true because somebody, however exalted, says it is. And what careful observation of a wide range of evidence shows is that there are disagreements even about the most basic claims of religions. So there will always be canonical

believers (those who take one revealed tradition to be inerrant and final)
as well as liberal believers (those who are prepared to revise the tradition
in the light of new insights and experiences). But we can trace in post-
sixteenth-century Europe an almost inevitable move away from unrevisable propositional views towards an experiential view of revelation,
engendered by tendencies rooted in Christian faith itself.

The experiential view of revelation is perhaps better able than a propositional view to account for the diversity of alleged revelations in religion.
They will not just be contradictory dictations from God, and they will not
all be false except one, which is held to be inerrantly dictated. Rather, the
Spiritual will disclose itself to people of very different cultures and temperaments. Their responses will vary, as will the rational worldviews in
terms of which they interpret the revelatory disclosures. The cumulative
traditions that build upon the primal disclosures will develop in distinctive
ways – though we might hope that in the end all traditions will converge
upon the truth. And personal experiences, being shaped by the tradition in
which they occur, will tend to confirm at least basic aspects of that tradition.

Where truth-claims conflict, it is clear that not all can be true. An
experiential view does not imply that all responses and interpretations
are of equal worth or adequacy. What the experiential view does help to
explain is how people come to have such different views and experiences.
The reason is that spiritual reality appears in many different contexts and
is interpreted in terms of many existent prior beliefs.

This explains why we should tolerate and respect views other
than our own. For many diverse views seem equally justifiable to their
adherents, in terms of the experiences and interpretations which form
their basis. We should not condemn others for conscientiously holding
the view they believe to be best justified. And we should not be too certain that we have formulated the truth as adequately as possible. It could
well be that diverse views flourish precisely because the way we formulate ours is so inadequate, and because it omits aspects of spiritual practice and experience which other traditions may emphasise. In this way
different traditions may have much to learn from each other.

Holding a generally pluralistic view of religions, we may stand outside mainstream traditions altogether, feeling free to select helpful insights from many traditions, which are all taken to be a blend of insights and errors, and think that religious truth is most likely to be found in a dialectical interaction of many traditions, in which truth is always provisional, and not confined to one leading tradition. Sometimes this is characterised as a move from religion to spirituality, from allegiance to one exclusive and institutionalised set of dogmas to a fluid and constantly changing pattern of practices conducive to positive relationship to spiritual reality, enriched by elements from many different faith traditions. Of course, this in effect forms a new tradition, superseding all previous ones, though it also uses past traditions as vehicles of partial and valued insights. But the difference is that this tradition has no unchanging text or normative authority. It is provisional, not final, and it does not claim theoretical certainty.

We may also, however, take a global view that wishes to stay with one particular tradition, though that tradition will seek to reflect all others from its own distinctive viewpoint. Global faith will then not be seen as a new world religion, superseding all others. It will rather be an attitude which can be taken by an adherent of any tradition, but which seeks to deepen its understanding of faith by attention to other traditions, and by reformulating its own principles in the light of the criticisms other traditions may make. Diversity will be celebrated, though we will also seek for commonalities among religions at a deep level, as the plurality of partial human understandings is held together with a shared concern to seek a truth that must in the end be the same for all.

Given the fact that disagreement and difference seem to be integral parts of human nature, and that diverse religious traditions will continue to exist for the foreseeable future, this is the view that I think suggests the most hopeful way forward for the future of religious belief. It comes into inevitable conflict with views which affirm the unique and absolute self-sufficiency of one religious tradition over all others, and which seek to eliminate diversity and change. But we can stand in an orthodox tradition, and see part of that orthodoxy as requiring us to respect and reflect in our own way the whole religious inheritance of the human race. We will not advocate the globalisation (the flattening out) of religion, but we will be committed to forming a truly global perspective from the viewpoint of our own tradition, in our own cultural setting.

In a sense, the global view is a return to the local view of myths and rituals as varied ways of sustaining empowering contact with the spiritual realm. But it has passed through the rationalisation and moralisation that claims to discern the unity and moral challenge of one supreme objective value beneath the diverse appearances of religion. It has passed through the critical processes of historical and moral examination that discriminate myths and traditions from claims to universal spiritual truth. So it has come to see the many religions of the world as ways of learning to transcend self by participation in a Supreme Objective Good, and to find the heart of faith in tradition-specific disclosures of transcendent value which empower for good the lives of those who are thereby enabled to participate in it. A convergent spirituality becomes possible in the modern world, which is not an agreement on doctrines or practices, but is an acceptance that many diverse paths of prayer and meditation converge upon one supreme reality of wisdom, compassion and bliss. That, it may be felt, is the heart of true religion.

There is a Buddhist parable, from the Hua-yen school of Buddhism, found in the Avatamsaka sutra, which speaks of the net of Indra. The great god Indra possesses a net in which there are many brilliant jewels. The net is infinite in extent, and there are an infinite number of such jewels. Each of them reflects in itself every other jewel in the net, and in this infinite reflection and co-reflection the whole cosmos scintillates with ever-changing beauty. In its context that is a parable for the interconnectedness of all things. It has also been used for the growing interconnectedness of information on the global electronic World Wide Web. But it is an apt metaphor for the global stage of religion. No religious tradition, as it is actually received and understood, includes all possible truth about God and human destiny. Each has its own unique contribution to make, but that contribution is only elicited as the reflections of other traditions are integrated in its own distinctive and unrepeatable pattern. From its depths new understandings can arise, which can only be evoked by encounter with other viewpoints – fortunately not quite an infinite number! – and by a recovery of its own history, which is largely a history of such encounters, acknowledged or concealed, in all their complexity and ambiguity.

At their best most religions offer a distinctive emphasis which can be reflected by others, and thereby given a different tone and colouring in its many new contexts. The compassion for all beings which Buddhism and Jainism affirm so strongly, the reverence for humanity that characterises Christianity, the love of life of Judaism, the total dependence on the divine will of Islam, the inner harmony and mindfulness of East Asian spirituality and the profound sense of the unity of all things in the cosmic self which is found to such a degree in Hinduism – all these, and many more, are facets of spiritual reality which are discerned in the diverse faiths of the world.

We should each be the poorer for lacking knowledge of these discernments. It is natural that each tradition should think of its own discernment as fundamental and normative for a final understanding of the divine. Since different religious narratives really do have differing ideas of supernatural states or beings, they cannot all be correct. They cannot even all be more or less equally correct. Some must be wrong, even if none are absolutely right. As a matter of fact, it might be more accurate to say that religious positions spread out to fill every possible space in the array of modes of relationship between the Transcendent and the physical cosmos than to claim that they all agree.

Nevertheless, there is a general descriptive core, which fits many ideas of the Transcendent. In many traditions there is said to be a supreme reality, which embodies perfection, and that perfection includes such characteristics as wisdom, freedom, compassion and bliss. Virtually all theistic faiths, as well as the renouncing traditions of Buddhism and Jainism, would affirm that there is such a reality, whether it is God or the state of finally liberated souls. The goal of the religious life is accessing that reality, and in general the goal is to be achieved by overcoming egoism, hatred, greed and ignorance.

It seems reasonable to assent to John Hick's 'pluralistic hypothesis', in its weaker form. We can then say that in many religions people are justified in believing what they do on the basis of their experience and of the plausibility of the tradition as they see it. Presumably some set of propositions expressing religious truths is the most adequate, but we may not know what it is, or even have articulated it yet.

It is impossible, however, to remain at the very general level of the 'common core', as I have formulated it. Some more specific description of the relation of the Transcendent to the physical cosmos and to human life must be attempted, if the religious life is to have substantive content. Yet religious traditions live mainly by images and metaphors, which spring from the originative experiences and teachings of major religious figures. So, as Hick argues, the question of theoretical truth may be less important in practice than the personal efficacy of the images in leading one from egoism towards union with the Reality of compassion and bliss. We may consistently be committed to one tradition of images as efficacious and illuminating, while allowing that other traditions may be so for other people, and that it is not known for certain which set of truths – if any of those known to us – is most adequate. A certain degree of humility and respect for the best in other traditions seems to be in order. The demand is not the impossible one that everyone should know all about every religious tradition. It is rather that no one should regard their own tradition as containing a complete and wholly adequate understanding of the divine, that we should be able to place our own tradition as part of a universal history of religions, and that we should tolerate, respect and, where appropriate, learn from others where they are conscientiously seeking morally acceptable ways of relating to tran-scendent Reality. To do that is to have a global understanding of religion.

It is not wise to be too sanguine about the future of humanity. Human societies may disintegrate into mutually uncomprehending and hostile cultures, religions may degenerate into exclusive and literalistic competitive ideologies, and the world may end in violent catastrophe. But if humanity has a future, the growth of scientific knowledge and communication, the economic pressures for global coexistence, an increased sensitivity to the injustice of radical and avoidable economic inequality in the world, and the increasing intermingling of individuals from diverse ethnic and cultural groups will co-operate to favour forms of religious faith which are critical, experiential, personalist and global.

Local, canonical, liberal and global forms of faith will coexist, and it is not realistic to expect them to merge into one super-faith, as though everyone would one day miraculously agree. That, as Orthodox Jews might say, will only happen when the Messiah comes and perhaps not everyone might agree about exactly what has happened even then! But all these forms of faith, however orthodox and traditional they may be, will be changed by their new situation in the increasingly self-aware global community of communities, which will be our future world, if there is to be a future at all.

They will be critical, in the sense that the methods of historiography and the well-established findings of the sciences will be accepted as legitimate aids in finding more adequate interpretations of faith. The consequence will be, not the forcing of a liberal interpretation on all, but the perception that a diversity of conscientious and scholarly interpretations of each tradition is possible, and an acceptance that we have to argue our own interpretation, not as obvious to all and certain, but as one interpretation among others. Insofar as it becomes better informed about its own history and the sources of its beliefs, each tradition will accept a diversity of interpretations, an internal plurality of belief. A greater tolerance, humility and patience will be appropriate to a clearer perception of the mystery and diversity of human faith.

Religious traditions will be experiential, seeing the heart of faith in distinctive experiences of Transcendence, rather than in political or metaphysical beliefs. The orthodox will continue to maintain that their scriptures or teachings are divinely revealed, but that revelation will exist to safeguard and evoke the central apprehensions of spiritual reality that transform human lives for good. It is in the depth of that apprehension and the quality of that transformation that religion is to be commended.

Religious traditions will be personalist, committed to realising the flourishing of human persons and, insofar as it is possible, of all created or finite beings. That concern is well rooted in virtually all the major traditions anyway, though it has sometimes been overlaid by tendencies to violence and repression, which have been justified by claims to hegemony or exclusive religious dominance. Such claims have been rendered obsolete by the socio-economic interconnectedness of the modern world. Ironically, the ending of claims to sole religious leadership leads to a recovery of the only real leadership religions can claim, which is that of discovering ways of protecting the equal human flourishing of all, as a religious requirement.

Finally, religious traditions, however orthodox they are, will be pluralist, in the restricted sense that they accept their place as one among many paths of relating to the spiritual Reality, even if they claim the truest recognition of and most authentic relationship to it. Freedom of conscience and of the practice of religion will be guaranteed in a world in which friendship and unity of spiritual commitment is valued, even or especially among those who differ in the ways of realising that commitment.

There will, regrettably, always be forms of religion that cannot fully accept these ideals. But orthodox canonical forms of faith as well as liberal or critical forms can and will do so. If the world survives, the drive to implement these ideals seems to be inbuilt into the processes of world development. To pursue these ideals fully now is the best way in which religions can help to ensure that the world does survive.

*　　*　　*

I have looked for a global religious perspective on the phenomena of the religious history of humanity. I have intended to follow in the footsteps of Max Müller, perhaps the foundation scholar of comparative religion, and of many who followed him, among the best known being Wilfred Cantwell Smith, Huston Smith, Ninian Smart and John Hick. These are all scholars who take seriously the religious claim to apprehension of a transcendent spiritual Reality, and who are concerned to arrive at an assessment of the place of religion in human life and thought which does not regard it as mere ignorance and folly.

There may always remain a fundamental divide in human thought between those who see nature as a self-contained impersonal system and those who see nature as a possibly obscured appearance of an underlying spiritual reality of overriding value. Religions seek to evoke an intuition of such a spiritual reality, and to participate in and mediate its power in human life. To understand religions is to understand the attraction and intelligibility of such a search, as well as its ambiguities, failures and dangers. It is not for the study of religions to say whether the search has ever succeeded, or whether it ever could. But we can be sure that it will never be renounced, and that the religious goal of fulfilment in relation to a Transcendent Reality of supreme power and value will remain an object of both fascination and, for some, of loathing for as long as human life endures.

Find out more . . .

An excellent introduction to the field, and the classic formulation of the pluralistic hypothesis, is John Hick, *An Interpretation of Religion* (Basingstoke: Macmillan, 1989). In one sense, this chapter is a series of footnotes to Hick!

Alan Race, *Christians and Religious Pluralism* (London: SCM Press, 1983), formulates the 'exclusivist', 'inclusivist', 'pluralist' trichotomy.

Paul Knitter, *No Other Name?* (London: SCM Press, 1985), is a very readable survey of Christian attitudes towards the world religions.

Wilfred Cantwell Smith, *Towards a World Theology* (London: Macmillan, 1981), is a sketch of global religion from a Christian perspective.

Frithjof Schuon, *The Transcendent Unity of Religions* (New York: Harper & Row, 1975), presents a view of an esoteric, hidden, unity of world religions.

Martin Forward (ed.), *Ultimate Visions* (Oxford: Oneworld, 1995), is a collection of fascinating and informative essays by leading scholars from many religions, expressing a global perspective on religion.

D. Krieger, *The New Universalism* (New York: Orbis, 1991), is a difficult but worthwhile study of a global vision of religion.

NOTES

1. W.C. Smith, *The Meaning and End of Religion* (New York: Macmillan, 1962), p. 120.
2. Edward Herbert, *De Religione Gentilium* [1663], trans. John Anthony Butler as *Pagan Religion* (Toronto: Dovehouse, 1996), p. 5. A good account is to be found in Peter Byrne, *Natural Religion and the Nature of Religion* (London: Routledge, 1989).
3. See Edward Said, *Orientalism* (Harmondsworth: Penguin, 1985).
4. See Ninian Smart, *The World's Religions*, 2nd edn (Cambridge: Cambridge University Press, 1988), introduction.
5. E.B. Tylor, *Primitive Culture* (London: Murray, 1873), p. 424.
6. Ibid., p. 447.
7. Emile Durkheim, *The Elementary Forms of Religious Life*, trans. J. Swain (London: Allen & Unwin, 1963), p. 422.
8. Ibid., p. 419.
9. M.E. Spiro, 'Religion: Problems of Definition and Explanation', in *Anthropological Approaches to the Study of Religion*, ed. M. Banton (London: Tavistock Publications, 1966), p. 96.
10. Max Müller, *Natural Religion* (London: Longman, 1889), p. 188.
11. Clifford Geertz, 'Religion as a Cultural System', in *The Interpretation of Cultures* (New York: Basic Books, 1973), p. 90.
12. Ibid.
13. David Hume, 'Natural History of Religion' in *Dialogues and Natural History of Religion*, ed. J.C.A. Gaskin ([1757] and Oxford: Oxford University Press, 1993), p. 135.
14. Ibid., p. 139.
15. Ibid., p. 176.
16. Ibid., p. 145.
17. Ibid., p. 163.
18. Ibid., p. 159.
19. Ibid., p. 184.
20. Ibid.

21. James Frazer, *The Golden Bough* ([1922] and Harmondsworth: Penguin, 1996), p. 853.
22. Ibid., p. 13.
23. Ibid., p. 853.
24. Ibid., p. 65.
25. Ibid., p. 59.
26. Ibid., p. 60.
27. Ibid., p. 851.
28. Ibid., p. 66.
29. Durkheim, *Elementary Forms*, p. 7.
30. Ibid.
31. Deut. 20:16.
32. Ezek. 18:4.
33. E.B. Tylor, *Anthropology* (London: Murray, 1881), p. 20.
34. Frazer, *The Golden Bough*, p. 855.
35. Ibid., p. 856.
36. E. Evans-Pritchard, *Nuer Religion* (Oxford: Clarendon Press, 1956).
37. Ibid., p. 322.
38. Donald Hughes, *American Indian Ecology*, excerpted in *This Sacred Earth*, ed. Roger Gottlieb (New York: Routledge, 1996), p. 133.
39. Ibid., p. 139.
40. Ibid., p. 140.
41. Ibid., p. 144.
42. Durkheim, *Elementary Forms*, p. 2.
43. Ibid., p. 10.
44. Ibid., p. 47.
45. Ibid., p. 188.
46. Ibid., p. 295.
47. Ibid., p. 206.
48. Ibid., p. 378.
49. Ibid., p. 414.
50. Ibid., p. 264.
51. Ibid., p. 206.
52. Ludwig Feuerbach, *Lectures on the Essence of Religion*, trans. R. Manheim (New York: Harper and Row, 1967), p. 136.
53. Karl Marx, 'Critique of Hegel's Philosophy of Right' in *Reinhold Niebuhr, Karl Marx and Friedrich Engels on Religion* (New York: Schocken Books, 1964), p. 42.
54. Sigmund Freud, *Moses and Monotheism*, trans. Katherine Jones (London: Hogarth Press, 1951), p. 192.
55. Sigmund Freud, *Totem and Taboo*, trans. James Strachey (London: Routledge, 1961), p. 145.
56. Sigmund Freud, *The Future of an Illusion*, trans. W.D. Robson-Scott (London: Hogarth Press, 1949), p. 52.
57. Ibid., p. 11.
58. Ibid., p. 55.
59. William James, *The Varieties of Religious Experience* (London: Fontana, 1971), p. 50.
60. Ibid., p. 430.
61. Ibid., p. 439.

62. Michael Argyle, *Psychology and Religion* (London: Routledge, 2000), p. 56. Chapter 4 deals with religious experience.
63. Olga Pupyin and Simon Brodbeck, 'Religious Experience in London', Occasional Paper 27 (Lampeter: Religious Experience Research Centre, 2001).
64. James, *Varieties of Religious Experience*, p. 466.
65. James, *Varieties of Religious Experience*, p. 481.
66. R.C. Zaehner, *Mysticism, Sacred and Profane* (Oxford: Oxford University Press, 1957).
67. Steven T. Katz, 'Language, Epistemology, and Mysticism', in *Mysticism and Philosophical Analysis* (Oxford: Oxford University Press, 1978).
68. Jacques LeGoff, *The Birth of Purgatory* (Chicago: University of Chicago Press, 1984), p. 135.
69. James, *Varieties of Religious Experience*, p. 483.
70. Ibid., p. 285.
71. Ibid., p. 234.
72. Ibid., p. 490.
73. Ibid., p. 488.
74. Carl Gustav Jung, *The Collected Works of C.G. Jung*, vol. 13, ed. Sir Herbert Read, trans. R.F.C. Hull, Bollingen Series 20 (Princeton: Princeton University Press, 1953–77), p. 51.
75. Ibid., vol. 11, p. 294.
76. Argyle, *Psychology and Religion*, p. 108.
77. Carl Gustav Jung, *Man and his Symbols* (New York: Dell, 1964), p. 42.
78. James, *Varieties of Religious Experience*, p. 464.
79. Carl Gustav Jung, *Memories, Dreams and Reflections*, ed. Aniela Jaffe, trans. Richard and Clara Winston (New York: Random House, 1963), p. 338.
80. Carl Gustav Jung, *Letters*, vol. 2, ed. Gerhard Adler, trans. R.F.C. Hull, Bollingen Series 95 (Princeton: Princeton University Press, 1975), p. 436.
81. Jung, *Collected Works*, vol. 11, p. 489.
82. It can be found in *The Babylonian Genesis*, ed. and trans. A. Heidel (Chicago: University of Chicago Press, 1963).
83. Karl Jaspers, *The Origin and Goal of History*, trans. Michael Bullock (New Haven: Yale University Press, 1953).
84. See Isa. 62:4.
85. Isa. 42:6.
86. 'Let there be no compulsion in religion ... whoever rejects evil and believes in God hath grasped the most trustworthy hand-hold, that never breaks' (Qur'an, Baqara, 256).
87. 'If thy Lord had willed, He verily would have made mankind one nation, yet they cease not differing' (Qur'an, Hud, 118).
88. W.K. Clifford, 'The Ethics of Belief', in *Lectures and Essays* (London: Macmillan, 1879), p. 240.
89. See Søren Kierkegaard, *Concluding Unscientific Postscript*, ed. and trans. H.V. and E.H. Hong (Princeton: Princeton University Press, 1992), p. 203.
90. René Descartes, *Discourse on Method*, vol. 2, trans. Arthur Wollaston (Harmondsworth: Penguin, 1960). See p. 50.
91. George Lindbeck, *The Nature of Doctrine* (Philadelphia: Westminster Press, 1984).
92. E.g. Mark 2: 27: 'The Sabbath was made for man, not man for the Sabbath.'

93. Rom. 13:9.
94. 2 Cor. 3:6.
95. Matt. 5:38–42.
96. Eph. 5:22.
97. Charles Taylor, *Sources of the Self* (Cambridge: Cambridge University Press, 1989).
98. The positive imperfect duty of 'perfecting human nature', and of developing the power to realise all one's purposes, are outlined in *The Metaphysics of Morals*, trans. Mary Gregor (New York: Harper Torchbooks, 1964), see 'The Doctrine of Virtue', p. 82.
99. Alasdair MacIntyre, *After Virtue* (London: Duckworth, 1981), chap. 5.
100. See Keith Ward, *The Development of Kant's View of Ethics* (Oxford: Basil Blackwell, 1972).
101. Immanuel Kant, *Lectures on Ethics*, trans. Louis Infield (New York: Harper Torchbooks, 1963), p. 123.
102. 'God is the morally practical self-legislative reason': *Opus Postumum* (Berlin: German Academy of Sciences, 1902–1938), vol. 21, p. 145.
103. *Religion Within the Limits of Reason*, trans. T.M. Greene and H.H. Hudson (New York: Harper, 1960), p. 142.
104. Paul Tillich, *Systematic Theology* (Welwyn: Nisbet, 1968), vol. 3, p. 265.
105. John Hick, *An Interpretation of Religion* (London: Macmillan, 1989), p. 235.

INDEX